Return from Purple Earth

Eliel Luma Fionn

RESOURCE *Publications* · Eugene, Oregon

This book is a work of fiction. Places, events, and situations in this story are purely fictional. Any resemblance to actual persons, living or dead, is coincidental

Resource Publications
A division of Wipf and Stock Publishers
199 W 8th Ave, Suite 3
Eugene, OR 97401

Return from Purple Earth
By Fionn, Eliel Luma
Copyright©2008 by Fionn, Eliel Luma
ISBN 13: 978-1-55635-812-8
ISBN 10: 1-55635-812-1
Publication date 1/17/2008

Chapter 1

"We made it, Torin!" Rebecca said, after they had materialized neatly onto the thick blue carpet of her bedroom. Their feet sank nearly ankle deep, prompting Torin to look down in surprise. Rebecca dropped her backsack, gazing about in satisfaction. Everything looked just as she had left it. The space was immense, nearly twenty paces in either direction. Along one wall was her huge white and blue canopy bed with colorful pillows, next to it a carved rosewood end table and dresser. Opposite the bed, a teak entertainment center held a small T.V. and CD player, as well as stacks of CDs and movies.

On the other side of the room stood a large oak bookshelf, overflowing with books, pictures, stuffed animals, and a collection of art glass. A mini refrigerator hummed in the corner near a white desk and chair. The cream textured walls held family photos and framed art prints from the Metropolitan Museum of Art. Piles of books lay on the floor by the bed, sprawled over her beanbag chair, and tucked away on another built-in bookshelf.

There was a deep closet for clothes and a blue-tiled bathroom complete with a Jacuzzi tub. It was certainly different than any room Torin had ever seen at home on Thianely. There, dwellings grew directly out of the ground; carpets were woven from plant vines, and light either came from the pink sun outside or from house crystals.

"It's enormous," he commented, noting that her room was half the size of his grandfather Imanayon's entire house. Torin walked around curiously, chuckling at some of the baby pictures propped on the bookshelf. He poked tentatively at the beanbag, not quite sure what it was, then, pushing the books aside, settled into it with a sigh.

Rebecca was struck by the contrast of her childhood room, decorated blue and white, and the tall, blond haired, green-eyed Thianelian occupying her blue beanbag chair. Even on Earth, Torin glowed.

While Torin watched, sinking even further into the chair, Rebecca rummaged through her closet and dresser drawers.

"I must not have been gone too long; everything looks exactly like I left it, books everywhere, closet cluttered. Mom must have dusted for me. Oh, I can't wait to see Mom and Dad!"

She sat on the bed, wiggling her toes inside her thin slippers. It was strange to be back home, when only minutes before she'd been on

Thianely, a whole world away. She would miss the pink sky, the purple earth, and her friends there. She thought of Leva of the Tree Folk, Liliar, a marvelous singer and member of the Bollux clan, and Tehy, Liliar's half Griffin, half human mate. She wondered how long she'd been gone, as time was not only measured differently on Thianely; it was barely measured at all. So much had changed for her since she'd first left New York, she could only imagine what had happened at home during her absence.

She knew she had a great deal of explaining to do. Her parents must have been frantic when she'd disappeared. It was bad enough to lose a child, let alone have no idea what had happened to her. Now that she had returned she could introduce them to so many new ideas, and also to Torin of the Fire Folk, a native Thianelian and her mate.

At least with Torin along she'd have proof of where she'd been. Knowing her dad, he'd have a hard time believing her adventures. She'd had a difficult time herself, even as she'd been experiencing life on another world. She had left home right before her sixteenth birthday and now here she was, she didn't know how many months later, practically married to a fellow from another planet. She hoped her father would be so happy to see her he wouldn't get too upset about Torin.

Rebecca noticed a slight pressure building in her head as if she had the beginning of a headache. The back of her neck throbbed, and then ached sharply. The pain increased, moving quickly down her body, pushing hard against her arms, her stomach, her legs. The relentless force knocked her over and pressed her into the coverlet, reminding her of one of those horror movies with the walls closing in. Rebecca winced as the pressure beat against her head and her chest, making it difficult to breathe. Thousands of voices tumbled through her mind like fast-forward on a tape recorder; and suddenly Torin was there, placing his hands gently on her forehead. She heard the familiar deep resonance of his voice creating a barrier of sound between her and the piercing pain.

"Rebecca," he said, "try to sit up now and I'll show you how to protect yourself here. You have to create a shield around yourself that blocks out people's thoughts and emotions."

Rebecca made an effort to sit up, resisting what felt like tons of gravity. She rested her feet on the floor, took a deep breath, and listened as Torin described how to create an energy shield. First she imagined herself inside a container of light, and then she strengthened it with vibrant colors. After she added layers upon layers of energy around herself like a huge cocoon, the heaviness subsided, but for some reason her headache persisted.

"I think you've got the beginnings of separation sickness," Torin said. "It develops in places where people are divided from their innermost selves. On Thianely, we live in small clusters of Folk trained to respect each other's mental and emotional boundaries, so it is easier to stay open there, more connected. This city houses many people who are unaware of energetic respect. Along with an energy shield you must close your mind here in a way that was unnecessary on Thianely. Picture your mind as a series of large doorways. Add thick screens over the doors so that nothing can get through unless it is necessary for you to know. I shut certain aspects of my mind as soon as we arrived, but I was unsure how you would react to your planet until we got here."

Rebecca imagined her mind as a large room with many doors, all of them closing. She pictured a series of dense screens encompassing each door, each a different color and texture. All at once the headache began to lessen. She felt immediate relief, but also a foggy blankness where once she'd heard Torin's thoughts.

"What happened?" she demanded. "I can barely hear you now. I mean, that noise was terrible, but I miss you."

Torin sighed in commiseration. "I know, Rebecca, and I am sorry that such defense is necessary. One problem about being so closed is that it makes teling more difficult. If you want to mind speak, you'll have to tune into my thoughts as if they were one of your radio stations. Once you know my frequency, you can open to me without being bombarded by everyone else's."

Rebecca winced. On Torin's planet, speaking mind to mind had been natural, nearly effortless. Here, it was more like her radio station had gone off the air. All she got was static. She attempted to follow his instructions, but finally shook her head.

"This is going to take some practice. I tried to do what you said, but when I left one door open the sledgehammers in my head came back. It's strange though, on Thianely, even when we were talking aloud, I could still feel you. We were talking and connected at once. Here words seem so thin, superficial, like layers of meaning are gone. No wonder different cultures have such a hard time

3

communicating! And I spent, what, about three months on Thianely without much trouble, but now ten minutes on earth makes me sick. How could I have not noticed the denseness, the overwhelming mind noise before?"

Torin shrugged. "You were born here. You could not have survived for long without closing off some of your perceptions. Now that you're more open, you will have to protect yourself differently."

He put his arm over her shoulders and hugged her close. "Remember on Thianely when you yelled at us in your mind?"

Rebecca smiled, recalling herself in the middle of a council meeting addressing the Fire Folk in a very loud tone of thought.

"We had little idea what it was to experience our world from an outsider's perspective. As you know, many of us have visited Earth, but not often have your Folk visited us. My Folk have taught those of us who travel interplanetarily many survival skills. I am grateful that I could be helpful. Do not judge yourself, Rebecca, you have never had to experience your own planet from another perspective before, particularly from off world."

Rebecca sighed, resting her head on Torin's shoulder for a moment. There was something incredibly comforting about him. She'd seen him shoot fire out of his palms to cook food, confront all sorts of nasty creatures, and even kill an enormous slug-like Bellorasp, yet she'd never felt safer in another's company. She wondered if she would ever get used to his kindness, and wished at that moment that she would never take him for granted.

Torin sat holding Rebecca, thinking idly about how well she fit in his arms, and how it would probably a good idea to sit further away from her. On Thianely, they would have been well and truly mated by now, but Rebecca was from Earth, and most young people did not choose mates for life at quite so young an age. He stood up, disengaging her arms as Rebecca glanced up at the wall clock over her dresser.

"Torin, it's only 2:00 p.m. and my parents won't be home from work for another few hours, so I can show you around. Oh, are you getting hungry? How about lunch?"

"Lead the way," Torin agreed. He followed Rebecca out her door and down the hallway, noticing that even though she was radiant on Thianely, the effect was exaggerated here, as though the darkness of the earth's atmosphere lent her even more light in contrast. They passed two other doors, but when Torin looked inquisitive, Rebecca waved him on. "I'm too hungry. Let's go downstairs first."

Rebecca led him down a flight of smooth hardwood stairs. The spiral stairway curved over a large, open living room. The room was divided into a play area and a relaxation area, with a pool table and bookshelf on one side and a sofa, chairs and entertainment center on the other. The walls were cream colored, with a border of mauve wallpaper at the bottom. There were large patterned rugs on the floors and cream lace curtains framing the windows. French doors led out to what Rebecca described as a large back yard.

An ornate silver framed mirror hung directly opposite the foot of the stairs. Rebecca glanced back to see what Torin thought of her home so far and noticed him staring at her. "What is it?' she asked.

Torin merely gestured at her to stop. He pulled her in front of the full-length mirror on the wall facing them. Rebecca stood in shock for a moment.

"That's me?" she asked wonderingly, realizing that it had been a long time since she'd really looked at herself.

The young woman who stared back at her was taller than she remembered, while her long wavy brown hair appeared thicker and more abundant. Her deep blue eyes held an inner light that radiated from her face and the rest of her body. She looked as if she'd seen much, knew even more, and was wise with the knowing.

Torin came to stand beside her. She'd noticed before that he emanated a lot of light, and though she had seen him nearly every day since she'd been to Thianely, Rebecca observed that the maturity in his face, his air of authority, had increased since they'd first met. He put an arm around her, drawing her close.

"You are changed," Torin said. "We have both grown a little. Your radiance is more noticeable than when you first arrived on Thianely."

Rebecca nodded speechlessly, struck also by the way they looked so natural standing side by side, as if they totally belonged together.

"I hope my parents are okay with this," she finally said, tugging Torin away from the mirror. She led him down the hallway and into the kitchen. "Let's go find something to eat."

Rebecca headed straight for the refrigerator, while Torin took in the huge, cheerfully decorated kitchen. The peach and cream walls matched the appliances, while peach patterned curtains let in sunlight from the two windows. A large oval table with six chairs stood in the center of the gleaming wood floor. Framed artwork hung on the walls nearby a bookshelf dedicated wholly to cookbooks and a gleaming wood hutch for special china.

Rebecca started piling bread, cheese, tomatoes, lettuce, and turkey meat on the table. She grabbed a knife, jars of mayonnaise and mustard, and a couple of plates, motioning for Torin to join her.

Torin passed up the meat, explaining that he was unaccustomed to eating living things besides plants. Rebecca, her mouth full, chewed slowly, savoring her favorite turkey sandwich.

"You know," she said, "I noticed a lot of Thianelians are vegetarians, and although we ate well when we were there, I really missed this stuff."

Torin nodded, swallowing a bite of sandwich. "Can you guess what food I most enjoy here?"

"I don't know, pizza, soda pop?"

Torin shook his head. "Actually, your soda does to me what the rain on Thianely does to you; I become completely drunk. No, I love your chocolate the most. Hot chocolate to drink, and chocolate bars to eat. I have noticed they help me maintain my shielding, and my strength."

"A lot of other people would probably agree with you, and chocolate happens to be one of my favorite foods in the world. Maybe it does help prevent separation sickness. One more great reason to eat chocolate! Isn't it funny how quickly you can get accustomed to strange food? While we're here, I'll probably miss the fruits, nuts, and vegetables from Thianely. They tasted so juicy and fresh."

"Tell me about your parents," Torin prompted, after they had finished their snack.

"I forgot I haven't really told you that much. Okay. Mom is Auran Elizabeth Bloom. My grandmother, that's Hazel Imogene Forest, wanted to name her Maureen, after my great grandmother, but my grandfather, Matthew Danbury Forest, hated the name. He told me he refused to name any child Maureen after his nasty mother in law. So while grandmother was still recovering from having my mom, my grandfather filled out the birth certificate himself, dumping some letters, changing a few. My grandmother signed it when she was half asleep.

6

Can you believe my grandmother still calls Mom 'Maureen,' even though it's not really her name? She's very stubborn, my grandmother. She's also much more formal than Grandpa. I call her Grandmother, but Grandpa is just 'Fort'. He's really a lot of fun and kind of balances Grandmother out. Anyway, Mom said that when she was a teenager her name was considered really cool. Auras are the glow around your body, you know."

"We describe what you call auras as the shine of the soul," Torin said, "but I know what you mean."

"Mom designs the interiors of houses and offices, sometimes even museums. She loves her job. She's really active, creative, and happy most of the time. That's kind of rare here, especially in New York. Most grownups I know seem really frazzled. Dad is Griffin Augustin Bloom, but he doesn't use his middle name at all. Mom calls him Griff."

Torin grinned across the table at her. "Your father is a Griffin?"

"He sure is," Rebecca replied. "He's not as large or fierce-looking as Griffins on Thianely, but he does get really loud sometimes. Especially if something doesn't go well at work. He's an architect that expects builders to do what he wants and they usually do. He's funny and kind and a great dad. I've really missed them both.

And we live in Murray Hill, the best part of Manhattan. There are hardly any residential neighborhoods here besides ours. You can barely hear the traffic, compared to the rest of the City."

She paused to listen, already used to the dull background noise of cars, people, and planes that was such a part of New York. It was odd to think that on Thianely the only consistent background was silence, unless one was fortunate enough to hear the songs of the trees growing.

"Maybe we can go on a walk sometime and I'll show you around. New York is kind of a whole world in itself; there's always so much going on, and the people are something else. I know you've been here before, but there's always something new to do."

They headed back down the hallway, where they toured the downstairs bathroom, a dusky pink powder room with pedestal sink, mauve carpet, fluffy pink towels and gold accents. The guest bedroom next door was decorated in shades of browns, beige, and gold. It had a large closet, a queen-sized bed and a small T.V.

After wandering back through the living room, Rebecca led Torin through the French doors into the back yard. A large deck with a sunken hot tub took up a quarter of the area. Two oak trees supported a hammock nearby. Flowerbeds added color to the edges of the still green lawn, a lovely sight against the brown of the fence and the blue of the sky. Maple trees dropped their leaves in shades of yellow, brown, and rust, dotting the green expanse. While they stood on the deck taking in the crisp air of early autumn, Rebecca noticed that the simple act of breathing required effort. Whereas on Thianely the air seemed to buoy her up, on earth it weighed her down. She felt slower and heavier, less energetic.

Torin, fascinated with the spa, tested the temperature of the hot tub and fiddled with the jet mechanism. As the water began to bubble furiously, Rebecca sank her awareness into the deck beneath her feet. She reached through the wood, down into the thin spires of grass, deep into the ground below. The dark soil reached up to her like an old friend, welcoming her home. For the first time since she'd arrived back, Rebecca felt she truly belonged on Earth. She stepped down onto the grass and wiggled her toes inside her thin slippers. She bent down to sniff the roses, which flourished in variegated colors at the edges of the yard.

Suddenly, the air hummed with activity. A whole flock of tiny faeries arose from the flowers, clustering about Rebecca, buzzing excitedly in her ears. As she tried to make out what they were saying, she spied two fat dwarves chasing each other around an oak tree, directly below the height of the hammock, while a lovely, green skinned dryad draped herself decorously against a maple trunk. A luminous white unicorn, its spiraling golden horn glistening in the sunlight, climbed gracefully onto the deck. Torin, who had been completely absorbed in watching bubbles arise in the hot tub, looked up and laughed.

Rebecca looked at him in bewilderment. "Where did they all come from?"

Torin reached over to scratch beneath the unicorn's horn, a difficult place for the beast to reach. It sank contentedly down on all fours, angling its head for easier access. Torin sat down next to the creature, smoothing its white coat.

"You've welcomed all of the beings back to this small garden, or yarden, Rebecca. They have always been here on some level anyway, but now they are closer to this third dimensional space. Most of your Folk would still be unable to perceive them, though throughout the history of your people there have been those who have had such vision. Because these beings are as real to us as we are to them, we may touch them and have them touch us. We exist in the same time and space. Come, this unicorn is called Gilden, and he loves to have his coat scratched and stroked. Unicorns, and those humans who have once been in unicorn form, are extremely sensitive to the touch."

Rebecca ran one hand down the silky hide of the unicorn. "I read a story once about a unicorn in a garden. I never figured it would happen to me. I have to say, though, it's comforting to know that nature spirits and the little people are still here. I thought they only survived on Thianely."

"Most beings retain the ability to travel inter-dimensionally. The creatures of your myths have simply transferred to safer spaces until such time as they felt comfortable in returning. This yarden is a very safe place."

"I guess so," Rebecca agreed. She paused, listening as two fauns, sprawled carelessly on the lawn, played panpipes for a circle of dancing wind nymphs. The swaying maidens, barely dressed in diaphanous breezes, swirled about, lifting the first of the fallen autumn leaves into the air. Rebecca watched the activity, softly stroking the unicorn's satiny coat.

"Gilden tells me he prefers to eat fruit," Torin informed her. "The faeries sip dew from flowers, while the fauns enjoy eating the soft cracklings of new-fallen leaves. The dryads on your planet are nourished directly from the roots of their trees. Most of the dwarves and gnomes you see here gather nuts, seeds, and fruit much as we do on Thianely. You are able to speak with them as well, you know."

"I know," Rebecca admitted, "but it's one thing to be talking to creatures on a different planet, and another to be doing it in my own back yard. I keep thinking that most people can't perceive any of this, and so it doesn't even exist. It's kind of sobering to realize that most of what is real to me doesn't exist for others. How am I supposed to live here? Pretend to be like everyone else?"

"It is one thing to be aware and not to speak of what you know, and quite another to pretend you do not know at all," Torin said. "What purpose would such pretense serve?"

"Well, it would keep people from feeling frightened by what they don't understand. There is a lot of fear of the unknown here, Torin. I'd hate to contribute to any more of it."

"So you will prevent such fear by worrying about it before it happens? By being afraid of your own awareness?"

Before Rebecca had a chance to respond, Gilden raised his head and roared with laughter, nearly impaling Rebecca on his horn in the process. "He has you there, Amalfina Kal. Now look into my unicorn eyes and tell me you do not know me."

Rebecca smiled sheepishly. "I know you, Gilden Ahtt, as well as I know my own unicorn name."

As the unicorn blinked his wide lids, his eyes, bright turquoise in color, twinkled kindly. "You'll find it's not so bad to be yourself, my dear, even on this planet. I thank you for our welcome here. It is pleasurable to be more solid of form once more."

"That's it," the unicorn murmured contentedly to Torin. "Scratch right above the base of the horn there, Dolwin Renn."

"We certainly have an abundance of names," Rebecca said, reminded of her mermaid and troll names on Thianely. "Luckily I like all of them so far."

"A name for each lifetime," Torin remarked. "As you remember more of your selves, names tend to follow. They are like keys to the doorways of old memories, a quick entry to other times. Naming has always been important, even in the faery stories of your world."

Rebecca nodded. She was growing sleepy, lulled by the softness of Gilden's smooth skin under her palm, the grace of the creatures moving about the yard, or yarden as Torin referred to it. According to Torin, on Thianely large gardens were called gardens, while small ones were yardens. She thought fondly of Imanayon's beautiful, spiraling garden on Thianely. It was very calming, and Rebecca had spent quite a bit of time there.

"One thing though," Rebecca said between yawns. "I don't think any of these guys should come in the house. Mom and Dad are going to have enough to deal with without faery folk strolling through the living room. Not that they'll even know the faery folk are there, but just in case."

Gilden tossed his head, narrowly missing Torin with his horn. "Do not assume that your parents suffer from constricted awareness,

Amalfina. Though you need not worry, none of us will enter your home without invitation except in case of some urgency."

"Thanks, Gilden. Goodness, I can't believe I'm so tired already! I suppose I ought to head back inside before I fall asleep on the deck," Rebecca announced. "Sorry Gilden, I'll have to scratch that particular spot later."

Torin gave Gilden one last pat between his ears, and followed Rebecca back inside where she continued Torin's tour. They wandered upstairs through her parents' bedroom, the sewing room, the home office, and into her room again. Torin appeared to be perfectly at home in an Earth house, although some of the appliances puzzled him. He hadn't seen a CD player before, and though he'd heard of computers, he'd never had the opportunity to use one.

"I want to turn on the T.V. and watch the news for awhile," Rebecca said finally, as Torin plopped back down in her beanbag again. "I still don't know what day it is. I forgot to look at the calendar downstairs in the kitchen."

She grabbed the remote, sat down next to Torin in the beanbag chair, and clicked on her T.V. She sat in stunned dismay as the news anchor mentioned the day's date.

"A year!" she said disbelievingly. "I've been gone over a year! Torin, my parents must be devastated. They probably figured I was dead, yet my room is the same, dusted and everything. This is too weird!"

"I am sorry, Rebecca," Torin said, pulling her onto his lap. "The difference in time between our planets must have grown longer. It is curious that your room is the same, though perhaps it is a benefit. You will feel much more at home in familiar surroundings despite separation sickness. Traveling between worlds can be difficult, causing, what is the term your folk use, jetlag."

"I suppose if I had tried to imagine returning the very moment when I left...but I didn't think of that. If I'd sent myself back to that time, would I have remembered everything that happened afterwards? Maybe it wouldn't have happened at all. I might not have learned anything."

Torin gave her a hug, resting his chin on the top of her head. "Rebecca, it does not matter. Here we are. Your parents will be happy to have you back no matter what length of time has passed. At least we

11

have returned safely, and look, the man on the screen is predicting warm skies."

Rebecca hugged him back. Then she stared at him in astonishment. "Torin, can you understand his English? I mean, are we speaking English right now? I can't even tell anymore."

"No, Rebecca, we are still speaking the Old Tongue, though we instantly translate the fragment of language you call English. A single language on your planet would no longer meet the needs of your mind. There are too many levels of understanding missing.

When the Great Separation occurred on this planet many times ago, the Old Tongue splintered into separate threads of speech, or what your Folk call different languages. Folk on this planet will understand what we say. Every being in creation understands the Old Tongue, even age-old trolls that sleep inside mountains."

Rebecca nodded, remembering the experience of talking to a newly awakened troll, her old friend Gomfrey Risco.

"Your parents will probably think we sound a little strange," Torin continued, "as if we had a foreign accent, but they will understand what we say. You comprehend me especially well because we're mates. You are also used to the different levels of meaning in mind speech, or what in mates you might term heart speak."

"Sometimes I can't believe all of this stuff. It seems impossible, yet it's so natural. Oh well, at least my parents will understand me. That's something. Want a soda?"

Torin shook his head. He realized that having Rebecca sit on his lap while talking about mates was not exactly helping his restraint. And he was more tired from traveling between worlds than he had thought. Giving Rebecca a little nudge, he stood up, plopped down upon her bed, and before he could finish saying "good nap," promptly fell asleep.

Rebecca eyed him for a moment, finally deciding she might as well have a short nap herself since she'd need the extra energy later when her parents returned home. She emptied out her tunic pockets, arranging everything she'd brought from Thianely on her dresser top, and lay down next to Torin. As he muttered something unintelligible, throwing one arm over her sleepily, Rebecca closed her eyes, wondering how their friends were faring on Thianely. She hoped they were all safe.

Chapter 2

Rebecca awoke to the sound of the garage door opening. She sat up quickly, shaking Torin by the shoulder to rouse him. Taking a deep breath, she shut her eyes for a moment, relaxing as Torin put his arms around her reassuringly.

"Do you want to go down first by yourself?" he asked, kissing her on the nose. Rebecca gave him a tremulous smile.

"I think that would be best. Here," she motioned to her bookshelves. "Tons of books to read. Or you can always watch T.V. and play with the remote."

Torin gave her a little push towards the door. "Go. I will be right here. All will be well, Rebecca."

Rebecca paused at the door, her hand on the knob. "Thanks, Torin. I'll be back soon."

She walked out into the hallway, down the stairs toward the kitchen. There she heard the familiar voice of her mother, scolding her father for leaving out sandwich supplies.

"I told you, Auran," her father protested. "I didn't come home for lunch. Remember I had that meeting about the blueprints? Besides, I don't like mustard anyway."

Rebecca could hear her mother sigh. "I know, but that was Rebecca's favorite kind. I'm sorry I got so angry, Griff; I miss her so much. I'll put it away. Who knows, maybe I was sleepwalking and did it myself."

Rebecca stood in the kitchen doorway, watching as her father gave her mother a pat on the back and kissed her cheek.

"Maybe you should let me put it away, Mom," Rebecca suggested, "since I'm the one that took it out."

Her parents froze in place as if they were afraid to turn around and find out she wasn't real. Auran got only a brief glimpse of Rebecca's face before passing out cold. Caught between running to his daughter and catching his wife, Griffin hesitated only a moment. He grabbed Auran right before she hit the floor, and stared at Rebecca in disbelief. Rebecca knelt down next to him as her mother came around.

"Mom, are you okay? It's really me. I'm sorry this is such a shock. I didn't realize I'd been away so long."

Auran sat up, shook off Griffin's supportive arm and hugged her daughter fiercely. Griffin silently held them both as tears of relief ran down all of their faces.

Auran turned to Rebecca. "Where have you been? Are you really okay? You weren't hurt? I thought we'd never see you again. That crazy Mrs. Meyer said you'd sunk right into the street and no one else had seen you at all. Oh, Rebecca, where have you been?"

Rebecca stared at her mother, noticing lines in her face that hadn't been there before, traces of sorrow etched into her skin. Her father looked older too, as if he'd been under great strain.

"I'm so sorry, Mom and Dad. I wish I could have told you I was okay so you wouldn't have worried so much. I was somewhere very far away, and I couldn't reach you from there. I've been fine, in fact, more than fine. I will explain it all, though I'm not sure how much sense it'll make. I love you both very much, and I really am okay. No one hurt me. I wasn't kidnapped and I didn't run away."

Rebecca's father rubbed his hand wearily over his face. "The important thing is that we have you back," he said finally, "and you weren't hurt. We've been imagining all sorts of terrible things, and poor Mrs. Meyer was interrogated for weeks. She and your friend Lucy moved away; they couldn't take the publicity anymore. We have looked everywhere for you, my girl. The FBI is still out hunting for you. You've been gone a whole year! I keep thinking I'll blink and you'll disappear. God, it's so good to see you! Those idiotic policemen thought you were some sort of runaway. You're sure no one hurt you?"

As Rebecca nodded, Griffin nudged Auran and Rebecca to their feet.

"Ladies," he said gruffly, "why don't we move into the living room? The couch is a lot more comfortable than the floor." He led the way to the sofa, one arm around Auran, one around Rebecca.

Rebecca gazed around the living room. She hadn't really looked at it closely before, when she and Torin had gone outside. Nothing had really changed much. The white and rose patterned sofa still took up too much space against one wall, the easy chairs in white and green weave on either side. The entertainment center held a larger T.V. than she remembered, but her parent's Indian art collection still covered most of the bookshelves. Rebecca sank more deeply into the sofa and put her feet up on the coffee table. Her mother immediately pushed her feet down.

"You know they don't belong on the table, Rebecca." She giggled. "Actually, I'm so happy to see you even if it's just to scold you. Let me look at you."

Rebecca obediently turned her face to her mother, as her father sat quietly, leaning back on the sofa as if it had been a long time since he'd simply relaxed. He clasped his daughter's shoulders loosely, waiting as her mother examined her.

"Just as I thought," her mother said, her artist's eye already taking in the changes, "you look older and stronger, more assured. Rebecca, your skin looks different. Also," her mother pursed her lips in puzzlement, "you look lighter somehow, like you've been happy, well, not happy, but deeper than that. And where did you get these clothes? The colors are fantastic; the style is certainly unusual. I can't quite place the material." She rubbed the cuff of Rebecca's tunic between her fingers. "What is this?"

"I promise I'll tell you all about it," Rebecca said, turning to her father. "Well, Dad, what do you think?"

Rebecca's father tightened his arm around her, drawing her closer and giving her a squeeze. "You look like a young lady who's been somewhere and seen a lot. I want to know where and what and how and everything, but first I just want to hold you for a while."

For a long time, the three of them sat cuddling on the sofa together. Finally Rebecca pulled away a little. "Mom, Dad, I can't explain what happened without a little help. The help happens to be upstairs. Could you come up to my room with me?"

As she led them upstairs, Auran and Griffin each held onto one of her hands, still unwilling to let go of her. When she pushed open the door, Torin immediately rose from her beanbag chair. He bowed low, first to Rebecca's mother, then to her father.

"I am most pleased to meet you," he said formally. "I am Torin, of the Fire Folk."

Auran and Griffin Bloom turned to Rebecca in shock.

"Mom, Dad," she said, "I'd like you to meet my..." she stumbled a bit over the words as Torin smiled encouragingly, "my mate."

As Auran gasped, Griffin Bloom completely lost his temper.

15

"Rebecca," he yelled, "what the hell is going on? You and this young man are what? Did he take you away from home? He may be old enough, but you certainly are not! As far as I know you still need your parent's permission to get married in this country."

"Excuse me," said Torin firmly, stepping up to face Rebecca's father calmly.

"We are not wed, and certainly will not be without one of your ceremonies. Nor have we done anything for which you need be concerned. Although the will to mate can be intense, we are not yet mated physically, only in spirit. And," he continued, looking Griffin right in the eye, "I will do everything in my power to keep Rebecca from harm, although she needs such help less every day. You have my word in deed upon this."

Griffin took a deep breath and mentally counted to ten. He shook his head as if to clear it, then rubbed his chin.

"All right," he said at last, "you seem like a sensible fellow, but you can't blame us for thinking the worst." He turned to Rebecca. "Where have you been, Rebecca, if you didn't run off or get kidnapped? Why didn't you call us? What is going on? I want you two to sit down and tell us what this is all about. Young man, your accent definitely sounds foreign. I'd also like to know where the hell you come from that you have these sorts of manners. It sure isn't the U.S."

"No, it isn't," Rebecca agreed, joining her mother on her bed. "Why don't we all sit down? We'll tell you what happened from the time I left up to now."

Griffin shrugged, and went to sit beside Auran, while Torin resumed his place in the beanbag chair. While Rebecca's parents listened in astonishment, Rebecca and Torin told a simplified version of what had transpired from the moment Torin had pulled her through a rain puddle to Thianely. They recounted her adventures with the Fire Folk, at the Threshold of the Trees, with the Merfolk, the Air Folk, the Earthen Folk, and the trouble with the Bolluxes.

"Let me get this straight," Griffin interrupted. "One of your friends, Tehy, is half-griffin (the kind of mythical creatures that are part eagle, part lion) and half Air Folk, people who can levitate at will. Another one, Leva, has green skin and lives in a tree, but also is related to people who live underground. Your other friend, Liliar, can create things just by singing. Torin can do strange things with fire and the Bolluxes, interesting name, are creepy nutcases that sound like they escaped from a jail for hardened criminals. And there really are mermaids on other planets. Have I got it right so far?"

"Pretty much, Dad," Rebecca admitted. "Although the way you said it doesn't sound very believable."

"Not too much from where I'm sitting either," Griffin commented. Auran patted his knee and leaned forward, eager to hear more.

Rebecca let Torin describe the difficulties occurring on Thianely, but they both instinctively left out Rebecca's abilities to shift her form and travel by thought. In fact, Rebecca left out a great deal about her inward adventures, including the fact that she'd absorbed information from the large record-keeping crystals at the roots of The Great Tree, the repository of wisdom on Thianely. Griffin choked a bit on the idea that his daughter had spent the better part of a year on an entirely different planet, but Auran shushed him when he tried to interrupt.

The telling took hours. Rebecca showed them the leaf she'd been given from the Threshold of the Trees, the golden root from the Great Tree, her crystal necklace, and the leaf pad of pictures Torin had drawn. They took a long break for dinner. Griffin showed Torin how to play pool while Auran and Rebecca cooked the meal. Torin had quietly offered to heat the food with his palms, but Rebecca had stopped him before he could try it. "I don't think they're ready for that yet," she'd explained.

After eating they all moved back into the living room. Finally, with minimal interruptions due to the fact that Auran and Griffin were completely flabbergasted, the tale was told. By then it was nearly midnight, and they'd all been yawning for a while.

"Well," said Griffin Bloom, looking at his daughter and the young man who seemed to have such a presence about him. "I think that's about all my poor brain can handle at this point. Do me a favor, Rebecca, and draw me a map and a genealogy chart, I got a little lost with all the names of those Bollux creatures and who is related to whom in the other Folk you mentioned. I also don't have a clue how we'll handle this with the authorities, but I suppose we can worry about that tomorrow. Why don't we go get some sleep?"

Rebecca rose to her feet, motioning for Torin to come upstairs.

"Wait a minute, young lady," said her father. "I think we can make up the guest room for your friend Torin here. You can bring down his knapsack. I'll loan him some extra clothes, in case he needs some. You go on up."

Rebecca sighed, realizing that even though she and Torin had spent many nights together already, customs here dictated a little more distance between them. Too tired to argue, she hugged her parents good night. Pulling Torin aside, she whispered in his ear, "It may take them a while to get used to us."

"It is not unexpected," he replied. "This is much for anyone to accept in one day."

Rebecca went upstairs to retrieve Torin's belongings while her father escorted him to the guest room. Instead of entering her own bedroom, Auran followed Rebecca to her room.

"Rebecca," she said, "I can't say I really understand all of what you've told us, but I want you to know that I approve of your fellow. He obviously adores you. He seems very strong and wise, kind too. He's really, well, handsome doesn't even cover it, and you two look so... together with each other. If there's anything you need help with, like birth control or anything, I want you to let me know."

Rebecca blushed. "Mom, we've been a little too busy with other things to get that physically involved. So don't worry, okay? On Thianely they don't even need birth control."

Auran gave her another squeeze. "You're home now, Rebecca. Things don't work the same way here as they do there. Let me know if you change your mind. I would think you're much too young, except you don't seem that young any more. Good night, sweetheart. Don't worry if we come in and check on you a few times during the night. We can't quite believe that you're home. Please don't go anywhere without telling us first, okay?"

Rebecca put her arms around her mom, holding her tightly. "I really missed you guys a lot. The whole time I kept wondering how you were, but I had no idea how hard it must have been for you."

Auran looked at her wryly. "One positive outcome of this whole situation is that my mother has been almost cordial to your dad. She'll probably revert back to her crusty old self when she finds out you're back, but it's definitely been an improvement. She even slipped up and called me Auran once."

Rebecca laughed. "How's Grandpa been?" she asked, thinking about her grandpa Fort. He'd always been one of her favorite people. He'd taught her to swim, play cards, and had taken her to the library for the first time. He and her grandmother lived about an hour away, but they'd visited fairly regularly.

Auran's face fell. "Oh, Rebecca, he's not been well. He took your disappearance really hard. He had a stroke a few months ago and still isn't back to normal. He and Mother moved closer to us so that we could help out more; they live just twenty minutes away now. I'm sorry, kiddo, but it's been rough. Seeing your face should help immensely though. I'll call them soon to tell them the good news. Now try to get some sleep."

After peeling off her Thianelian clothes, Rebecca got in her bed, thinking sadly of her grandpa. It was hard to imagine him ill or old, let alone incapacitated. She hoped she could somehow help him.

She lay awake for a while, enjoying the feeling of being back in her room again. She could still feel the pressure of the earth's pain on her mind shield, but at least it was bearable. Though she missed Torin's presence beside her, she soon drifted off to sleep.

Auran went into her own room, shut the door, and sat wearily on the end of the bed. When Griffin finally joined her, she looked at him, suddenly no longer tired. "Do you believe them, Griff?" she asked, as they undressed and crawled under the covers.

"Beats me," he shrugged, pulling her comfortably against him. "It's a little hard to swallow, especially after all those things I yelled at Mrs. Meyer. I think the least derogatory phrase I used was a 'blankety blank lunatic'. Now I'm not sure what to think, except that Torin, well, I could swear that he doesn't even know how to lie. I do believe he is from somewhere so far from our culture that it may as well be a different planet. You know what he said when I inquired about his sleeping arrangements with Rebecca?"

Auran looked at him questioningly.

"He said that he loved her, but that he has only her protection in mind, and that where he comes from respect for one another is taught from birth. He said they are used to sharing a sleeping place, but as long as she is safe here he will remain in the guest room. He bowed to me again. And did you see his hands? He has the strangest palms I've ever seen, with sort of spiraling designs on them. Not tattoos, just his own skin. I don't know, but at least Rebecca's home, even if she looks like a different person."

"She truly has changed, hasn't she Griff? Her eyes are different, like open doors. I always knew she would grow up, but I never thought about her growing open." They lay awake for a while, contemplating their daughter's return, too keyed up to sleep.

Torin, in the bedroom downstairs, sat on the floor creating a ring of fire around the house, in case mind shields weren't enough protection. He lay in darkness, thinking of the tasks ahead, Rebecca upstairs, and the oddness of a place where people's minds were so noisy. Then he too, slept.

Chapter 3

The next morning Rebecca woke early, as the dawn was beginning to brighten her curtains. Dressing quickly, she hurried downstairs to find that Torin was already awake.

"Morning," she said. Torin was sorting objects from his backsack on the floor. He rose to his feet, greeting her with a kiss. Rebecca smoothed the still rumpled covers on the guest bed. "How did you sleep?"

"Like someone who has traveled between worlds and met the parents of his mate for the first time. I rested very well, considering I missed your presence. I have to agree with your father though. I am not sure how well our containment would work if we spent much time in the same sleeping space. I am already noticing the effects of the atmosphere here. When Folk live in fear of their own survival, it results in a much greater urge to procreate. Rebecca," he grinned, "as usual the topic of mating has brought color to your cheeks." He sat back down on the floor, pulling her with him.

"I wanted to ground my presence here more fully to find out how much interference the increasing separation will cause, but I found many layers of materials between us and the ground," he explained. "It must be very difficult for your Folk to remain connected to the earth. I can feel the consciousness of trees deep below us, but above them there is a very dense substance, like the sidewalks I have seen before."

"Concrete is pretty hard," Rebecca agreed. "Under these area rugs we have hardwood floors. Below that are framing, concrete foundation, and then the ground. What are you trying to do?"

"On Thianely, our elemental abilities are effortless, or at least they used to be. Here, we must first contact the ground before we attempt to open our minds and discover what abilities work here. We need the extra support, because your planet has very uneven energetic stability."

Rebecca nodded agreeably. "Okay. What do you want to do first? But let's not spend too much time at it. I'm hungry again."

"It will take only a few of your minutes," Torin assured her, holding out a small red stone. "Concentrate on this firestone for a moment. Feel down into the ground below us, much as you did in your yarden."

Rebecca held the smooth, reddish brown stone on her left palm, closed her eyes, and imagined being inside the earth under the floor of the house. She shook slightly as a column of energy raced up her spine, shot out the top of her head, and hit the ceiling. The house shook like there'd been a minor earthquake. Torin quickly removed the firestone from her grasp, abruptly breaking off her connection. Rebecca shook her head in dismay, still dizzy from the experience.

Torin reached out a steadying hand. "Are you well, Rebecca?"

"I'm fine, Torin, but the ground here isn't very stable at all, except for the spot in the back yard. Under the house, down the street, and even within a few miles it looks like an accordion, all folded over in places with interrupted energy flow. There's no particular cohesion. I could feel the whole planet shifting. I got a bird's eye view of pockets of places with strong earth energy next to places drained of all force, like I was looking through an x-ray vision telescope. I'm surprised the Earth's crust can even handle the stress without completely cracking. What are we going to do about singing Balance here? The sound waves might cause terrible damage."

Torin pushed back a lock of hair that had fallen into his eyes, looking at her thoughtfully. "Rebecca, do you think you could scan the planet and mark the places where the earth force is strongest and weakest? If we are going to sing a clearing song and encourage the earth to let go of the atmosphere of suffering that enshrouds it, it will be more effective if sung in a very stable ground place. We might also have to use skip tones to avoid the weaker spots."

"I'd sure better find out the state of the ground before we sing," Rebecca agreed. "One tremor is enough. I think my parents have a world map that I can use as a template. And Liliar did teach me something about skip tones, how they move and undulate in stepwaves of sound. But let's wait until after breakfast. Either having all of that energy run through me increased my appetite, or I feel hungrier here in general."

"When your physical body or subtle bodies are missing the awareness you normally experience, it is perceived as a lack. I've noticed that many of the Folk on your planet feel very hungry for the energy that food cannot provide. They are never fully satisfied on any level and always feel that something is missing. Separation sickness creates ill health on many levels. And after that energetic episode you will probably need food right away.

I wanted to let you know that I put a fire shield around the house for extra protection. It seems to be working so far, as I was able to ground myself in the fire of my own nature. I also took a fire bath, and didn't singe anything. Perhaps your abilities will come more easily if you ground yourself in the water that flows within your body, at least until we find stable sources of the earth element here."

"Speaking of the physical, what would you like for breakfast?" Rebecca asked as they made their way into the kitchen. "Maybe if we cook something with our palms we could see how my fire technique holds up here."

"Do you think we should wait for your parents?"

Rebecca shook her head. "It's still pretty early. I hope that little tremor didn't wake them; they're really going to need their sleep. I know what a strain it was for me to get used to the idea of travel between planets. I remember actually feeling my brain ache when I first got to Thianely. Besides, I'm not sure how much of our story sunk in. I don't know how they'd feel about watching me shoot fire out of my palms. The first time I saw you do it, it completely freaked me out."

She opened the refrigerator. "What shall we have? Scrambled eggs, cheese omelets, hot oatmeal?"

Torin came up behind her to peer over her shoulder. "Hmm. Nothing from animals without their permission."

Rebecca turned around, closing the refrigerator door. "You may have to get used to eating oatmeal then. Maybe later we can stop by the organic grocery and pick up some less traumatized food."

She got out a pan, added oatmeal, and raised her eyebrows questioningly. "Where shall we cook it, Torin? I'm used to you flaming things out of doors, or else over a hearth. The last thing we need is to start the house on fire."

Torin took the pan from her, placing it on the table. "Here, this will work fine. Send heat to the food while keeping it from the pan. That will keep the surrounding area safe."

Rebecca measured filtered water into the pan, and then added oatmeal. Taking a deep breath, she concentrated on feeling the presence of water in her tissues, the flow of blood in her veins. She imagined heat pooling in her palms. Placing her hands over the pan, she focused on heating the oatmeal. Steam had just begun to rise from

23

the cereal when her parents walked in. Rebecca hesitated, but Torin urged her on.

"Keep going, you are doing fine, Rebecca." He turned to Griffin and Auran to bid them good morning, but they were too stunned to reply. They stood watching their daughter, blue flames shooting from her palms like a torch. When the oatmeal began to boil, Rebecca quickly took her hands away. Torin reached over to feel the coolness of the pan.

"You did it!" he said. Rebecca grinned, then noticed her parents' expressions. Auran had turned pale, while Griffin stared as if he couldn't quite trust his eyes.

"Rebecca, I thought in the bright light of morning things would seem different. But I didn't think they'd look this different! How the hell are we supposed to handle this anyway? I've been racking my brains to think of a way to tell the police, not to mention friends and family about your return, but this is beyond understanding. If we do try to explain it, you're going to be treated like some sort of lab experiment. Even if you refrain from doing things like this in public, you still look too damn different for people not to notice. Can't you at least do something about that glow around you?"

Rebecca shuddered once, and it seemed to Torin that she crumpled a little. She opened her mouth to speak, but Auran forestalled her.

"Don't you dare apologize for whatever has made you so happy," Auran ordered. "As for you, Griffin Bloom, you take your bad temper and even worse manners out of here until you can behave yourself. Who cares what we tell people? This isn't about them. What really matters is that Rebecca is home, and she's amazing."

While Griffin stood absorbing the force of Auran's anger, Rebecca said shakily, "Dad, Mom, I know this is a lot to take in; it was a lot for me too. I'm sorry if this all seems really frightening to you, but I can't make it go away. I wouldn't want to even if I could. I know it's hard to understand that there could possibly be a place where people do things that we think of as magic, but there it's as normal as our flipping a light switch or pushing a button to watch T.V. If this is too much, maybe Torin and I should go somewhere else. I mean, it's not like I could go back to school, anyway. Maybe we shouldn't tell anyone I'm back. I don't want to scare anyone."

Auran moved forward to put her hands on her daughter's shoulders, looking straight into her eyes. "Rebecca, for the rest of our lives, you are always welcome here, even if you turn purple and glow in the dark. And you too, young man," she said to Torin. She turned to Griffin, elbowing him sharply in the ribs. "Griffin," Auran said sharply, "I mean it. Apologize like an adult and then sit down and have some oatmeal. Think of the savings on the gas bill if we don't have to use the stove." She turned away to get bowls and spoons, quickly setting the table while Rebecca and Torin took their seats.

Griffin sat down somewhat sheepishly. "I'm sorry, you two, I am incredibly grateful to have you both here. I'm also completely overwhelmed by all of this. It's one thing to watch this kind of stuff on T.V. and another to see your own kid do the impossible. It's not just you having flaming palms, Rebecca, it's that you look so different and I missed it. I missed twelve months out of your life and it pisses me off. Hell, the only reason that your room was still the same is that neither of us believed you were really gone. I'm proud of you, I want you to know that. I guess I thought I'd dreamed last night. I am truly grateful you're home."

"It's okay, Dad. Here, have some oatmeal."

They put off discussing anything serious until after the meal was over and they'd all cleaned up. Rebecca's parents called in to work, taking the rest of the day off. Griffin explained to Torin it was one of the benefits of running one's own business as they sat down together in the living room to plan a strategy.

"For the time being," Auran suggested, "why don't we agree that we won't tell anyone else that you're home, unless it becomes necessary. With the exception of my mother and father, of course."

"The old harpy will probably go right back to treating me like carpet fuzz," muttered Griffin dolefully.

"Come on, Dad, think positively," Rebecca giggled. "Maybe she'll be so happy to see me her good mood will leak over onto you."

"She's almost worse when she's being nice," Griffin insisted. "She pats me on the shoulder and calls me 'Poor man,' then she makes a weird moaning noise in the back of her throat. The first time she did it I thought she was choking on something. It's ghastly."

"I'll call them soon," Auran insisted. "You can go hide in the office when they come over, Griff. I'll need help with Dad's wheelchair though."

Rebecca winced at the thought of her vibrant grandfather in a wheelchair.

"Thanks, Mom. I can't wait to see Grandpa, and Grandmother too, of course. By the way, besides creating fire, I also have some skill in healing. We were going to try some experiments to see which of our abilities work here and which don't. I didn't really get to that part of the story, my abilities, I mean. I was going to explain that part more gradually."

Griffin sat up interestedly. "I think my mind has already been blown pretty thoroughly, so why don't you tell us what else you can do. After the demonstration this morning, what could be more shocking?"

Rebecca exchanged a glance with Torin. "Plenty," she said. "I'll stick to generalities for awhile. Believe me, some of this can make your brain hurt."

"My head's already killing me," Griffin admitted. "That little earthquake this morning didn't help. You two must have felt it. It's strange that I didn't see it on the news."

Rebecca hesitated, not quite sure if she should claim responsibility. Torin shook his head slightly, and said, "On Thianely, we learn most of the information we need to know over a long period of time. Too much at once can stress the system. Your physical laws work differently here, and it takes time to become accustomed to experiences that stretch your idea of reality. Rebecca may at least be able to relieve your head pain."

Rebecca reached over to place her hands on Griffin's head. He sat patiently, muttering, "Now don't burn any holes in my skull, sweetie, I'm going to need those cells working to take this all in." He smiled as a cooling sensation trickled into his head.

"The pain's gone! Auran, it worked! Just think, if Rebecca puts her hands on your mother's head, maybe she could grow her a new personality."

Auran made a face. "Torin, don't listen to him. My mother isn't as bad as he makes her sound. She's just a little conservative. Griffin conveniently forgets to mention that he had hair down to his behind the first time they met. It took her a little while to get used to him is all."

"Yeah, about thirty years going on eternity," Griffin grumbled. "If she makes any comments about the length of your hair," he added, noting that Torin's was nearly to his shoulders, "tell the old bat that it's none of her business."

"Just for that, I'm going to go call them right now," Auran insisted, getting up off the sofa to use the hall phone. Rebecca sighed, relaxing into the sofa. "Now I really feel home again, Dad," she said, grinning. "Hearing you gripe about Grandmother is about as normal as Mom telling me to get my feet off the coffee table."

Griffin patted her knee. "Before they show up, why don't you two tell me a little more about your supernatural abilities, or I suppose I mean natural abilities? I know you told us part of why you were called to Thianely, Rebecca, to help balance things there, and you described the friends you've met. But I also have about fifty thousand questions about Thianely in general. Torin, how do you all get along with such amazing gifts? How does your economy work? Do you ever lie? Who are your world leaders?"

Rebecca reached over to kiss Griffin on the cheek. "Remember I told you, Dad, that Thianelians ask for what they need. They don't really have an economy the way you mean it. No one works for anyone else, and they don't have a form of money either. Kids learn from their parents and community, do a kind of walkabout, and remember knowledge of ages past by hanging around the Great Tree. Or at least they did before it was uprooted. It's so totally different there. No pollution, no theft or crime, no bad guys except for the Bolluxes, Drenics, and Bellorasps."

"You mentioned something about the Bolluxes. Funny that the name sounds like a U.K. curse word," Griffin mused. "But what are the Drenics and Bellorasps?"

"The Drenics are ice creatures that destroy everything they touch with their breath, and the Bellorasps suck the sound and soul out of any being with the misfortune to meet them," Rebecca explained.

"Their names sound as nasty as they do," Griffin commented. "Does everyone there speak the same language? I'm asking because your speech sounds slightly accented, Torin. How is it that you speak English so well?"

Rebecca glanced over at Torin. "I'm going to the bathroom while you explain this one," she said, patting Torin on the shoulder as she left. She passed Auran in the hall, still talking to her mother on the phone.

"I'm not exaggerating, Mother," Auran said in frustration. "It's important that you bring Dad over now. It's vital! No, you don't need to wash your hair; it's not a visit from the damn president. Okay, I apologize for swearing, but could you please come over right away?"

She listened for another moment, rolling her eyes. She put the phone down against one hip, motioning for Rebecca to go on past. "She's in her guilt trip mode," Auran explained. "I'll let her run on for a while to calm her down. She'll bring your grandfather over after she finishes complaining. Sorry sweetie, but it might take some time."

Rebecca had to laugh. "Some things never change. It's okay, Mom. Torin is in there entertaining Dad with Thianelian customs while I go to the bathroom. I'll meet you back in the living room."

Rebecca soon returned to her spot on the sofa, where her father sat with Torin, looking nonplused.

"Is this true?" he asked Rebecca, gesturing towards Torin. "He's really speaking a foreign language that I can somehow understand?"

"We both are," Rebecca admitted. "It was strange to me at first too, Dad, but I finally got the hang of it. It's really handy to think that every human being on Earth, everything in creation actually, understands the Old Tongue. In that way it's not really a foreign language at all. Think how communication between different cultures would improve if everyone remembered again."

"It is very convenient for speaking with other beings as well," Torin added. "Trees, rocks, this table here for instance." He motioned to the coffee table upon which Rebecca had automatically rested her feet. It began to float upward into the air a few inches, and then settled back down.

Griffin winced. "Besides the fact that I just saw the coffee table levitate, and get your feet off there, Rebecca, you're telling me that somehow my ears are hearing only English when you're speaking something else?"

Rebecca shook her head. "It's more like your ears are hearing a different language that your soul understands but your brain thinks is English."

"Okay, that's it," Griffin said, throwing up his hands. "That makes absolutely no sense to me at all. I've about reached my limit here. I'll have to hear about the rest of what you call normal later. Where's your mom?

"Grandmother was annoyed that mom wanted her to come over without telling her why," Rebecca explained. "You know she's never liked surprises much."

"Aren't you a lucky fellow," Griffin muttered to Torin. "You get to meet Rebecca's parents and grandparents all in one visit. We're not so bad, but don't let the old witch scare you off. Though I have to warn you she doesn't improve much on further acquaintance."

"It's okay, Dad," Rebecca reassured him. "Torin's used to dealing with much worse than Grandmother. Some of the Bolluxes make Grandmother look cuddly."

Auran stomped into the living room in disgust. "They'll be here, eventually. Mother wants to set her hair and change Dad's clothes. She's going to the grocery store too. She said if I won't tell her what's going on over the phone it must not be too important. Sorry, everyone, it looks like we'll have to wait for Mother to get over her snit."

"That's nothing new," Griffin said. "Remember when Rebecca disappeared and we wanted to tell your folks in person before they heard it on the news? The old witch wouldn't open the door until her hair dried properly, and she wouldn't interrupt your Dad's T.V. program so he could answer the door either. We had to wait outside on the porch for a half hour, and neither of us was in any shape to deal with her crap."

Auran sighed noisily. "Well, at least we have plenty of time to talk. Rebecca, could you tell us more about what you two need to do here? I know you need to plant that golden root somewhere to grow another Great Tree, but I didn't quite understand about the planetary singing thing. It sounds like quite an undertaking. There were some singing benefits for the victims of September 11th, but there have only been a couple other major concerts since then. Since 9/11 it would probably be easier to get people all over the world to shoot each other than to sing globally."

"What happened on September 11?" Rebecca asked curiously.

Griffin and Auran spent the next half hour describing the events resulting in the loss of the Twin Towers, and brought them up to date on current events around the world.

" As usual," Griffin commented, "many countries' human rights policies are appalling, not to mention the constant poverty, disease, and wars. You picked an ugly time to travel to earth, Torin,"

29

he added. "Although, come to think of it, our history is full of intensely brutish, violent times. We earth humans seem to be a trifle slow learning to get along with one another."

"Events are connected between our planets," Torin said. "On our planet time has become distorted and our abilities are being affected by the increasing separation. On your planet the suffering that has existed all over your world is becoming more frequent and more pervasive. Judging by your entertainment, violence is commonplace. It is difficult to heal wounds you have refused to acknowledge or become so accustomed to you rarely notice. Separation from each other has caused great pain here; your Folk need reminding of what they have forgotten. Yet each being must ultimately choose from his own will."

"To answer your question, Mom," Rebecca continued, "We need to help establish what's known on Thianely as a clearing song, The sound vibration actually sweeps away the dense pain and fear that shrouds the planet like a crumpled, smelly overcoat. Then we'll be singing a song of aemethra, or integrating song, that assists in reconnecting not only people here, but those on other worlds as well. Our friends on Thianely are already preparing to sing there, and we need to initiate it here. Torin and I were thinking about using maps to locate places of stability. Many places on earth are sort of energetically shaky, and not just fault lines either. I'm going to need to know about the weaker areas so as not to start earthquakes. And at some point, I have to find the right spot to plant the root from the Great Tree."

Griffin looked sadly over at Auran, and patted his daughter's knee. "You know, throughout the history of this planet there have been those who have come to kick us humans in the ass and tell us to wake up and get along. Most of our greatest teachers haven't fared too well. I want you both to know that I will do everything in my power to help you two, but forgive me if I don't hold out a lot of hope that our species is going to suddenly understand peace and love and brotherhood. You see before you a disillusioned ex-hippy.

Torin, I'm also having a difficult time knowing that you and my daughter have powers that, well, not only seem impossible, but also would be of great interest to our government. Unfortunately, our people here tend to use technology not only for gathering information, but also to achieve power over others. If these sort of people found out what you two can do so casually, without technology at all, well, I'm really worried about your safety."

"I understand your concern," Torin assured him. "We realize that what we do is not without the risk of discovery. We will try not to attract undue attention, but at some point, our efforts will be felt by every being on the planet that wishes to awaken. Rebecca has extraordinary abilities even on Thianely. She has proven that she can take care of herself, though many of her gifts will remain unknown until she needs them.

We are not yet certain how the state of this planet will affect our abilities, but I can tell you this, many of them exist beyond this present time. You have already heard my will to protect her as best I may. There are many constrictions and divisions here, and we will need to be able to stay centered even in these conditions; therefore, we must practice.

I also request access to your computer network, in order to contact those who would assist us. Many Folk will energetically hear the call of the clearing song, but there are those we must physically meet. Of the many Thianelians who have made the journey here before, some still remain."

Rebecca turned to him in surprise. "That's a great idea, Torin! The more help the better. I'd love to meet some earthbound Thianelians and hear their perspectives."

"I want to be here when you do," Griffin said. "This is like the science fiction books I used to read, aliens and everything, although you're not exactly short and green, Torin."

Auran laughed, and, excusing herself for a few moments, motioned to Rebecca to join her. She pulled Rebecca into the kitchen and shut the door.

"Okay, I have a few questions of my own, sweetie. You said that Thanelian women don't use birth control because they don't need it. I guess that means they don't go through menopause either. How does the whole thing work, and can I learn myself?"

Rebecca smiled at her mother's enthusiasm. "Well, Mom," she explained, "Thianelians are only fertile when they've decided to have children. The Tree Folk have regular reproductive seasons, the Griffin Folk I don't know about for sure, but the Fire, Air and Earthen Folk are more or less in charge of their own fertility. I asked my friend Leva, remember the tree person I told you about, if she had a period once and she thought it was the most bizarre thing she'd ever heard. She told me that Tree Folk only leak sap when injured or grieving. To her losing life force energy once a month seemed very inefficient and for some reason I went a whole year without even noticing I never had my period. It seemed normal there. But I don't know if it's something I could teach you since I'm not sure how I did it."

Auran sighed. "Well, it was worth a try. I got the idea from talking to your grandmother. She was so unpleasant during menopause, I'd just as soon skip it, although your father was convinced she was experiencing menopause from the moment he met her. Keep me posted, though, if you do figure it out."

"Okay, Mom, I will. Now, how about some lunch."

Chapter 4

"Griff, could you come here a moment?" Auran called. They'd all eaten lunch and were back in the living room waiting for Auran's parents to arrive. Griffin and Rebecca were teaching Torin how to play cards. Auran had seen some odd movement through the French doors and had gotten up to take a closer look. She leaned against the glass, peering out into the back yard.

"I thought I saw, well, I don't know exactly what it was."

Rebecca looked at Torin in surprise. She hadn't expected her mother to be able to see anything in the back yard, at least not yet. She and Torin followed Auran and Griffin out onto the deck, where Gilden the unicorn immediately bowed his horned head in respect. Griffin stepped backward in alarm, nearly treading on Torin's foot.

"Tell me there's not a unicorn by the hot tub," Griffin insisted.

Auran looked about in awe. "Faeries in the flowers, tree ladies and gnomes, a dwarf, a faun, and a unicorn! I'm not even on drugs and I see them all clearly."

"Why is there a unicorn by the hot tub?" Griffin repeated.

"We unicorns love bubbling hot springs," Gilden informed him calmly. "The heat is good for the horn and hooves, and your deck is uncluttered by fallen leaves. The dry leaves scratch my coat."

"Oh." Griffin looked around in bemusement. Auran was circling the perimeter, seeing if she'd missed any of the faery-tale creatures that had taken up residence in their back yard. Rebecca stood watching her parents to make sure neither of them collapsed in a faint. Meanwhile, Torin occupied himself by sitting down on the deck and scratching a particularly itchy spot by Gilden's left ear.

Griffin was saved from further contemplation of the impossible creatures frolicking in his yard by the incessant ringing of the doorbell.

"Hey everyone," he called, "the Wicked Witch of the East is here."

"Hush now, Griff," Auran admonished him, leaving the lawn somewhat reluctantly. "I already said you could go hide in the office if you don't want to see her."

"I wouldn't miss this meeting for anything," Griff grinned. "Your mother confronting proof of extraterrestrial life, this I have got to see! Rebecca, you and Torin can go sit in the kitchen until we

33

prepare your grandparents. We don't want to spring you on them unexpectedly and give anyone a heart attack."

While Rebecca and Torin headed for the kitchen, Griffin and Auran went to answer the door. "Let me do the talking, Griff," Auran insisted. "I think they'll take it better coming from me."

Griffin shrugged. "No problem. But let me help get your dad out of the car first."

Auran opened the door. Her mother stood outside, one finger still poised over the doorbell.

"What took you so long?" Hazel demanded, pushing past Auran into the hallway. She glanced over at Griffin. "Matthew could use a hand, whenever you're ready." She submitted to Auran's brief embrace, and then preceded her into the living room. Hazel placed her large black purse on the coffee table, sat down in Griffin's favorite chair near the sofa, and eyed her daughter sternly.

"Now what was so darned important that you couldn't spit it out over the phone?"

"If you wait until Dad gets here, I'll tell both of you at once," Auran said somewhat nervously. It never ceased to amaze her that she could still find her mother intimidating, even now that she was an adult. She wondered what it would have been like if Griffin's parents hadn't died when he was young. Perhaps her mother-in-law would have been easier to deal with than Hazel. It was hard to imagine anyone being more difficult than her mother. They waited in silence until Griffin had wheeled Matthew into the room and settled him near the sofa. Griffin sat down on the sofa while Auran bent over to give her father a kiss. Hazel waited impatiently.

"Don't tell me you're going to have another child at your age!" Hazel burst out. "When will you accept that the girl is gone and there's nothing you can do about it? Like I've told you before, you have to get over it and go on with your lives. But that doesn't mean for you to start over. People your age wind up having retarded kids."

"Thanks for all the support and encouragement," Griffin mumbled sarcastically. Luckily Hazel was slightly hard of hearing and, as usual, missed his commentary.

"Mother," Auran said loudly, "could you listen for a moment and not jump to conclusions? We're not having another baby. Something amazing has happened." She reached over and grasped her father's hand. "Mother, Dad, Rebecca is back. She's home."

Although Matthew had difficulty speaking, there was nothing wrong with his hearing. His eyes immediately began to tear up, and his grip on Auran's hand grew tighter.

"What are you talking about?" Hazel protested. "The girl's been gone for a year already. Are you saying that the FBI finally located her? Where has she been? Is she in the hospital?"

"No, Grandmother Hazel, I'm right here." Rebecca stood in the entryway of the living room, taking a few moments to simply stare at her grandparents. Grandmother Hazel looked even more forbidding than usual. Her white hair was pulled up in a tight bun on top of her head so that her skin stretched tautly over her face. The frown lines around her mouth were more pronounced, and her eyes had sunken into their sockets. She'd always been a large woman, and although not overweight, she appeared dense, unmovable. Griffin had often joked that she had the personality of an army tank with the bulk to match.

Rebecca almost gasped when she saw her once vigorous grandpa reduced to this old man in a wheelchair. His head slumped down to the left and his whole left side appeared shrunken. Once gray, his hair had turned completely white. But his blue eyes were clear, and even though tears trickled slowly down his cheeks, the crooked smile he gave her was the one she was used to, wide and full of joy.

Auran stepped aside as Rebecca walked to her grandfather and knelt down by his chair. "Hi, Fort," she said. "It's Sport. I'm back." She leaned over carefully so that he could hug her as hard as he was able. Holding onto one of his hands, she turned to address her grandmother.

"It's really me, Grandmother, how are you?"

"How am I?" her grandmother replied, leaning forward in her chair and shaking a finger at Rebecca. "I don't know what you mean by coming here and trying to deceive us all, young lady. My granddaughter is dead, probably killed by some maniac. How dare you, asking me how I am, taking advantage of our grief and manipulating our feelings! I know perfectly well you are not my granddaughter; you don't even look like her."

"Okay, that's it, you sanctimonious, unfeeling witch," Griffin said angrily. "If you're so stubborn you can't even see what's right in front of your eyes, it's hopeless even talking to you."

"It's okay, Dad," Rebecca said. "I look kind of odd to me too. How about if you ask me something only I would know, Grandmother.

35

You and Grandpa look different to me too. A lot can happen in one year."

Hazel pursed her lips and nodded. "All right," she said grudgingly. "What do you call your favorite chocolate cookies, the name you gave them when you were five?"

Rebecca smiled. "Snoreos, because Grandpa always ate them before bed and I thought they made him snore."

Hazel stood up and came around to where Rebecca sat holding Fort's hand. "I suppose it could be you," she admitted. She bent down to give Rebecca a kiss.

"Now tell me, where have you been for a whole year, scaring us half to death. No phone calls, no letters. Look at poor Matthew; if it weren't for you, he'd still be..."

At this point, inside her mind Rebecca could hear the familiar refrain of a song she and her parents had created for moments like these.

> "Guilt trips, guilt trips, guilt trips for me and you...
> I did this for you; you did nothing for me,
> Guilt trips, guilt trips, guilt trips for me and you...
> After all we've done for you, the least you could do...
> Guilt trips, guilt trips, guilt trips for me and you..."

She looked up to see Griffin drumming his fingers on the coffee table in rhythm to the song. He grinned, winking slyly.

"I'd better go get Torin," Auran interjected. "This explanation requires a bit of help. Mother, Rebecca, why don't you two have a seat. I'll be right back."

Rebecca made herself comfortable on the floor next to Fort's wheelchair, while her grandmother chose a place on the sofa close to Rebecca. Seeing his favorite chair unoccupied at last, Griffin quickly claimed it. Auran returned with Torin, introduced him to her parents, then sat down on Griffin's lap. Torin, settling himself on the floor next to Rebecca, soon found himself being scrutinized by a white haired old lady with a deep frown on her face.

"So young man, what have you got to say for yourself?" Hazel demanded.

Torin stared at Hazel politely. "I do not understand the question, but from the energy of the asking, it appears you are angry with me."

"Nonsense," Hazel dismissed him. "I don't know you well enough to bother about you one way or the other. I want to know what you mean by keeping my granddaughter away for a year and frightening us all half to death and giving my poor husband a stroke."

Griffin rolled his eyes, but before he could say anything, Torin began to laugh. Hazel glared at him disapprovingly.

"I understand your grief at losing Rebecca," Torin finally said when he'd finished chuckling. "I was amused at the idea that I could have kept Rebecca anywhere she chose not to be and that your husband's stroke was caused by another. His body responded to a sense of unease in the only way available to him at the time. Rebecca may describe these healing matters much more clearly than I. Perhaps she will also be able to explain how difficult it is to speak with those who listen only with the ears of their egos rather than the ease of their hearts."

"That's telling her," Griffin called from his chair across the room.

Rebecca leaned over to Torin and kissed him on the cheek. "Thanks," she whispered in his ear, "but I don't think anyone can explain anything to Grandmother that she doesn't want to hear."

"Mother, Dad," Auran said. "You're going to have a hard time believing where Rebecca has been for so long. We'll get into that in a minute. But first Griff and I have been trying to figure out what we're going to do about the ongoing FBI investigation into her disappearance. For very good reasons we don't want anyone to know she's back. As you can see she's very different than before, and she can do things that are not considered, well, possible. For the time being we're going to ask you both to keep quiet about what you're going to hear."

Fort nodded as best he could from his wheelchair, although Hazel just snorted. The expression on her mother's face reminded Auran of when she was a child, had done something wrong, and was trying to defend herself. It was Hazel's "this better be good" face.

Rebecca started by recounting her adventures on Thianely, beginning with Torin tugging her there through the puddle in the street. She described her experiences with the Fire Folk, the Tree

Devas, meeting Leva the tree maiden, Tehy of the Air and Griffin Folk, the Merfolk, Liliar of the Bolluxes, and an abridged version of her journey across Thianely. Hazel sat quietly for the most part, harrumphing here and there when something seemed particularly unbelievable. She insisted on examining Torin's hands and merely shrugged when his palms lit up in alternating colored spirals of flame.

Fort listened with increasing excitement, leaning so far in his chair that Rebecca had to catch him before he toppled over. As Rebecca spoke she maintained physical contact with her grandfather, holding his hand, patting his knee gently. Fort began to feel a tingling radiating up his body, starting at his feet and rising to his head.

For the first time in months, he could feel sensation in the left side of his body. A strange sense of wonder filled him. Here was Rebecca, back from an incredible adventure, yet it seemed almost commonplace compared to the changes he felt in his own body. Nerves that had been asleep began to awaken. His skin could feel the pressure of the air. The solid bulk of his chair pressed against his hips and thighs. He wiggled his toes, stretched out one foot, and began to move facial muscles that had been frozen. Inside his head the tingling raced from one side of his brain to the other, igniting memories of earlier times, ideas he hadn't thought of in years.

"Absolute hogwash," Hazel concluded, as Rebecca finished her travelogue. Torin offered to get the items they'd brought from Thianely to show her, but before he could rise, they heard a loud guffaw from the wheelchair.

"Hazel, darling," Fort said loudly, "shut up and listen to what Sport is telling you. The touch of her hand has done more for me than all those doctors could do in a year. It's got to be real, otherwise I wouldn't be here telling you to be quiet."

As Hazel gaped in astonishment and promptly collapsed into tears, Auran and Griffin leaped from their seats.

"Oh Grandpa, I'm so glad to be able to talk to you again," Rebecca said, throwing her arms around her grandfather and hugging him fiercely. They all crowded around until Fort told them all to back off so that he could try walking again. He needed support on both sides, but for the first time in a year, he could stand upright and even take a few steps.

"Rebecca," he crowed, "if we could bottle whatever it is you just did, the world would be a much happier place. I feel like a man again, instead of a withered lump in a wheelchair! It's been so frustrating not being able to walk or speak. I understand that we have to keep a lid on things, but it seems a shame not to be able to share what you've learned."

"Well, Fort," Rebecca began, "we didn't quite get to that part yet. Torin came back with me to help the planet. We're going to initiate a clearing song here, a tonal vibration that will complement the one on Thianely. Everyone who's willing gets to assist us, in his or her own way. It's hard to explain, but we're working together with other planets as well, to maintain a kind of balance."

Fort shrugged. "I don't really know what you're talking about, sweetie, but I'll help however I can. Let me know what you need; you've got it." He reached over to shake Torin's hand. "I guess you think pretty highly of Rebecca, or you wouldn't have come with her to this god-awful mess we've made of things here. I want to thank you for keeping her safe and bringing her back to us. And now, if you don't mind, I'm going to take my wife home. Griffin, you give us a call any time you need us and we'll be right over. Hazel, let's go."

Hazel, overcome with emotion, for once couldn't speak. She took her husband's arm, and with Griffin's assistance, helped him walk out to the car. Griffin returned a few minutes later, sighing with satisfaction.

"Who would've thought the old broad could ever be rendered speechless? It was priceless, sweetheart, just priceless."

"Oh, Rebecca," Auran hugged her, "I'm so happy! Thank you so much for Dad. My mother doesn't mean to be so difficult," she added to Torin. "She's not usually quite so rude, but it's been a really tough year."

"Well, I'm completely fried," Griffin said, plopping down onto his chair. "What time is it anyway? I suppose someone should go see if those creatures are still hanging around the backyard. You don't suppose that unicorn will dig up the grass with his horn do you?"

"We'll go check, Dad," Rebecca offered. "Why don't you and Mom take a break? I know this has all been a lot to deal with."

"Unicorns, faeries, your grandmother, and a miracle all in one day. I'll say it's a lot. Pinch me if I seem to be going crazy." Griffin leaned back in his chair and closed his eyes. Auran stretched out on the sofa and did the same, while Torin and Rebecca headed out the French doors to check on the visitors in the back yard. They spent the rest of the day lounging in the yarden listening to the songs of the wind faeries, the stories of the fauns, and recovering from her grandparents' visit.

"My grandmother has always been hard to deal with," Rebecca commented, as she and Torin swung slowly back and forth in the hammock. "But this time listening to her really wiped me out."

"She is a very angry person," Torin agreed. "And she does not keep her feelings to herself."

"That's for sure."

"When I was young and very angry I once burnt part of Grandfather's garden by not keeping my energy contained. Although the Devas helped the plants heal, and I made my amends, the pain sounds of the plants and trees haunted me for months. All the trees of Thianely felt what I had done. I became what you call infamous. Though I was only three years old at the time, the name Fire Boy came to be known all over Thianely. That is why my friends there are well acquainted with my temper, even though Grandfather taught me how to manage it. I have never forgotten the sounds of the pain I caused either, although the garden forgave me long ago. I think your Grandmother is very frightened and uses anger to hide it. She longs for balance like many of your Folk. It is the nature of creation to seek connection with all that exists. It is difficult to do that here sometimes."

"I'll say!" Rebecca agreed. "But Torin, I never would have thought of you having such a temper, even though you've mentioned it before. Most of the time you seem so calm."

"I have my Grandfather and his garden to thank for that," Torin said. "I also learned about emotions in my visits to the Great Tree, although I received few answers to questions of my parentage. It makes sense that I would have to learn a greater amount of control being the Fire Lord's son. As you have had to learn patience being Hazel's granddaughter."

Rebecca snorted. "I'll have to try that one out on Dad; I'm sure he'll appreciate it. It is strange to think how messy people here are with their emotions. Depending on the culture, of course, but it still seems like most of us are not taught how to be anything but repressed or explosive. A world of extremes." She yawned, turning to cuddle Torin in the gently swaying hammock.

"I can't believe I'm tired again!" she said in annoyance. "I either need more sleep, or megavitamins."

"Rest now," Torin suggested, pulling her even closer as she settled into sleep. Breathing in the fragrance of her hair, the softness of her skin, he drifted into a sort of half dream. The movement of the hammock lulled him. An occasional breeze sifted the scents of flowers about them, as faeries sprinkled rose petals across their legs. While still maintaining awareness of the creatures in the garden, the sun warming his face, Torin held Rebecca close.

Chapter 5

After a brief dinner, as everyone was still recovering from the events of the day, they all turned in early. Torin felt a pang of longing as Rebecca went upstairs to her room, but exhaustion soon claimed him in a deep sleep. Rebecca could hear her father snoring from the room across the hall, so she knew her parents had dropped off quickly. Every time Rebecca closed her eyes, however, pictures of her friends on Thianely kept moving across her inner vision.

Tehy, his wings folded behind him and tail uncoiled upon the purple ground, stood with his arm about his mate, Liliar. They were accompanied by many of the Griffin clan, more of the fierce warriors making ready to fly to the Earthen Folk's village to protect the singers gathered there. Next she saw Imanayon, Torin's grandfather, gathering his Fire Folk into large groups to defend their village.

The scene shifted to the purple waters of Thianely. Hundreds of the Merfolk, tails moving in glistening waves, hurried home to the deepest levels of the ocean. She watched the churning of their tails, the movement like fervent schools of fish, and then the image changed. She was back at the Threshold of the Trees, watching as the oldest Tree Folk began to shift their tree roots to form a protective outer perimeter around the youngest. Their leader, Meridwen, smiled at Rebecca as if she was able to see her, but when Meridwen spoke, Rebecca could not make out the words.

Rebecca sat up, wondering if she were truly seeing Thianely in present time, or was somehow being caught up on events that had already occurred. She lay down again, idly wondering how Leva, their half Tree Folk, half Earthen Folk friend was doing. As soon as she had the thought, Rebecca could see Leva, about to enter the Time Gate on the outskirts of the Earthen village. Rebecca watched as Leva disappeared from view for an instant, and then reappeared inside the shimmering, nearly transparent energy gate. Suddenly, Rebecca saw two dark figures appear as well, and gasped in horror as they enveloped Leva in a black vapor. Leva crumpled to the ground as the two figures fragmented into thousands of tiny pieces.

Rebecca was up, out of the bed, and dressed before Torin had had time to poke his head through her door. At her look of relief, he slipped into her room quietly, trying not to wake her parents across the hall.

"Liliar woke me," he said. "The Earthen Folk are taking Leva back to her grandmother Imelina's house. But they don't know exactly what happened or what to do for her. How did you find out?"

Rebecca sat down morosely on the edge of her bed.

"Torin, I lay down to go to sleep and saw the whole thing. Leva stood inside the Time Gate and all of a sudden two dark creatures showed up. When they shrouded her in some kind of cloudy stuff, she fell. I also saw Tehy, Liliar, Imanayon, Meridwen, and the Merfolk. I wasn't sure if I was seeing events now, or what happened previously. Some of it seemed disjointed. I thought the Gate was already being guarded by the Griffin Folk, but I didn't see any of them with Leva there."

"Liliar said that several of the Griffin guards at the Gate were killed by Bolluxes," Torin explained sadly. "And Leva was attacked by Drenics. You know that the Bellorasps and Bolluxes are attacking all over Thianely. They have polluted the rivers to drive the Merfolk into the ocean and off patrol of the tributaries. The Ice Lord of the northern region, Skelric, has also been assisting the Bolluxes. Skelric's mate, Drenica, is Queen of the Drenics. I've heard of the Drenics, but never have come in contact with one. From what little I know, the poisonous odor of Ice Drenics is fatal. Imelina says that Leva is still alive, probably because some of the energy in the Gate protected her. I didn't even know Drenics could survive that far south."

"I don't think they can," Rebecca said, stroking his arm gently. "The ones I saw in the Time Gate splintered like black icicles. What do you think, should we go back?"

Torin shook his head. "Liliar says we're needed here, and they have the best healers on Thianely looking after Leva. I already knew she was in danger, Rebecca; I saw her lifeline. Her palm showed a break in the line, back before we even left the Threshold of the Trees."

Rebecca sat beside Torin for a moment, feeling helpless, but at last she jumped to her feet. "The Life Water! I need to save some for planting the next Great Tree, but there should be enough to give Leva. Torin, I need your help to transport it to Thianely. I'll be right back."

Rebecca grabbed the small flask of water that she'd brought from Thianely and ran to the bathroom to get a plastic bottle. Carefully pouring a tiny amount of the precious liquid into the bottle, she motioned Torin to the floor.

"I'm going to try something beyond sending this between thought," she said, placing the bottle between them on the carpet. "I want you to concentrate with me so that I can send it to a time right before the Drenics got her. Can you let Liliar know it's coming? For some reason I can't contact anyone unless I'm almost asleep, and even then it's kind of haphazard."

"It is normal for people of your Earth to experience much of their awareness in the dream state," Torin said kindly. "On Earth I dream more as well, although I have a strong connection with Liliar whether awake or asleep. I will send her the message now."

He briefly closed his eyes and pictured Liliar, the Bollux singstress who'd become their friend. He sent her the picture of the flask and tried to include the idea of it arriving earlier than current time, but he wasn't quite sure that Liliar knew what he meant.

"Now what would you have me do?" he asked. Rebecca clasped his hands with hers and visualized the flask arriving on Thianely before Leva collapsed. She let her mind go blank, and directed her will to catapult the small bottle through time. As she felt a burst of heat and light from Torin's palms, she focused their combined energy on the flask of water between them. As soon as the energy contacted the bottle, it turned several brilliant colors that shimmered, shifted and shot up toward the ceiling like a fireworks display. When the colors finally subsided, they saw that the little bottle had vanished.

Rebecca and Torin looked at each other in amazement, finally turning their gazes upward. A huge singe mark streaked the ceiling, slowly dropping ash onto the carpet. Torin immediately checked in with Liliar to see if the water had been received, while Rebecca collapsed on the bed, vaguely wondering what to do about the discoloration on the ceiling.

"They got it!" Torin announced in satisfaction. "Liliar said it already worked. Leva remains somewhat weak, but she is well enough. Liliar says that Leva's being and body stayed connected by only a thin cord. The Life Water has brought her back to herself."

Suddenly Torin felt a curious weakness overtake him and barely managed to make it up to Rebecca's bed, where he immediately fell asleep. Rebecca lay down beside him, somewhat weary herself. She glanced over at the clock to see that it was 1:00 a.m. Not only was it very late, but that burst of intention had severely depleted them both.

"I guess everything takes more energy here," she mused. "We'd better get up early though. I have a feeling we'll be spending the day cleaning." She set the alarm for several hours later and joined Torin in slumber.

Chapter 6

Rebecca and Torin were both awakened by a knock on the door.

"Rebecca," Auran called. "It's past ten, and you should probably be up soon. Torin's not answering his door either so maybe you can wake him after you get up. Breakfast will be ready in about twenty minutes."

Rebecca rolled over and sat up, while Torin sleepily rubbed his eyes.

"I must've turned off the alarm earlier," Rebecca muttered. "I didn't mean for us to sleep quite this long."

"We needed the rest," Torin assured her, sitting up as well. "It takes effort to send objects such a long distance. Remember when you couldn't recall how to do it, and Liliar had to sing the Queen Egg back to the stronghold of the Griffins?"

"Oh, yes," Rebecca said. "I forgot about that. It is harder here to do many things, so I guess I should be happy we succeeded, especially for Leva's sake. Whew! That was tiring. You didn't even make it back downstairs." She pointed up at the ceiling. "And it was a little messy, too."

Torin leaned over to kiss her good morning. Somehow, they both forgot that Auran was making breakfast and Torin was supposed to be downstairs in the guest room. Rebecca felt a rush of energy from her head to her toes, and without even thinking about it, she pulled Torin closer. He looked down at Rebecca, seeing her blue eyes glowing brightly up at him without hesitancy, and he felt his restraint weaken and fade. All of those months on Thianely he'd waited, since Rebecca had not felt the same urgency of the mating instinct there.

She reached up to him, running her hands through his long hair, feeling his strong jaw and the smooth skin of his face with her fingertips. The ends of his hair brushed across her cheeks as he leaned closer. She'd never felt ready to touch him fully, and now each time she felt his skin against hers thousand of tiny energy ripples moved through her body. It felt exciting and comfortable at the same time, very familiar.

"We've done this many times before," she said, watching the pupils of his green eyes widen and feeling the center spiral of his chest heat up.

"Rebecca," Torin said, trying to calm his breathing and hold onto the last vestiges of his control, "I need your help. Before, you were not fully open to me, and now that you are, your lack of containment is dissolving mine. You must learn to moderate your responses to me here. On Thianely you were not ready, and here your parents are not. We do not yet have the time I would wish for us to spend together. Also, when we mate, all our previous lives as mates will become more present. And the last time, we were of the Dragon Folk. It may be that we would take such forms again, and there would be more from such a mating than singe marks on the ceiling."

Rebecca laughed, turning slightly pink. "I forgot. You're right; we have enough to explain without burning the house down. You'd better get up before I grab you again. This containment thing is tough. It was easier when I was too embarrassed to even think about it. Now I feel tingly all over, like you have a magnet inside you pulling me."

Torin sighed and got up. "That is a good description of what it feels like to meet one's mate. It intensifies with age and experience. The more lives two people have together, the deeper the bond. Come, let us both get up. I had already agreed we would not be sharing a sleeping space, but we have. Now we know that your parents were right to be concerned. I do not know if intentions to avoid reproducing work well here, Rebecca. Most of our Folk do not have a problem while they are here, but you are from the Earth."

"Do you want to use the shower?" Rebecca asked, as Torin ran a hand through his hair.

Torin closed his eyes for a moment as rippling waves of blue flame undulated up and down his body. He opened his eyes and smiled. "This is faster. Would you prefer a fire bath as well?"

"I always forget about fire bathing," Rebecca admitted as she came to stand beside him. "It really saves on changing one's clothes, that's for sure."

By the time they arrived in the kitchen, Auran and Griffin were well on their way through a stack of pancakes. Rebecca and Torin soon joined them, and for a while the only sounds were of food being consumed.

"Mom, I'm afraid we made a little mess on the ceiling last night," Rebecca began, putting down her fork and relaxing into her chair.

"Let me guess," Griffin said, "You were having a Mary Poppins tea party and spilled jam up there or something."

"Not exactly," Rebecca said, and went on to explain the night's adventures.

Griffin shook his head in dismay. "Well, that's one I wouldn't have guessed. But your friend's all right, that's the important thing. And regarding the singe, I think after we clean it up we have extra paint to cover the mark. I can take a look later."

Auran was looking at Rebecca intently. "Do you mean to tell me that you sent an object to another planet and it arrived at the moment it was needed?"

"Something like that," Rebecca agreed.

"So, couldn't you have sent a message to warn Leva before it even happened? Like, do you think you could go back to before September 11th, say, and tell someone in the government? Or even move the terrorists to another place, like a jail cell?"

Rebecca exchanged a glance with Torin. "I don't think so, Mom. First of all, interfering with events that affect so many lives has too much of an effect on the way history goes. I don't feel qualified to make those kinds of decisions. Besides, telling stuff to most people here wouldn't work because they'd only believe you afterwards. Even though Leva did have a kind of advance warning from Torin that she was in danger, she still chose to do what she did. Also, Torin and I were both exhausted sending a small bottle. I don't think I could handle sending a terrorist anywhere, especially one whose intention was so opposed to mine. Intention takes energy, you know. Opposing another's intention takes even more."

"This is the kind of speculation that I could see the government doing, if they ever got their hands on you two," Griffin broke in. "That reminds me, what are we going to do about the FBI? If anyone sees and recognizes you, Rebecca, there will be media coverage and all kinds of investigation."

"We don't want to keep you both cooped up in the house," Auran said. "We're just not sure what to do. I know it seems silly to talk about the future in regular terms, Rebecca, but we had planned on you going to college. We don't see how it could work though."

Rebecca understood how her parents felt, but the idea of going to college when she had absorbed so much information from the record keeping crystals on Thianely seemed absurd. Plans she'd made

48

as a child about what she'd be when she grew up sounded like faery tales to her now. So many of the values she'd had before were irrelevant to her; they were too associated with old ways of thinking.

"How about next week we take a trip out to the lake?" Griffin suggested. "We could even take your parents, Auran, if they want to come. Now don't go all cross-eyed on me, I've suggested excursions with your parents before. Oh, okay, maybe I haven't. Things are different now, though. Torin can fry your mother with his flaming palms if she misbehaves."

Auran nodded. "I think a vacation is a great idea, Griff. We can take a few weeks and mull things over. It's so calm and peaceful out there, I'm sure we'll be able to come up with some sort of plan. We won't have to worry about anyone spotting Rebecca either."

"You're in for a real treat," Griffin said to Torin. "There's boating and fishing, but no one else lives around the lake since it's a protected area. A client of mine helped build the lake, it's manmade, and so he had a small cabin close by. He sold it to me for a pittance. It's at Lake Sacandaga. Auran and I need to check in at the office, but we can probably leave in four or five days."

"That sounds great, Dad," Rebecca said. "I think it may be a good location for singing aemethra."

"What was that for again?" Griffin asked.

"Aemethra is a word the Thianelians use to describe a bridal knot woven from crystal. It symbolizes the weaving together of two souls in marriage, separate crystals, but connected at many points. In this case, aemethra means the interconnection of all of the planets together to increase the Balance on each. It also symbolizes the interconnectedness of all of creation that we are reaffirming through song. First we sing a clearing song here like the ones sung on Thianely and her neighboring planets, Hevald and Torildian, and then all the different planets sing aemethra together. After that things should get really interesting."

"Things aren't exactly dull right now," Griffin commented.

"Rebecca," Auran said, "I don't want you two to be stuck in the house, but I'm not sure if it would be appropriate for you two to be seen in the neighborhood. You missed your last birthday, so your father and I wanted you to go pick out something. Maybe if you go shopping in out of the way places and use your abilities to poof yourself places?"

49

"I like that, Mom," Rebecca said, "We'll poof ourselves around."

At that moment they all heard a clatter of hooves across the wood floor. Gilden the unicorn stood politely in the kitchen doorway.

"Excuse the interruption," he said quietly, "I would not normally take the initiative to enter your home without invitation, but there is a creature just arrived who wishes to converse with Rebecca. It appears to be of some import."

They quickly followed Gilden out to the back yard where they immediately saw who he meant. Ringed by every fantastical creature in the vicinity was an enormous dragon, its sandy colored scales being brushed by satyrs holding willow wands, its lavender eyelids stroked by wind nymphs. Two dwarves trimmed the beast's long claws, while all manner of faeries played tag along its broad back.

Auran and Griffin stared in awe. Without even opening its eyes the dragon turned its head slightly, acknowledging them in a rasping dragon voice.

"Well met, Old Friends, your presence has been greatly anticipated. If you gaze aloft, you will see why I, Gandonel of the Earth Dragon Clan, have come."

Torin, Rebecca, Auran, and Griffin looked up. Far away they could make out what looked like two dark clouds amassing on opposite sides of the sky. As they all watched, the indistinct shapes hurtled toward one another, attacking furiously. The shapes became more distinct as the battle progressed until they became recognizable as enormous dragons, thousands of them, warring in the sky. On one side the dragons were green, brown, or gold, on the other they were red or black.

Griffin shook his head slowly. "This will certainly liven up the evening news. 'Large Dragon Armies Clobber Each Other Over the New York Skyline, more at 11:00.' I only hope the air traffic controllers don't freak out."

"How absolutely beautiful," Auran murmured, dividing her time between looking up and staring at the dragon lounging in the grass.

"Don't worry, Dad," Rebecca assured him. "No one can see them but us. It's just some of the old Guardians showing up. They must be really bored if this is what they're spending their time doing." She caught Torin's eye and sighed. "Well, I suppose we'd better go

50

talk to them. Or maybe I ought to. Mom, Dad, I have to go change. I hope it doesn't bother you."

Griffin paused in his perusal of the sky to look at her disbelievingly. "I'm witnessing a whole firmament full of mythical creatures battling each other and you're worried about changing your clothes?"

Torin shook his head, about to explain, but Rebecca couldn't wait any longer. She stood up, and stepping down from the deck, walked over to the dragon in the yard. She reached over, humming a sort of rumbling chant, and touched the dragon's scaly back.

"Thank you, Gandonel," she said, and began to change. The shape of her head shifted, her features becoming indistinct. Her body softened, spreading out and dissolving into a blurry, amorphous cloud. All at once edges began to form, and the whole mass lengthened and stretched into the silvery, transparent outline of an immense dragon with huge lapis-colored eyes. The silver dragon that was Rebecca grew legs and claws, and large iridescent wings. She flapped her huge wings slowly and rose up into the air, becoming more solid as she did so. She flew higher and higher until finally she was so distant, she became just another one of the dragon-shaped forms. Soon, they could barely make her out.

Griffin turned to Torin. "Can you do that too?" he asked, motioning after his dragon daughter.

Torin nodded. "It is one of many forms I've had before. Gandonel helped her remember dragonness, but because of the promise I made to you I could not accompany her."

"What was that?" Griffin asked in bemusement, watching as Auran made her way over to the large dragon on the lawn. She knelt down by one large forefoot and began to scrape her nails over the back of it. Gandonel rumbled in contentment.

"Rebecca and I were mates during our last incarnation as dragons. If we both regained our previous forms, the urge to mate would be dragon sized."

Griffin flushed slightly in embarrassment. "Oh."

For Rebecca the change to dragon felt like a warm bath in bubbles of clouds. Moving her great wings was a relief after having such tiny, cramped little shoulder blades. She headed straight for the middle of the dragon battle, though at first the enormous creatures were too busy clawing and breathing fire to take much notice. When

51

Rebecca shouted at the top of her mind in dragon speech, the great beasts stopped their fury in surprise. Soon both dragon leaders, one green and the other red, flew up to her somewhat sheepishly, taking care to blow her flames of welcome and respect.

The green dragon with golden eyes let out puffs of gold flame, hovering in mid air. "I am Darnellian of the Golden Air Drakes, Leader of the Cloud-spinner Clan. I command the Dragons of Air and Earth." Rebecca nodded and blew a green fire in greeting.

The other dragon, a vermillion red with soot black eyes, gave a quick puff in bright yellow, and announced his title as well. "I am Forellan of the Fire Drakes, Leader of the Starflame Clan. I command the Dragons of Fire and Star."

Rebecca acknowledged his presence with a blue flame, and stared at them disapprovingly with piercing azure eyes.

"Where is Tyreli?" She asked shortly, and swept her gaze through the dragon-crowded sky. The two dragons eyed each other. Finally Darnellian spoke. "Tyreli told us that when we were ready to fly as one clan, if we hadn't extinguished ourselves completely, we could call on him, but until then he would encloud himself."

Rebecca shook her head slowly. "What has happened to you, my friends? The dragons have been known for their tradition of community from the beginning of time. How long have you been warring over which clan is strongest? It must be eons now. Now, go and wake Tyreli, it is time to join together with the Water Dragon and Wood Drake Clans." When neither dragon moved Rebecca bared her silver teeth. "I am Reahria, the Singer of Dragons, and you will not disobey me."

Both dragons turned quickly, returning to their folk. After they'd admonished their clans, the two warring sides began to disperse, and Rebecca was left alone. She had to wait for only a few moments until Darnellian and Forellan returned with a third dragon between them. The three paused before Rebecca, and the center dragon, a strange, white-skinned creature with fur instead of scales, and enormous clear eyes, chortled at them in dragon speech, emitting wisps of purple smoke.

"Finally the clashing clans have ceased," he roared, shooting a dragon flame of purple delight. "Too bad you didn't show up a few million years ago, Reahria. Did you tell them you could sing them into oblivion with one note? They're youngsters, never even seen one of your kind before. Pleased you made it, my dear. I hope Gandonel was of some help. It's been too long. But where is your mate, Lorian? I haven't seen him lately."

Rebecca pointed down with one scaly forefoot, indicating Torin, far below.

Tyreli craned his neck, nodding in understanding. "I'll see you both again not too long from now. Now at last it's time to bring the clans together."

Rebecca glanced at Darnellian and Forellan. "Lest you forget," she said, and from her dragon's mouth poured an ancient ballad from the earliest times of Dragonkind. It was a chant, the beginning of Earth itself and Dragonkind's place in its creation. She sang of the community specific to Dragons, where all were valued and none forgotten. She spoke of the courageous ones, those who'd become human themselves in order to teach others and provide an example for humankind to follow.

At last, living among humans, the dragons had become vulnerable to separation themselves. All of Dragonkind suffered, and the healer dragons went underground in order to wait for the time in which their wisdom would be heeded. She reminded her dragon brethren of their history, the bravery of their ancestors, and mostly of the old dragon communities, where knowledge and wisdom were shared, where each knew his or her place and where even the leaders ruled by the will of the whole.

By the time Rebecca finished, all three dragons were oozing great golden tears at the loss of such beauty, at the loss of the very heart of Dragonkind's strength. She explained her intent to help the earth rebalance herself, and of the need for all dragons to remember their voices when it was time. In the meantime, she said, they must help in clearing away the beings that fed on fear and despair, and try to coordinate their efforts together, for that would bring the greatest healing of all.

"When you hear the cleansing notes I will sing, may you all join in to rid the earth of such suffering as may dissolve in sound," Rebecca reminded them.

Rebecca bade them goodbye, promising to bring Torin to visit, and she began her descent back to the yard. She felt the rush of air past her wings, the glide of her body down-sky, and she allowed her love of Dragonkind to wash over her, willing it to remain with her long after she'd resumed her human form. Rebecca returned to the yard in her human body, landing gently on the grass.

Torin and Griffin hurried to her side, while Auran sat blissfully by Gandonel, eyes closed, still raking the dragon's foot with her nails.

"Are you okay, sweetie?" Griffin demanded, while Torin looked at Rebecca longingly.

"I'm fine, Dad. Tyreli said hello, Torin," Rebecca added. "Maybe next time you can come with."

"Let's make that a while from now, Rebecca," Griffin interjected. "Torin explained to me what happens if you're both dragon at once. Maybe you could wait a few years. By the way, what's going on with your mother? If it weren't a huge scaly beast with long teeth and fangs, I might be jealous."

Rebecca laughed, smoothing one pants leg where the change from dragon to human had rent the fabric slightly. "I think mom's been a dragon keeper. They're human folk who communed with dragons in ages past. She's also been able to summon all kinds of creatures, like unicorns and elves and faeries. She's happy remembering her connection with other times. She'll come out of it soon."

Rebecca stretched her arms wide for a moment, already missing her wingspan. "Torin, I talked to the Dragon Folk and they've agreed to work together, but I really need to get going on finding the right location to sing the clearing song. It's nearly time. I can feel the energy building up in me. Could you help me get down the old world maps and look?"

Torin smiled. "I need to wait for a few of your minutes, Rebecca. The dragon shift caught me by surprise. I need to work on my containment before we sit together."

"I can help you with that," Griffin said firmly, taking Torin by the arm. He was not quite sure exactly what Torin had meant, but he could see the way Torin was looking at Rebecca and decided a little time apart was just what they needed.

"Come on, Torin, and I'll show you how the Internet works. Then you can start contacting some of your fellow Thianelians. Rebecca, why don't you pry your mother off that overgrown lizard, and go rest in the hammock. It's not every day you turn into a dragon and stop sky wars. Well, maybe it is for you, but you must be tired anyway. I got exhausted just watching."

Chapter 7

"One thing we have in abundance here," said Griffin, pulling up an extra chair to his desk so that Torin could watch, "is the ability to access information about pretty much anything. Let me show you how this works, so you can use it anytime you want."

Griffin took his time, explaining operating procedures thoroughly, and Torin marveled at the idea of using a machine to access information that could easily be gleaned on Thianely by mind teling. Griffin demonstrated how to get on the Internet, and suggested a topic to search. He chose aliens half as a joke, and half out of curiosity to see if anything on Thianely came up.

Griffin frowned, running his finger down the numerous web sites that appeared. "Nothing here. We could always try something more specific, I suppose, like Thianely itself."

But when they entered Thianely, nothing popped up at all.

"When I need to contact Thianelians, I call to them in my mind. Here, I suppose I must put an ad in your newspaper," Torin said.

Griffin marveled at how quickly Torin had caught on to typing on the keyboard. "It's hard to believe your society exists without any sort of technology," he commented. "You don't have stock markets or jails, or even the need for money. It must be terribly strange to be on a planet with values that make so little sense. The closest thing we have to your world are those few tribes in out of the way places that haven't changed much in centuries, although that's rare nowadays. Most of them have modern clothes, though they may lack modern conveniences."

"I enjoy your technology," Torin admitted. "Fast cars especially. However, it is strange for me that your transportation not only poisons the air but also makes much noise."

"Look, I wanted to let you know, Torin, that of all the people Rebecca might have picked to be my son in law, you are certainly beyond what I hoped for, it's just that she's still so young. I mean, I think of her that way. I appreciate you respecting my comfort level, as far as Rebecca is concerned. Anyway, I hope my dragging you out of the back yard didn't offend you. You seem like a pretty good guy."

"I understand," Torin said, and then he grinned. "I like you as well, Griffin Bloom. I count Griffins among some of my closest friends."

They were interrupted by a shout. "Griff, Torin, come quickly, something's wrong with Rebecca! Hurry, we're in the yard."

Torin jumped up, and followed closely by Griffin, he ran outside onto the deck. The dragon Gandonel was gone, and most of the creatures were now clustered around Rebecca, who lay on the grass. Torin and Griffin hurried down onto the lawn.

"What happened?" Torin asked, kneeling down by Rebecca. He bent over, running his hands above her face, limbs, and body while a bright green light shimmered from his palms.

Auran turned to him and said shakily, "I don't know exactly what happened, but I saw her changing right in front of me, like her body started turning into all sorts of creatures and people. Suddenly she fell over and lay still."

Griffin sat down beside her, pulling Auran into his arms and holding her closely. "It's all right Auran, shh," he said soothingly. He looked at Torin questioningly.

"Rebecca will be fine," Torin said reassuringly. He glanced around the yard as if looking for something.

"Ah," he announced, standing up purposefully and moving over to a lilac bush. He bent down to grab something between his thumb and forefingers. He returned to the spot where Rebecca lay, holding the squirming creature firmly between his fingers.

"What is it?" asked Griffin, who, no matter how he tried, could only make out a vague outline of something wiggling.

"It's a fal-gnebling," Torin replied, "a cousin to the goblin, quite a mischief maker. It must have come through the faery ring of trees here. Normally the faeries would have kept them out, but they were preoccupied with Gandonel; faeries love dragons. Fal-gneblings like to feed off shape shifters, like Rebecca, who has recently finished being in dragon form. They're like little energy suckers. There are many such beings on your planet."

He thought for a moment. "Right now," Torin said, "I need to send this creature home, but I do not want to cause you any discomfort. If you think this may disturb you, I could wait until you go inside. Rebecca will wake up soon, so you do not need to remain here."

Auran shook her head, some of the color returning to her face. "I'm not going anywhere. I want to watch."

"I don't think anything you do will bother me after what we've seen so far," Griffin said reassuringly.

They both watched in fascination as Torin began to hum a little fire tune. Out of the grass rose a single orange flame with what looked like small fire sprites dancing in it. Auran and Griffin noticed that although they could feel the heat of the flame even a few feet away, the grass remained completely unsinged. Torin held the little creature up in front of his face and sang,

> "Gneblings, goblins, ghosts, and ghouls
> Return to live in swamps and pools,
> Back to woods or stone or cave,
> Hill or mountain, sky or grave,
> Home back to your kindred swarms
> Return now in your present forms."

The flame grew larger and from the center appeared a blackened, hideously contorted face. When Torin tossed the Gnebling into the flame, the dark image's mouth opened, neatly catching it. From all around the garden appeared tiny gnat-like creatures, each drawn into the flame like the first. Opening its great mouth wide, the repulsive face ate every single one. Soon the area was completely clear. At last Torin clapped his hands together, creating purple sparks, and the flame with the dark face vanished.

"It is not really as unpleasant as it appears," he said, looking at Griffin and Auran's disgusted faces. "This is how Fal-gneblings return home, as well as many other sorts of beings." At that moment Rebecca woke up, pushing herself to a sitting position on the grass.

She noted her parent's worried faces. "I'm really fine," she assured them, taking Torin's hand as he pulled her to her feet. "I didn't mean to frighten you, Mom. I forgot I had to protect myself when moving in and out of different forms. I was checking to see how easily I could shift into other forms just for fun, and I accidentally attracted scavengers, beings who are attracted to energy changes. They drained so much energy, sort of like tiny vampires, that I must have passed out from exhaustion."

She turned to Torin in surprise, "Did you realize how many lost and misguided creatures there are all over Earth? Some of them need help finding their way home, while some are actually feeding off of people's pain, helping to perpetuate it. I'm going to have to include them in the clearing song to send them back where they belong. Sorry it took me so long to return to consciousness, but I had to recover my strength."

"I sent many of the ones in this yarden home," said Torin, "but there may be others. If you are well enough, I think you must sing the clearing song soon. Otherwise, we will have to deal with them on an individual basis, which is much more time consuming."

Rebecca had a thought. "Dad, Mom, you know how Professor Davidson drinks all the time and looks sort of blurry?" Griffin and Auran nodded.

"Well, besides the alcohol he's consuming, he's also surrounded by beings who prey on turmoil, who enjoy creating more fear. When people drink or take drugs too much they are no longer present in their bodies, and they leave themselves open for all kinds of attacks. They become sort of halfway houses for any being that wanders by. If I can take most of these scavengers out of the picture, then even though a person might still be a drunk, he'd have a much easier time deciding to sober up."

Griffin and Auran looked at each other and shrugged. "Makes a kind of sense to me, Rebecca," Griffin said finally. "We'll take your word for it. I'm beginning to realize that all those kids who see monsters under the bed are probably seeing monsters."

"Exactly," said Torin, "small children are still able to see the other realms, until they are told to grow out of it. Imagination is simply what your people call that which they cannot perceive."

"Oh no," Rebecca said suddenly. "I suddenly realized that old Mrs. Appleby probably really did see aliens in the cupboards. That poor old woman wound up in a home."

"I'm going inside to lay down," Auran said abruptly. "I've spent the greater part of the day with a dragon, a magical transforming daughter, and it's been a major mind warp. I need a break."

"Sounds good to me," agreed Griffin. "I think my idea of reality has had enough strain for one day too. My head feels a little odd."

"I think I'm ready to relax too," Rebecca said. "Let's go do something easy. While you guys nap, how about we go read some maps?"

Chapter 8

Back in the home office, Torin and Rebecca pulled down the huge world map, unrolling it on the carpet. After they knelt down, Rebecca ran her hands over the map, feeling her palms warm up over power spots, and cool down over weak places. Torin jotted down areas of greatest and weakest strength on a note pad. The two spent some time at the task, until Torin laid his pad aside with a sigh. "Come here," he said, motioning for Rebecca to join him. They headed back into the living room, curling up together on the sofa.

"I think your parents are taking this well," Torin commented, stroking her hair with one hand as she rested her head on his shoulder.

"Yes," she said, "my Mom told me when I was little that there were faeries in the garden. I used to make faery houses for them. Mom has a pretty good imagination, and Dad, well, he's got a great sense of humor. Torin, I keep wondering how it's going on Thianely. I feel deaf, dumb, and blind here sometimes. I can only seem to tune in when I'm half asleep."

"Liliar said that Leva is recovering and everyone else is well. Tehy leads his Griffin kin. They will be able to keep the Bolluxes at bay. Besides, Liliar has been handling her tribe from birth." He gave a mock shiver. "Not the easiest of relatives."

Rebecca laughed. "Do you know, I think that petrified bog sprite Haldane gave me will come in very handy here. It's for defending one's ground, which is why Bolluxes have bogs in the first place. And the bog sprite Haldane gave me will be perfect for protecting the Great Tree. I've just figured out where I'm going to have to plant the golden branch."

"And?" Torin prompted.

"Have you ever heard of Central Park?" Rebecca said, chuckling at his look of dismay. "Yes, I know it's probably an odd place, being so public, but the ground is strong there, and in fact there's a kind of spiral energy in the soil that would be perfect."

"All right," Torin agreed, "we had better decide on a spot to sing first, or we will be so occupied fending off nasty beings there will be no clear space to plant anything in your park. So, where do you suggest?"

"I was thinking," said Rebecca, "that we need to find a place by a large body of water. I'll look at a smaller map soon to get a better idea. Right now, how about we don't do anything for at least an hour. I'm tired, and my mind shield seems to take a lot of energy to maintain."

Torin nodded his assent, took a deep breath and settled back into the cushions. Rebecca reached over to get the remote from the coffee table, clicked on the T.V., and settled back. A few moments later she turned off the T.V. in disgust, as Torin sat stunned by the images that had flashed by.

"Rebecca," he said finally, "I have been to your world before, yet there are many things I do not understand. Why do people want to see others suffering or being harmed? I would assume most people are not like the Bolluxes and enjoy hurting others, yet television is full of such things. I saw only a few moments, but does it not create fear? Also, what is the purpose of making people think of mating so often? That woman was saying that if she wore that scent, she would find a mate. Did she truly believe this?"

Rebecca shrugged. "I don't know, Torin. All of those commercials are to sell products, and people will buy anything if they believe it will bring them love."

"Love?" Torin said. "This is what some of your people believe is love?" He looked at her quizzically. "Rebecca, you do not expect these behaviors from me do you? I mean, because I do not speak in these ways and comment on your body often does not mean I do not love you."

Rebecca smiled. "I know. I like the way you express yourself just fine."

Torin gazed at her seriously. "Rebecca, do you know all that it means for us to mate? It is not only for physical pleasure. It means that we will share many abilities, a sense of teling that cannot occur unless one is mated, a greater consciousness of previous lifetimes, and awareness of many other states of being. In my world one does not mate indiscriminately, for without the proper mate, one's boundaries are destroyed, and one may lose one's sense of self, and even one's entire consciousness. That is why on Thianely, with a few exceptions, most beings are only attracted to their mates."

Rebecca looked at him in surprise. "I wondered why you never acted grabby... I mean, boys here can be kind of pushy. Many people have sex only for fun."

Torin grinned. "It is not only for fun, but I am sure it will be. I think we can talk about this more at some later time. Your face is red."

Rebecca picked up a couch cushion and smacked him with it. "Thanks a lot," she said. For the next half hour they threw pillows back and forth both with and without using their hands, trying to outmaneuver each other with their minds. It was like friendly wrestling. At last they took a break for lunch, and Auran came downstairs to tell them that Griffin was still taking a nap.

"Rebecca, I'm going to snooze soon myself, but I thought you two might want to go do some shopping. Considering your own grandmother didn't know who you were, the likelihood of anyone recognizing you is pretty slim. And one good thing about New Yorkers is they don't slow down enough to notice each other much. Maybe Torin could get some clothes too. You can also stop at an organic grocery on the way back and pick up a few things Torin might like to eat. Try the one on fifteenth," she said. "I haven't been there in a long time since it's further away than Rosen's. I don't think you've been there but once, so there's less chance of you being noticed. I don't suppose you know how to make yourself invisible, by any chance?"

"I could on Thianely," Rebecca said, "but it was mostly by accident. I don't know how well it would work here. We'll be careful though, Mom. I sure wish I could take the car and practice my driving," she said wistfully. "It's been a while since I tried. Torin would like it if I drove really fast like a taxi, but I guess that will have to wait until I get my license."

Auran laughed, "I think I'd rather see you change into many strange creatures in front of my face than speed around New York like a taxi. I left some money on the side table in the hallway; there should be plenty."

Auran patted Rebecca on the arm. "Go ahead and have fun, sweetie, but be careful." She headed upstairs to join Griffin.

Rebecca stood quietly for a moment. "You know what, Torin, I don't want to go anywhere really public until we sing the clearing song," she said firmly. "I don't even want to imagine what sort of beings hang out in the subway, not to mention around all the shops. I don't have enough energy to deal with them right now. We can always go shopping another time. I think I'll take you somewhere a little bit more private, but you'll see when we get there; I'll let it be a surprise. If we travel by thought it's a lot quicker than even a taxi."

Torin nodded. "I appreciate your willingness to exercise your mind rather than your legs. I suppose we should find some place where not too many people will see us or hear us. Or perhaps some place so crowded that no one will pay us much attention. In any case, it must be a place you know well, because we do not want to leave any parts of our consciousness stranded between places."

Rebecca glanced at him in surprise. "Torin, I wasn't even thinking of that when I traveled thought. It was more like following threads of people's or a particular place's energy. I picture it, feel its essence, and then let it go. How could I lose anything when I'm always with myself?"

Torin stared at her wonderingly. "So, that is how you did it!" he exclaimed. "When we first arrived I thought that if your room had changed you wouldn't have been able to find it. But if you were following the energy, a change of a physical nature would not matter. I was always taught to be very careful when traveling elementally. I never even considered traveling from beyond the elements. I was trained to think of myself as mostly fire, and the properties of fire moving. It was very connected to the physical rather than the energetic. Home is a sense of place, not merely a physical location. Show me how you do it."

"Okay," Rebecca said, and she stood very close to him. "Now, feel my mind when I travel. I'll move across the room."

Torin reached out with his palms, concentrating on feeling Rebecca's mind. When he looked up she was standing across the room by the sink. He shook his head in confusion.

"Rebecca, do you realize that there is no sensation of movement at all? Your energy did not waver, yet there you are over there. Even when we travel elementally, it is still possible to detect our movement. I do not understand."

"I don't think," Rebecca said thoughtfully, coming to stand close to him once more, "that I would be able to travel elementally here at all. Feeling the instability of the ground and pollutants in the water made it hard for me to balance. I guess you could say I'm bypassing the elemental level completely. I will eventually need to contact all of the elemental forces in order to help establish balance, but I trust thought-travel more right now. You did it with me, so you can do it by yourself too. Without thinking about fire or its properties, or having to hold your consciousness, trust that your complete self is always there and let yourself move to the sink. Go on; don't think. Just go."

Torin closed his eyes and disappeared physically, although Rebecca could see a faint outline of his body moving across the room. When Torin opened his eyes, he was standing by the sink. He laughed triumphantly.

"Rebecca, it is most ironic! The only way to travel thought is not to think at all. It is having an intention, and letting it go. This is much faster!"

"I'm glad you like it," Rebecca said, smiling at his enthusiasm. "Moving through space, and I suppose time as well, is easier if you allow your physical body to simply melt into tiny particles of clear intention. Of course it is really handy being physical too. Speaking of physical, did you know I could see the shape of your body moving? Try letting go of the separation between your body and the space around it."

Torin eyed her in alarm. "I can see that I still have an attachment to what I was taught about elemental travel. I have always held a distinction between myself and space in order not to become lost to myself."

"Have the distinction, but don't become attached to it," Rebecca suggested. "If you hold to it too tightly, you separate yourself from the idea that your consciousness is safe in form. Like, have a container but don't stick to the walls of it."

Torin sighed. "It is difficult to let an established belief move out of my mind. I will think about this more."

Torin practiced transporting himself from side to side, dematerializing and rematerializing until Rebecca's neck got tired of watching him. The vague outline of his body had almost entirely disappeared.

"Hey," she said, "you're getting pretty good over there. Now do you want to hold hands and do this together, or do you want me to go first and follow my intention?"

Torin bowed. "You first, I need practice."

"Okay," Rebecca agreed, "but we might need sweaters. Where we're going can get pretty breezy."

Torin looked surprised. "This world may be unbalanced, and even suffering from an advanced case of separation, but if you are

63

unable to raise your body temperature to compensate for wind, I can certainly warm you myself."

Rebecca gulped. "Sorry, I'm still thinking like my old self. My mom has trained me well. Never go anywhere without warm clothes, tokens for subway fare, and change for a pay phone."

"I understand," Torin said. "Grandfather taught me to always ask before eating, shelter in trees during electrical storms because they repel lightning, and never thank a Bollux, because then you are beholden to him. I suppose such training depends upon the planet. Come now, let us go."

Rebecca scribbled a note for her parents, and then gave Torin a quick hug. Closing her eyes, she disappeared.

She opened her eyes to a cloudless day, nearly as blue as the sky in her backyard. She stood near a tall flame-shaped structure that rose above her head, completely surrounded by a fenced enclosure. She looked out over the water at the skyline of lower Manhattan and turned to greet Torin as he materialized next to her.

"Well, what do you think?" she asked, making a sweeping gesture out over the harbor. "Here we are on the torch of the Statue of Liberty, and you're getting the view of her no tourist ever sees. Mom said that public access is restricted all this week. We were thinking of taking you anyway. Sometime we'll come out here the regular way and I'll let you see the statue from base to crown."

Torin took in the view, eyes wide. "This is certainly a quiet place you have chosen. No crowds, and no one will hear or see us either."

He promptly sat down, shaking his head. "It is always amazing to me to see so many buildings in one place. The first time I came to earth I could not understand how so many human beings could live this closely together. The mind noise can be deafening. The statue is wonderful, though, right out here surrounded by water. How interesting that the most stable ground you could find is under water."

Rebecca nodded in agreement and sat down beside him. The area in which they sat was rather narrow, though they could walk all the way around the flame of the torch if they chose to. Rebecca noticed that the small hatch door that led down to the lower levels had been padlocked shut.

She grinned widely, clasping Torin's hands. "Isn't this fun?" He turned to face her, wincing slightly at the hardness of the concrete floor.

"Exciting view, but not so comfortable sitting down. Why don't we get started so we can stand and look at the city some more?"

He paused, as if listening inwardly. "Rebecca, something feels wrong. I can hear Liliar calling to me and I can smell a dark, putrid energy, almost like a Bollux..."

Rebecca gasped in alarm. Something was taking shape directly behind Torin's back. She grabbed him by the hand, quickly pulling him to his feet. He fire shielded them both as the creature materialized fully. It was a slender, seedy looking man, unkempt and straggly looking, although he wore his tattered clothes with an air of aplomb. He leered at them crookedly, revealing incongruously golden teeth.

"Lovely view, isn't it? I had these capped by one of those dentist fellows. I ate him afterwards for dessert, and a delicious little morsel he was."

He turned to the railing, ignoring them for a moment. "Ah, one of my favorite things in creation, a whole city of unwitting fools to prey upon, when they're not too busy preying upon each other. We Bolluxes could learn a few things from you humans, much as I hate to admit it. Look at this," he said, pulling at his ragged trousers, "the perfect disguise, a homeless person. Or," he added, looking very pleased with his own cleverness, "I can be dapper as the next fellow. High level executive complete with briefcase."

As he spoke, his clothes became a business suit and tie, with matching shoes and briefcase. "Here on Earth, it's not what's inside that counts, it's only what you appear to be. It's quite easy for an accomplished changeling such as myself. I could probably have been elected to office, but it's too boringly simple."

"Let me guess," said Torin in distaste, "you must be a Bollux we haven't met."

"Don't be more lack-witted than you actually are, my not dear fellow; of course we've met. Granted, it's been quite a few years, and you were just a little grubling at the time, say, no more than a few seasons old. It's a pity about your parents; they didn't bother to watch you grow up. Although the greater pity is that you were ever found at all. By rights you should be an ash-burned skeleton, or the dust of disintegrated bones. I'd have preferred nothingness to seeing you

65

again, but there you have it. Sometimes you can't have too much of a bad thing. Royden Bollux, at my service."

Torin glared at him and would have stepped forward, but for Rebecca's restraining hand.

"I suppose we don't have to ask what you're doing here," Rebecca said, thinking how much more difficult things were going to be with a Bollux on the loose in Manhattan.

"Well, now, let me see." Royden said, rubbing his pockmarked chin in mock confusion. "It could be that I've come to chide you for interfering where you unfortunately belong, or that I've come to avenge the death of my brother Jierdan, but I never cared for him anyway. Perhaps I have nothing better to do. Or perhaps it's the glorious view of these terrible structures piercing the sky," and he made a sweeping gesture with one hand, much as Rebecca had earlier.

"Let's say that you have something I want, like a little crystal wisdom. Perhaps we can do a swap, say the crystal powers for the safety of your friends, and my sickeningly charitable half sister. There was a slight accident and a few of them were harmed, not lethally, I might add, but enough for them to pay us an extended visit. We've captured the half hatchling and his mate, and a rather dirty tree maid. Go ahead," he said, noting their disbelief, "try checking in with them and you'll find that they are avocado, or was that incommunicado? I don't remember which, except that one of them is a particularly vile green-fleshed fruit."

Rebecca turned to Torin, who immediately tilted his head as if listening to far away voices. He shook his head worriedly.

"Unfortunately, unlike most of his clan, he speaks truly," Torin said. "I know something is wrong. I can feel Liliar trying to communicate, but she is unable."

Rebecca leaned closer so that Royden couldn't hear. "This must have happened just recently. I thought Leva was fine and the Griffins were guarding the gate again."

"I know," said Torin. "The time difference between here and Thianely must be distorting even further."

"Ash brat, Water Spit... or was that Sprite," Royden interrupted impatiently. "Whatever you are, do hurry up. I have a busy agenda. Places to defile, people to persecute. If you won't trade I'll have to arrange for particularly gruesome ends for your friends. Hmm." He paused thoughtfully. "I've never pulled the wings off a Griffin before;

66

that might be entertaining. Or I could try draining the sap out of that tree lass. She'd look lovely decorating my den. A petrified wood nymph."

"Maybe you could let them go, like Liliar would," Rebecca commented, stalling for time.

"Don't foul the air with that name!" snapped Royden. "Moronic suggestions aside, I really must have an answer, for, as always, my patience is as limited as my other virtues. That is to say, I have none. What a lovely place, this human world! A veritable feast of pestilence, choice sustenance for the atrocious appetite, with a side order of terror and contagion. So much competition, violence, and indifference, I tell you I am moved to the quick to have found myself so at home. Well now, what shall it be?"

"I shall give you what the crystals gave me," Rebecca announced, stilling Torin's protest with a glance, "in return for the safety of my friends, the tree maid, the half Griffin and Liliar, your own kin. How will I know you've kept your part of the bargain?"

Royden looked aghast. "I, not keep my word? I am swollen with pride at your lack of trust." He immediately puffed up to the dimensions of a grotesquely rotting corpse, smiling wickedly as they nearly gagged on the smell. At last the Bollux shrugged, resuming his normally offensive shape and odor, and pointed to Torin.

"He'll hear through my misbegotten sister. They are related, you know, both gotten by the same fire-shifting sire. Don't worry," he added, as Torin stiffened in shock. "You're absolutely no relation of mine. In return I will trust your complete absence of talent for guile, and take the crystal wisdom from you. Now, as soon as the crystal knowledge begins to enter me, your companions will be released. If I do not free them, you can stop dispensing information, and the transfer will be reversed."

"Agreed," Rebecca said reluctantly.

"Aren't you going to thank me for saving your friends, my dear?"

Rebecca eyed him coldly. "I know better than to thank a Bollux, except perhaps your sister."

Royden shrugged. "It was worth a try. Now, I will come stand by you. Drop that fire shield, Boy, or the deal's off. Think of it this way. I must make myself somewhat vulnerable in order to receive, a state which no Bollux enjoys. If I have misspoken, well, I will be at your mercy. Which reminds me. I need to hear the boy here swear an oath that he will not harm me during or after the transfer."

Torin sighed. "By Father Telches, Mother Rhiate and my clan of Fire Folk, I do honor this agreement not to harm you."

"Very well, let us proceed. Afterwards I will be of such knowledge as to unseat my father's place as head of the Bollux clan. Get used to dealing with me. I predict a long future with myself tormenting you all like an insistent mosquito, and you powerless to swat me. Don't you love insect analogies? There's a certain pestilential quality I adore."

The stringy Bollux moved close to Rebecca, who had a moment's urge to plug her nose at his stench, but restrained herself. Even in his business suit the Bollux reeked. Royden reached over to grasp her hand gingerly, as if he were experiencing cleanliness for the first time and finding it noxious. Rebecca closed her eyes, gathering strength. She allowed the crystal songs that Alphumerian had taught her to move through her mind freely.

Torin watched the Bollux turn bright pink, gradually shifting to dark green. Liliar called to Torin in his mind, informing him that they were being freed, and he nodded grimly. Royden changed color again, first blue, then purple, then brown. Finally he staggered, shot with rainbow colors, as his whole body began to quiver. With a gasp, the Bollux struggled to let go of Rebecca's hand, but she held on firmly, even as he began to writhe and shake.

Torin backed up as gushes of energy boiled from between Rebecca and the Bollux, hurtling against his body. Amazed at the force unleashed, Torin was pushed almost to the edge of the railing, barely able to hold his ground. As Rebecca stood in a column of golden light, the Bollux imploded, collapsing into himself until he was no more than a black hole hovering in space. Rebecca quickly reached out, and holding her palm in front of the blackness, she hummed a fast hard note. The dark spot that had been Royden blinked out completely.

Torin held onto the railing, recovering from the force of Royden's disintegration. Rebecca stood untouched, but she too shook slightly from the aftermath of the Bollux's death. As the huge golden flame subsided around her, she joined Torin at the railing. They held each other for a moment, until finally he asked, "Rebecca, what was that? I have never seen anything like it."

"It wasn't too different than when you lasered the Bellorasps," she replied soberly. "I only gave him what he asked for. His pinched, tiny consciousness couldn't handle the expansion at the rate at which I sent the information, so he collapsed in on himself. The opposite of a Bollux is wisdom, so I guess you could say he completely negated himself. It's too bad he had to die.

There aren't many who can process that much information so quickly. I haven't even brought it forward in my own mind. It's been in storage inside me. Torin, the other Bolluxes will know he's gone, and they'll know how it happened. Since they know they can't get the crystal wisdom through a transfer, the information is safe inside me, but they will probably try to attack us. We know Bolluxes can travel here, which will make everything even more difficult. They will do everything they can to prevent us planting the next Great Tree. Wisdom and balance anywhere they find distasteful, but especially on Earth. From what Royden said, Bolluxes treat this planet like their own personal playground of mayhem. The Great Tree will really discourage all of that."

Torin sighed. "I am not sure what more we can do besides take precautions, including teaching your parents some protective measures. Rebecca, I am a little stunned at the news about Liliar and me. I thought I had no living first relatives, yet Liliar is my sister! Grandfather found me, so he is my adopted kin, but I need to learn more about my father so I will know more about my abilities. It would be much easier to know ahead of time, before I turn into a human laser and ignite several Bellorasps, for example." He shook his head ruefully. "And I kept telling you that you did not know who you were."

"I didn't know at all," Rebecca said, taking Torin's hand in hers. "But I do have an idea how it feels to be surprised by your own abilities. I didn't expect that Royden would die, even if I understood why after it happened. I still feel kind of sick."

"I did too, after the Bellorasps burned to ashes," Torin said. "It is unpleasant to be involved in the violent end of any being."

"Let's sit for a while," suggested Rebecca. Torin obligingly made a place for her on his lap, wincing slightly at the hardness of the cement beneath him.

"I'll be right back," Rebecca said impishly, disappearing and reappearing in seconds with a very large sofa cushion. Torin looked at her questioningly.

"I will replace it, hopefully before Mom notices," Rebecca promised. Torin smiled, accepting the cushion with relief, and waited for Rebecca to reposition herself on his lap.

"That's better," Rebecca said. They sat in silence for a time, enjoying each other's nearness and letting their minds be still. Rebecca rested her head on Torin's shoulder, breathing in his scent, feeling peaceful. She realized that she trusted him completely. Torin held her closely as they both relaxed together.

"Torin," Rebecca said finally as her stomach growled loudly. "I'm feeling starved again."

Torin smiled at her. "I suspected that from the strange animal noises coming from your middle. What would you like to eat?"

"Something filling that will give me a boost," Rebecca said. "And I'm really tired. It seems like ever since we returned to earth I've been feeling either very hungry or very weary."

"I too," Torin agreed. "Also very interested in mating. I have noticed that is a common state here as well."

Rebecca stared into his green eyes and marveled that as hungry and exhausted as she was, she could still contemplate wrestling him to the hard cement at the top of the Statue of Liberty's torch. Torin's eyes widened and suddenly he pushed Rebecca off of his lap just as her stomach growled again.

"Food," Torin said somewhat shakily. He stood up and took a few steps away until his heart spiral calmed down somewhat. "I will get some," he offered, needing a break from having to restrain himself around Rebecca so much.

"It's only fair," Rebecca said, enjoying the effect she had on him. "You brought up the subject."

Torin glanced at her in amusement. "And you looked at me with such desire. However much time we spend here on Earth, my dear mate, it will seem very long to us both. But now I will travel thought to your home and find us something sustaining to eat. I will be back soon."

And with a wave of his hand, Torin disappeared.

After Torin had returned with two of Rebecca's favorite turkey sandwiches, a small wedge of cheese, several vegetarian sandwiches for himself, two apples and six chocolate cookies, they sat down and devoured everything.

"Ah, that's better," said Rebecca, although after all that food she felt like she needed a nap. She yawned hugely, as did Torin mere seconds after she did.

"Would you prefer to sing the clearing song another day?" he suggested. "Perhaps when we both have more energy?"

Rebecca shook her head. "I need to do something about it today; it feels like the right time. But since we are so exhausted, I thought maybe we'd try something a little different. My dad always says that the best ideas come about due to laziness and the urge to expend as little energy as possible for the greatest possible outcome. Some people call that efficiency, I guess. Anyway, instead of us having to do most of the work, why don't we let all of the folk here do it?"

She paused, looking out over the edge of the fence. "What I mean is, since the Earth's natural state is one of balance, even though not all the people may want to restore it, we can call on all the beings here that do, including the Earth herself. There are too many creatures here that are feeding off the planet and the people for me to be very effective in singing a traditional clearing song. And I'm worried that the sound vibration would cause earthquakes.

People have a hard time letting go of something that they think really is part of them. Even if people are aware of parasites, some of them still won't let go. We cannot choose for others, only provide another option. So," and she took a deep breath, "I'm going to send out a call to the Earth and all her Guardians, and whether they're awakened or not, they'll still respond. Like I responded when Thianely called. Then we'll have all dimensions of earth covered, and we won't have to work so hard. I won't have to sing skip notes, or worry about how the sound waves will affect the earth's crust. We'll let all the Guardians do their jobs."

"I am more fatigued than I anticipated," Torin admitted. "Being earthbound always takes much energy and there was a great deal of force released when you were doing the crystal transfer. But I can still give you support. I will guard the physical level while you are busy. Do you want me to fire shield, or will that get in your way?"

"I think I'll need it," Rebecca said. "Actually, we have a great body of water here, plenty of ground, a clear sky. Could you shield us with all the elements at once?"

Torin shrugged. "I have never tried it, but I suppose if I can travel thought, anything is possible."

While Rebecca stood in readiness, Torin sat down in front of her, closed his eyes, and spread his arms in a semicircle. Rebecca waited until she could see the shimmering shield of multicolored elements slowly revolving around them, then lifted her arms up high and sang in a voice that was loud from the sheer force of the words, rather than in volume:

"Lady, play your trumpet loud,
Call all angels far and near,
Sound the symbols; cheer the crowd,
Ring the prophet and the seer.

Sing the beasts from cave and mountain,
Trill the birds from nest and lake
Watch the forests flow like fountains
Hear the mighty oceans quake.

Wake the lightning; chime the fairies,
All awaken, dance and spin!
Leave the roosts and hives and come now
All are dancing, climbing in.

Spirals winding highward, snakeward,
Hear us all resounding loud
Trumpet blaring, souls ashaking,
All of earth and heaven proud.

Comes the question, comes the asking,
Play the answer; finally hear!
All of truth and blazing wonder
All are coming now and here.

Lady, play your trumpet softly,
As our task has now begun,

*All the parts we'll sing together
And weave the sound of everyone."*

Rebecca finished, swaying slightly, while Torin sat nearby, still maintaining the shielding. She gazed out over Manhattan and nudged Torin with one foot.

"Here," she said, a tone of awe in her voice, "I'll help with the shield, open your eyes and look." Torin swiveled around and there he saw, directly above and on all sides of them, thousands of angels winging their way in a sort of celestial gathering. Torin, who had never seen such beings, gaped at the sheer beauty of their colorful wings and energetic radiance.

"We have no such beings on Thianely; they dwell only on Hevald, Lord Dariel's planet," he murmured, standing up for a better view. "Though I have heard of them, I have not seen them in form."

Rebecca nodded. "They're special guardians of Earth as well. They bring many messages to people here, especially hope. Some of them are fierce, and many are singers, but one thing they all are is helpful." She sighed in satisfaction. "Now watch."

Far across the horizon and beyond, dark shapes began to lift from the ground, from the water, and right out of thin air. Some were indistinct, some more clearly defined. They rose to a certain level in the sky and, as Torin watched, they began to shift forms. Dark wraiths, round bulbous creatures, and ghoulish specters burst into balls of light, winked out abruptly, or, as Rebecca pointed out, chose to transform themselves completely. Many joined the angelic multitude higher up.

"There now," Rebecca said approvingly. "Things are beginning to move. Most of the beings you saw, like the really blobby ones, simply chose to go back where they belong, others resisted and blew up, and some of them chose a higher state of being. That's what's called 'turning a wraith.' Sometimes if you give lower vibrational beings a higher option, they actually choose it."

Torin thought for a moment. "Any such thing as turning a Bollux?"

"What about Haldane and Liliar? She seems to be offering him another way of being," Rebecca reminded him. "That's all anyone can do. She can't do it for him."

"Oh, like that phrase, 'you may show a Deva a flower, but you can not make her live in it, and if she is not homeless, forget it.'"

Rebecca eyed him skeptically. "Yeah, I guess so. There's a lot we can't help with at all, you know, without being asked. Like for instance, we can't do a thing about suckaloonies."

Torin blinked at her. "Sucka what?"

"Suckaloonies. They're these grey gelatinous masses that adhere to people and suck their energy, in return for feeding people's egos. They're really hard to get rid of, and the person has to be willing to look at their ego stuff and know who they are. Do you know, I think I used to see them on people when I was really young; I forgot about them until just this moment." She made a sweeping gesture; "In a world of people who are taught to forget themselves at the youngest possible age, you can see how extensive the problem is. You don't have suckaloonies on Thianely."

"I wonder if they are distantly related to the Bolluxes."

Rebecca stifled another yawn. "How about heading home? It looks like it's getting late, and my parents are probably waiting. Plus this will be going on for days, all over the planet. It gets kind of distracting to watch after a while." She paused for a moment. "You know, I don't know what day of the week this is. I don't even know the date."

"I would say you were right on schedule, whatever earth time it is." Torin bowed with a flourish to the angels and grasping her hand, he tugged her home.

Chapter 9

They arrived in the living room right in front of Griffin and Auran, who were comfortably ensconced on the sofa. Auran blinked in surprise, but recovered quickly.

"Well, don't tell me. From the lack of groceries and shopping bags, I'd say you didn't make it to the store."

Griffin seemed to catch his breath a little more slowly. "Well," he joked, "at least I don't have to suffer the perils of teaching you how to drive, Torin. Hey," he added hopefully, "I don't suppose you could give us lessons? Think of how much time and energy I could save on commuting!"

"Mom! Dad!" Rebecca admonished them, albeit smilingly, "I can't believe you two!"

"Why not?" said Griffin smugly, "if we can believe you two. Look at it this way. If I were to go to work tomorrow and tell our employees, they'd think I was nuts. Or imagine me trying to find a therapist who could assist me in being comfortable with all the impossible things I've seen lately. Can't you hear it? 'Excuse me, I'm having trouble adjusting to my daughter's supernormal abilities.' He'd think I was stuck in some magical thinking phase of childhood. I minored in psychology; I know how they think. So Rebecca, I'm going to make as many jokes as I possibly can, to get through this. Also we had a grand nap and I'm rested enough to have recovered some of my equilibrium. Besides, you two make all of this seem so normal, I figure, what the hell, I can handle it."

"Good," said Rebecca, clasping her hands in front of her while Torin lowered himself into one of the easy chairs with a grateful sigh. "Because, it looks like we're going to keep traveling the way we've been doing. We did get a little side tracked on our excursion and never made it to the store, but I promise we will." She sat down in the other easy chair, made as if to put her feet up on the coffee table, and caught Auran's expression. "Okay, Mom." She dropped her feet and looked over at Torin, who had fallen asleep in his chair.

"Big morning, huh?" her father commented, watching Torin shift in his sleep to get a better position.

Rebecca smiled sleepily. "It was pretty intense. Have either of you ever seen an angel?"

Griffin stared at her for a moment, and then shook his head. Auran looked away nervously. "Well," she said tentatively, "when I was little I used to think I saw an angel that came in my room at night and sang to me, but my mother said it was just my clothes draped on my rocking horse. After that I never saw it again. I used to wish I'd never told my mother; she had a way of taking the joy out of things."

"She certainly hasn't changed much," muttered Griffin. "That woman could take Christmas out of Santa Claus."

"Why did you ask, Rebecca?" Auran said, ignoring Griffin's comment.

"I wanted to let you know not to worry if some showed up here. I'm going to be working with them for awhile, and I told them they could reach me at home."

Griffin burst out laughing. "I bet Miss Manners would love this! She could write a chapter on 'Entertaining Celestial Visitors in Your Home,' how to accommodate their wingspans at the dinner table, and topics of conversations to avoid, like, do not inquire about fallen relatives."

Auran began to weep, a kind of soul wrenching sobbing that immediately brought Torin awake, and Rebecca to her side. Griffin tried to console her, but she merely cried harder. Finally, after they'd given her some tissues and a cup of water, she calmed down enough to speak.

"When you first disappeared," Auran said to Rebecca, "I thought about all of the things we wouldn't be able to do, the time we'd never share, and the life you wouldn't have. When you returned I was so happy, but Rebecca, it's like all of our dreams for you have died all over again. You'll never be able to go back to high school, you know too much. College would be a disaster. They'd either think you were crazy or they'd feel threatened. You don't exactly fit in the hierarchy of academia. You have abilities that would frighten most people, and yet you make it all seem natural. Where will you live, how will you fit? The worst of it is, in the short time you've been back, we've started to change too. If I learn how to see angels, will I still be able to work and have our old friends? What's going to happen to us?"

Rebecca leaned over to kiss Auran's cheek. "Despite everything, it's still me, Mom. I still have to eat and sleep and pee like everyone else. I know you're sad and scared, but I'm still me. Even though I know about things other people don't remember, it doesn't mean I know everything. Besides, half of the time I don't even realize I know something until I speak and it falls out.

Mom, you wouldn't have to learn to see angels, because you already know how. You only forgot because it isn't okay in our society. Think about all of the major religious traditions on the planet. Not only do they have helpful beings like angels, but they also include demons and malevolent spirits and a whole variety of others, including the little folk like leprechauns and elves and faeries and so on. Everything's just separate in our minds from everyday life. It doesn't mean it's not there simply because we ignore it. That's why we're going to have protect ourselves. If you look at the big picture, we're all safe because we're all part of the universal soup, but on the level of energy or physical or emotional bodies, we have to take care of ourselves if we want to stay in form. It's as necessary as brushing your teeth."

Torin, who'd gotten up and left the room for a few moments, returned carrying his leaf pad notebook.

"Oh, no, Torin," protested Rebecca, turning a deep shade of pink.

Torin placed the leaf pad on the table in front of Auran. "I wanted to remind you that Rebecca did not accept everything right away either, Auran. Remember when we showed you these pictures of Rebecca during her adventures on Thianely? And you should have seen me the first time I came to your world. I had to leave after only a few days." He began flipping pages while Griffin and Auran scooted forward on the sofa in order to see more clearly.

"I especially like the one of Rebecca yelling at the council," Auran concluded, wiping the last of the tears from her eyes, "although the one in the blue leaves of the tree is lovely." They looked at the leaf pad pictures for a little while longer, until Rebecca's stomach began to rumble.

"How about dinner?" Griffin suggested, glancing at his watch, "it's already almost 6:30."

They all helped cook, feasting on mashed potatoes, string beans and salad, with roast beef for everyone except Torin.

After the meal, Torin and Rebecca disappeared for a few minutes. When they returned to the living room to find Auran and Griffin, Griffin looked at them suspiciously.

"All right, what's up, you two? I know that look, Rebecca. It's the same look you had on your face when you set a Santa trap in the kitchen and caught me eating those cookies."

"Mom, Dad, Torin and I have been practicing and we want to take you on a little evening trip. I promise it will be something you both won't want to miss."

"Are you going to turn us into fat air or something first?" Griffin queried.

"Do you think we'll be safe?" Auran asked, looking both nervous and excited at once.

"Definitely," Rebecca assured them. "All you have to do is grab hold of our hands. We'll make a circle and we'll be there in no time."

Griffin and Auran stood up. "What are we supposed to do?" Griffin asked. "Are sarcastic thoughts going to get in the way?"

"All you need to be is willing to go with us."

"I'm game if you are, Auran. And if we wind up plastered all over some billboard somewhere, at least we'll have the satisfaction of knowing they'll never figure out how we got there."

Torin, Rebecca, Auran and Griffin all clasped hands, and as Griffin waited for some strange sensation of movement, Auran closed her eyes tightly.

"You can open your eyes now, Mom," Rebecca said. Auran gasped at the incredible view from the top of the Statue of Liberty's torch. The sky was still full of angels and the exodus of various beings leaving for home.

Rebecca checked to make sure that Auran wasn't going to pass out, and then dropped her hand. Griffin stood in stunned silence next to Torin, who was providing heat from his palms to keep them all warm. The sun had set and the breeze off the water was cool. They watched quietly as the angels grew brighter against the dark sky until it seemed to Rebecca that anyone with eyes at all must see them.

Torin stood close behind her, encircling her in his arms, resting his chin on the top of her head. Griffin and Auran drew close as well, and in the hush of the darkening, Rebecca could hear the angels singing. They stood silently listening for a while, and Auran spoke. "I truly thought I'd never hear them again. Thank you, Rebecca. Thank you, Torin."

Griffin couldn't speak at all. He could see the lights of lower Manhattan below and the lights of thousands of angels above, and he thought it was the most beautiful sight he could imagine. The sound of them all singing was wordless, but it shook something inside him and filled him up beyond measure.

Torin whispered in Rebecca's ear. "Such beauty is rare. Do you know what they sing?"

Rebecca turned around. "Not exactly," she whispered back. "It's even older than the Old Tongue; it must be some angelic dialect. They remind me of Liliar though. Have you heard from her?"

"Yes, she told me that her brother Haldane is in great trouble. After Royden died, while the Bolluxes were trying to recapture Leva, Liliar, and Tehy, Haldane let all the bog sprites out of the bogs. They got inside the Bollux compound, and devoured everything in sight. Apparently they are not too choosy about what they eat. Haldane also showed Liliar something to keep them safe from the Bolluxes in the future. Leva, Liliar, and Tehy escaped to the Griffin holdings. And remember the Bolluxes are still upset at the pure water that got into the bogs, courtesy of the Griffin Folk. The bog sprites were almost relieved to escape the clear water threatening them in the bogs, which is why is was not difficult for Haldane to let them out. Anyway, Haldane is in lock down somewhere and keeps hollering loudly in Liliar's mind so that she cannot rest. I suppose they will have to rescue him next."

Torin looked serious, though Rebecca could not see him very clearly, only the luminance outlining his body and his hands glowing faintly with heat. "The Bolluxes have also vowed to disturb you in your own world. They are angry over Royden's failure to get the crystal knowledge, although they seem unconcerned over his death."

"So what you're saying is I really pissed them off?"

"I agree with the sentiment even if I'm unfamiliar with the phrase," Torin confirmed.

Rebecca slumped a little in his arms. "I thought things were hairy on Thianely. What are we going to tell my parents?" She looked over at them, still enraptured with the night. "What can we do to protect them?"

Torin kissed her gently on the top of her head. "Perhaps it will be safer at your lake cabin with fewer people there. We must stay close, but Auran and Griffin are very powerful, you know. I think they may surprise you in their ability to defend themselves."

Rebecca suddenly cocked her head, inwardly conversing with an enormous blue-winged angel who floated gracefully down in front of them. Rebecca listened for a few moments, bowed, then reached out with a gesture of thanks. The angel swiftly winged back to her brethren.

"We've got to take care," she said to Torin, as Auran and Griffin joined them. "The Bolluxes definitely plan to interfere with me planting the tree. The angel, her name is Lariel, said that you must find your father's gifts, for they will help us. We ought to go home and protect the house. You can do research tomorrow. I know, let's do an all-elemental shield again, rather than only the fire shield. That should at least hold till morning."

Griffin reached out in the dark, finding Rebecca's hand by the glow of Torin's. "I want you both to know that I will never forget this night."

Rebecca smiled. "Aren't they glorious, Dad?"

When they'd arrived back in the living room, Rebecca and Torin gazed at each other meaningfully. "We have to do some things to protect the house," Rebecca explained to her parents. "We have to create an energy shield and tomorrow we'll show you guys some other precautions."

Auran went to check the answering machine, while Griffin headed outside to lie in the hammock and look at the sky. "I'm going to go angel gazing," he announced happily.

Torin and Rebecca went to the guest room and sat down by the bed to summon a shield. Torin called upon fire and air while Rebecca called upon earth and water. Though the elemental forces were not as stable as they were on Thianely, they were only too willing to help. Afterwards, both Rebecca and Torin could feel the thick layer of protective energy surrounding the house.

"That will be well enough for now," Torin said. "I think we have experienced enough for one day. I am ready to sleep." He eyed the bed and nudged Rebecca gently. "I miss holding you," he said, "but I think it is time for you to rest upstairs."

Rebecca nodded sleepily and bade him goodnight. On her way upstairs she saw Auran hanging up the phone.

"I called your grandparents. Dad is doing great. He's insisted on taking long walks and I think he's worn your grandmother out completely. They want to come over tomorrow, sweetie, after Pops goes for another walk. They'd love to come to the lake, by the way. Griff will be thrilled. Where is your dad, Rebecca?"

"Last I heard he was going outside to lay in the hammock and look for more angels."

"They are something," Auran said. "Totally awe inspiring. Well, goodnight. Your dad and I will probably be awake for a little while longer since we napped, but try not to wake us up later in the middle of the night with any explosions or singed ceilings."

"I won't, Mom," Rebecca assured her, heading immediately off to bed.

Auran grabbed an afghan out of the hall closet and went out to join Griffin. She could barely make him out swinging gently in the hammock, for the night was dark but for the faint glow of Gilden's horn. Gilden the unicorn lay beside the hammock while Griffin idly scratched around the base of his horn.

"So what do you use that horn for, fella?"

"Impaling wraiths, disemboweling demons, penetrating darkness, healing illness," replied the unicorn gravely. "Oh, I also use it to stake vampires, but that's a rare occasion."

Griffin froze, pulling back his hand, but Gilden beckoned him to keep scratching. "It is safe enough," he assured Griffin. "I have no reason to impale you."

"Well, that's a comfort," Griffin said dryly. He moved over to make room for Auran to lie down beside him. She draped the afghan over them both and cuddled close.

"I thought your kind only allowed virgins near them," Griffin commented to Gilden.

"Sometimes one must make allowances," replied the unicorn. "Though we prefer the company of children in general. They are somewhat less violent than the adults of your kind. Humans have created many legends with the usual human motivations behind them. The myth of the virgin is doubtless a religious-based attempt to keep women from certain behaviors. Witches are thought to lose their power if they engage in mating rituals, but what is more powerful than bringing forth life? Mothers are more powerful than maids."

"I never thought of it that way," Auran mused.

"You, Lady of the Fey, will come into your understanding and awareness more each year, just as do many others of your kind. Elders of both sexes used to be honored on your planet, and still are in some cultures. However, wisdom is not understood as a great power, so your people focus on other forms."

"Why do you call me that, Lady of the Fey?" asked Auran.

"You have had many lifetimes as a faery creature, naiad, mermaid, nymph, nature spirit, and a queen or leader of such creatures. They will come if you call. You might remind Rebecca that you are able to help protect your home by drawing from your own experience."

"I'm not sure I understand what you mean," Auran said, "but I'm already quite fond of the little people in the yard. I suppose if Rebecca could have been a dragon, I could have been a faery. One of the faery folk told me her name was Panissa Mariblossom, and she gave me some pansy nectar. It was quite tasty. Oh my goodness, Griff, I really was a faery! I just remembered coming out of my chrysalis, damp with dew, new-winged, with the taste of nectar on my lips. How could I have forgotten?"

"You were born human," Gilden said. "That's how most beings forget. I have heard it is the most difficult form in which to remember oneself. I have not tried it, however I did incarnate as a giant once. Though I trod on a few humans by accident, at least I did not forget myself. I never was very graceful on two legs, but that is the closest I've ever come to being human."

"Stepping on one?" Griffin repeated in disbelief. "I don't think that really counts. How about me, what sorts of creatures have I been?"

Gilden eyed him for a moment. "Merman, Griffin, Centaur, Gnome, Selkie...Do you want to hear about the dark creatures as well? Most beings have learned from their shadow selves in many lifetimes. You humans often forget that the soul learns from all aspects of consciousness, not only the pretty forms."

"I'm having enough trouble getting my mind around the idea of me with a fish tail. I don't want to hear about what a creep I've been through the centuries."

"It is not as important what form you held," the unicorn reminded him. "As it is what you learned."

"Does it count if you forgot it all later?" Griffin asked. "I don't seem to remember if I learned anything or not."

Gilden made a sound that reminded Griffin and Auran of a lawn mower, and it took them a moment to realize he was laughing.

"I have always enjoyed your humor, Griffin Bloom," the unicorn said finally. "Now I am going to call my Folk in to help keep watch. Rest well." Gilden rose from his place by the hammock and thrust his horn high into the air.

Griffin and Auran watched as Gilden's golden horn began to glow white in the darkness. The light was soon reflected by other glowing horns, most golden or white, a few blue or green, all descending from the sky into the yard. Auran and Griffin soon basked in the luminance of the whole herd of unicorns.

"This is better than tiki torches," Griffin whispered, as the unicorns lined up in rows, dancing gracefully upon their hind legs.

"You can tell what sort of unicorn they are by the horn glow," Auran whispered back. "The blue ones heal with sound, the green are more connected to physical nature, the golden ones heal soul wounds, and the white ones, like Gilden, penetrate spiritual darkness. Oh wow, how did I know that?"

"I don't know, but it's getting a little nippy out here. How about we head on inside and see if we can find anything really trivial and mindlessly boring on T.V. I keep worrying at odd moments that I've gone nuts. Then I remember that you have too, so at least I'll have company."

"I know what you mean," Auran admitted. "After angels and unicorns and remembering having wings, I could use something profoundly superficial to watch as well. And Mom and Dad are coming over tomorrow. We'll need to get lots of rest."

"I'll head over to the office to check on things tomorrow," Griffin volunteered. "Give me a call and tell me when they're gone."

Auran elbowed him in the ribs, nearly knocking him out of the hammock. "All right, you goof, you're off the hook this time, but what are you going to do with my Mother for three weeks at the lake?"

"Suffer?"

Chapter 10

"Mom, do we have any sea salt anywhere?" Rebecca called from the kitchen door. "I've been ransacking the cupboards, but I didn't find any."

"Hang on a minute, Re," Auran said, hanging up the hall phone before joining her. "I had to finish my phone call first. If the salt's not here, it's upstairs in the bath. I had to use it instead of Epsom salts. What do we need it for?"

"Torin's on the net trying to locate other Thianelians. Dad snuck off to the office this morning early, so I thought you and I could set up some other safety precautions around the house."

"Gilden did mention something about that last night," Auran said. "And Griff did warn me he'd be leaving, so it's not exactly sneaking."

"He looked pretty sneaky to me, Mom," Rebecca laughed. "He had that guilty I'm-avoiding-Hazel look on his face."

Auran smiled, as she and Rebecca started upstairs to locate the salt. "How is Torin handling all of this?" she asked curiously. "He seems to be very calm most of the time, and even when he's pointing out your grandmother's lack of manners he does it very politely."

"He loses his temper now and then, but not hardly so you'd notice," Rebecca said. "Usually it's when there are Bolluxes about, or if he thinks I'm being threatened. It's got to be pretty weird being here though. I'm having a hard time and I'm a native."

Auran paused outside her bedroom door. "I have to admit, if I hadn't experienced most of this first hand, I wouldn't believe it at all."

She pushed open the door to her bedroom and immediately spied something buzzing in the large geranium pot by the window.

"How did flies get in here?" she muttered, as Rebecca went into the bathroom to find the sea salt. Auran bent down to examine the plant more closely.

"Rebecca," she said. "How come there are small faeries living in the geraniums? I thought nothing was allowed in here without our permission."

Rebecca came quickly, sea salt in hand. "I asked for help from all of the guardians on the planet when I sang yesterday. I think these are faery guards. I saw three naiads in your bathtub, and the orchids in your bathroom are full of flower Devas. Six angels followed Dad to the office and seven of them are here guarding the house. I think a bunch of unicorns showed up too."

Auran nodded. "Griffin and I saw them last night. We certainly have a house full. Do you really think it's necessary?"

"I'm afraid so, Mom. You know how we have burglar alarms to keep out crooks? There are other levels of defense needed when you have to keep out beings who can shift form or materialize at will. By the way, do you still have those quartz crystals that I gave you from the bookstore?"

"All of them, sweetie. I keep them in the dresser drawer over here."

Auran pulled out several large clear quartz crystals, as well as a pink rose quartz and a deep purple amethyst wand. She set them all on top of the dresser. Finally, she held out a round black globe.

"One of the employees gave me this round obsidian ball, too, when you first disappeared. She said it was for finding anything missing on the planet." She chuckled. "No wonder it didn't work. You weren't on the planet at all."

"These are great, Mom," Rebecca assured her. "We're going to set up an energy grid to keep out harmful influences. We can do it in the living room on the coffee table."

"Okay," Auran agreed, "but then you'll really have to keep your feet off the coffee table. And I have some fresh rosemary and other herbs to make herb amulets to spread throughout the house. Frankincense resin also works well to clear out nasty creatures." She paused in disbelief.

"There I go again. I didn't even know that I knew this stuff, and I loathe New Ageism."

"Now you know how I feel," Rebecca said in commiseration. "It takes a little getting used to."

They gathered everything they needed into the living room and laid out a cloth on the coffee table. Once Auran had made a circle of salt to represent the house and yard, Rebecca placed the crystals inside the circle. Auran handed her several squares of linen piled with herbs: rosemary, juniper, and sage, with little bits of frankincense. After tying the bundles with thread, they put one in each room of the house.

Returning to the living room, Rebecca and Auran clasped hands and charged the crystals to protect the house. Auran could feel energy running between their hands into the crystals. Her feet tingled and her back grew warm. Afterwards, she felt a strange rippling effect across her shoulder blades.

Rebecca eyed her curiously. "Did you know you have large white wings popping out on your back? Not physically, Mom, etherically. Look, I can run my hand right through them."

Auran blushed, feeling strangely naked, as if she'd sung on a public street, or been caught thinking aloud. She turned to look, and could barely make out the faint outline of thick white wingspans, the tips reaching all the way up to the ceiling.

"No wonder you saw angels when you were a kid," Rebecca commented. "You spent a lot of time as one."

Auran trembled, causing her wings to immediately retract. "Rebecca, that is quite possibly the nicest thing anyone has ever said to me. I don't think I'm quite ready for wings though. But how is it that we have a whole troop of unicorns lounging in the yard, dragons sailing through the sky, angels perched on the roof, and no one sees them?"

"Some people might," replied Rebecca. "Little kids and some adults who haven't forgotten how. Others might look at a unicorn and see only a horse. When Gilden looks at you, for instance, he sees everything you've ever been as part of all that you are. Human, faery, mermaid, angel, and so on.

On Thianely, it was so strange to be reminded of all that I have been by everyone I met. It kind of messes with your self-perception. It's really hard to have low self-esteem when everything around you validates your entire existence. Now that your vision has expanded because your brain is open to interpreting information differently, you'll never forget you've had wings. I wonder if Dad will be able to see Grandmother differently some day. Not simply as an annoying old witch, which she incidentally has been, but as all she's ever been and will be as well."

"I wouldn't hold my breath on that one if I were you, sweetie," Auran said, still slightly reeling from seeing her own wings. "Some habits are hard to change."

"That's kind of an interesting way to look at it," Rebecca mused. "Old perceptions are like habitual thoughts. I suppose you have to replace them with new thoughts to break the old perceptions."

Auran sat down on the sofa. "Sometimes you sound like you're three hundred years old rather than seventeen, Rebecca. After I sit for a few minutes I'm going to go do something completely normal, like make a batch of cookies."

"I'll go see how Torin's investigating is going," Rebecca said. "Let me know when Grandmother and Fort get here."

Rebecca found Torin happily ensconced with Griffin's computer, his fingers flying over the keyboard. He'd managed to change the desktop color in addition to adding small green lizards skateboarding across. He turned his head as Rebecca peered closely over his shoulder and planted a quick kiss on her nose.

"Have any luck?" she asked, leaning over and resting her chin on his shoulder.

"Yes," he said in satisfaction. "It appears you did as well. I could feel the extra barrier you and Auran created around the house. As you do, she grows stronger in power and awareness every moment." He rotated the mouse, checking Griffin's inbox for incoming mail.

Rebecca looked at the screen in surprise. "Forty two return messages? Which web site did you contact?"

"Telmind.com," he replied, amused. "Though mindtel is difficult here, the long distance telers used it anyway, in a manner of speaking."

"Clever," Rebecca nodded. "What did you say?"

"I left a message that the Guardians have been called to awaken and that any Thianelians in a position to meet us within ten days time contact me at Griffin's e-mail address. It only helps that his address has Griffin in it. They will assume he is also Thianelian, as most Thianelians have always been aware of the link between our planets."

"What are you planning? To have them all show up at the lake to help sing aemethra?"

"It appears to be a safe place to gather," Torin admitted, "so I thought to discuss it with your parents before I reply to the e-mails."

"Sounds like a plan," Rebecca said, suddenly yawning. "Whew, I'm tired again. I'm going to go lie down until my grandparents get here." She watched for a moment longer as Torin shifted to a computer game and began to play cards. She patted him on the shoulder, thinking how even offworlders could get addicted to computer technology.

"Rebecca," Torin called softly before she headed completely out the door. "I understand now why your people spend so much time distracting themselves." He looked up at her, his eyes very green. "When I focus on the games, I do not contemplate lives such as our dragon ones."

"You just had to get me to turn red before I left, didn't you," she admonished him, shaking her finger slightly. "I'll see you later, Torin. I think I need to save up some energy to deal with Grandmother."

Rebecca walked to her room slowly, feeling rather strange. Hugging her pillow, she snuggled down on her bed, realizing that part of her wasn't quite ready to let go of her old idea of her parents. There had always been the comfort of knowing how they would behave, how they would think in different situations. Now her mother was growing wings and her father was making angel jokes. She sighed, knowing that it was all going much more smoothly than she'd anticipated, but she felt wistful nonetheless.

And she had to admit she still felt sickened by what had happened to Royden. No matter what the circumstances, taking a life was dreadful. It seemed somehow worse that he would be completely unmourned by his relatives, except perhaps by Liliar.

"I could have let go of his hand," she thought, even while knowing that she hadn't had much choice if their friends were to have been freed. Still, she was saddened by the necessity to defend herself, her friends and family, and to seal the house. The density of fear that most people experienced on earth felt overwhelming to her. Finally she closed her eyes, drifting into sleep.

She was back on Thianely, under the deep pink sky. Under her feet was a carpet of thick, leathery blue leaves and on all sides she could feel the towering presence of the inhabitants of the Threshold of the Trees. Before her stood the largest tree of all, the Great Tree, whose bark shifted from brown to blue to green at will. "That's odd," she thought. "The Great Tree was uprooted long ago. I must be dreaming. Oh well, I'll go inside anyway."

As it had many times before, the bark of the Great Tree parted for her, opening into a smooth, crystal lit passageway. Expecting to see Meridwen of the Tree Folk, Rebecca was surprised to see the essence being of the tree, Alphumerian herself. She was thin and weathered, old beyond imagining. She met Rebecca with open arms, catching her up and swinging her around like a child. Rebecca, astounded at the strength of such a small person, blurted out the first thing that came into her head.

"But you're dead. I saw you."

"Of course," Alphumerian nodded approvingly. She set Rebecca back down on the ground. "What has that to do with anything?"

Rebecca opened her mouth to reply, then thought better of it. "I'm very happy to see you," she said finally.

Alphumerian smiled, creasing her cheeks into rivulets of wrinkles. "I wanted to tell you that you are doing a wonderful job securing the wisdom of the crystals, Rebecca. Do not worry; the information can only be given to a living tree, no other. It is safe inside you, because the crystals willed it so. Come along through here," and she pushed open a thick door that Rebecca had never seen before. Inside was a large circular room with smooth green walls that pulsed, as if the heart of the tree beat through the wood. As Alphumerian pointed downwards, two mushroom-shaped stools formed out of the floor. She sat down on one, indicating that Rebecca sit on the other.

"Is this really the Great Tree?" Rebecca wondered aloud.

"In a manner of thinking," replied the essence being. "Now listen, I am here to help you access the information you need to plant the next tree properly, as well as any other tidbits that may come in handy."

Rebecca glanced at her suspiciously. "You don't talk like Alphumerian did."

"What do you expect from a dead person? Now that I am no longer bound by my last form, I may express myself any way I wish. If you are not so attached to people's personalities, you will be more at ease when they shift."

"Oh," Rebecca said, thinking about her parents.

"Now, focus your mind, child, and follow the light of the crystals inside you."

Rebecca closed her eyes, imagining the crystals, the enormous stones emanating wisdom and strength. Each glowed separately in her mind, and for the first time she realized that each had a specific kind of information. The clear crystal housed information from the beginning of creation, of past, present, future, and the state of awareness and presence where time did not exist at all. The pink crystal recorded the evolution of consciousness manifested in form and formlessness. The purple crystal catalogued all sensory-based information in every dimension that had such distinctions. Although the information of each crystal was contained in her mind, Rebecca realized that at some level, she was contained inside it as well.

"Very well thought," Alphumerian said. "Now, to access each kind of wisdom separately without going mad, you must be as specific with your intention as possible. If you allowed the wisdom to stream through too freely, you would lose all sense of self and be completely useless, so far as this lifetime goes. In other thoughts, ask exactly what you need to know, addressing one crystal at a time. This is only a technique to clarify information, for the crystals themselves are only symbols of the information itself. Picturing them separately allows you to contain the wisdom properly."

Rebecca smiled wryly. "Just as you are only a symbol of the knowledge of how to access the information." "I knew you would understand quickly," Alphumerian said. "I will be here whenever you need me." She immediately vanished, leaving Rebecca sitting on the little tree stool, wondering if she should have kept her mouth shut.

"Rebecca, wake up." Rebecca wondered for a moment how Torin had arrived in her dream, but soon the chamber in The Great Tree faded. She opened her eyes to find Torin gently shaking her shoulders.

"Your mother asked that I wake you," he explained. "Your grandparents are here to see you. Did you sleep well?"

Rebecca sat up and hugged him. "I was back in the Great Tree, receiving instructions from Alphumerian. I have to access the crystal wisdom more directly in order to plant the new tree. It was so comforting being there, Torin. For a little while it was safe without my mind shields."

Torin held her closely. "Rebecca, how are your mind shields holding up?"

Rebecca made a face. "I miss Thianely. I miss the song of the ground supporting me, the pink sky, even the smell of the air. I feel burdened here, as if everything takes effort. I never needed naps before. There must be more gravity or something. I don't feel particularly nourished by the food or water, and to tell you the truth, it was better being a dragon."

"You are homesick for wholeness," Torin said knowingly. "I will bring you some of the root cakes Imelina gave us; that might help. Didn't Leva give you some leaves and sap from the Threshold Trees as well?"

While he went to get the food, Rebecca went to the dresser. There in plain view were the blue leaves from Leva. Feeling the thick strength of the leaves helped, and Rebecca remembered Leva telling her once, as they sat nestled high in a limb at the Threshold of the Trees, that all leaves on Thianely carried the energy of their home tree. The leaves and sap had healing properties for dispelling sorrow and brought strength when one was away from one's tree. Many Thianelians incorporated the fibrous leaves into their clothing and carried them close to their bodies.

"I guess this counts as being away from my tree, a whole planet of them," she said, fingering a leaf. As she stroked the leafy veins, she felt the familiar sounds and smells of Thianely settle into her. Her feet sank deeply into the carpet, as if searching for ground.

Torin returned, and held to her lips the acorn cakes Leva's grandmother had made. Rebecca took a bite, chewing slowly. She felt fed on more levels than only her body, and she realized that the sweetness, the clear sharp taste, seemed to pierce the sadness inside her and melt it away. Again she realized how far she'd come from her old Earth self, and yet how easy it was for her to slip into sorrow when constantly surrounded by despair. How much harder it would be for most people to stay clear of suffering, having never experienced anything other than such vast separation, except perhaps as babies.

She stopped her contemplation as Torin handed her a little food parcel, wrapped in a woven vine cloth.

He looked at her closely. "You seem a little more refreshed," he commented. "Keep the rest for later, whenever you may have need of it."

"What about you, Torin? How are you doing in this strange place I call home?"

Torin hesitated, thinking for a moment. "I miss sharing a sleeping space with you, but my grounding holds well, if not my containment. I do not feel much weight of pain here, though, like you, I tire more easily. But come, your grandfather wishes to speak with you further."

They made their way downstairs. Fort was pacing up and down the hallway waiting for Rebecca. When she inquired about her grandmother, Auran told her that Hazel was collapsed in an arm chair in the living room, having been walked to exhaustion by Fort, whose energy level appeared more than recovered.

"Rebecca, kiddo, whatever you did, it worked great!" Fort gave her a bone-crushing embrace and shook Torin's hand vigorously. "Now that I have my strength back, I want you to tell me all the things you left out of the first version you gave us."

Rebecca and Torin took turns explaining more about Thianely and their adventures there. At first Rebecca felt awkward talking about her part in things. There were so many experiences difficult to put into words. And this was her grandfather, who'd known her since she was first born. But Auran nodded at her reassuringly whenever she hesitated, which made it easier, and Torin filled in the parts she skimmed over.

Fort eyed her over his coffee cup. They'd left Hazel snoring on the sofa while they sat around the kitchen table snacking on brownies Auran had made.

"I probably wouldn't believe your story if you didn't look so obviously different, Sport, not to mention what happened in my own body. As for you, Torin, I'm proud to know you. Now what?"

"This might be a good time to talk about extra guests at the lake, Torin," Rebecca suggested.

Torin turned to Auran. "I have forty two e-mails from Thianelians nearby, at least within several hours driving distance. I thought to ask your permission to invite them to meet us at the lake. I need details on day and time, and directions for maps."

Before Auran could open her mouth, Fort said eagerly, "More folks like you? I can't wait! Who would have thought there really were aliens living in New York! Although, now that I think about it, it's probably the easiest place for them to blend in."

"It sounds fine to me," Auran said. "We still haven't firmed up the exact departure day. I'll talk to Griff when he gets back from work. You ought to be able to reply to the e-mails tomorrow though, Torin."

"I should probably take Hazel home and put her to bed," Fort said. "She seems to be very tired lately."

"I think she's worn out more than physically," Rebecca informed him. "In order for you to heal, your whole vibratory pattern speeded up. For her it's kind of exhausting being around that quickness of energy; it'll take her a while to catch up."

"What are you all up to for the rest of the day?" Fort asked.

"I thought we could make a trip to the library," Torin replied. "I found some books on the net that are not available to be downloaded. One is called, *Lore of the Fire Lord,* by Tyor Kehn, probably a Thianelian. The library has it in, as well as several others I would like to read."

"I came up with a shopping list for the organic grocery. Why don't you spend the money I gave you for a birthday gift, Rebecca," Auran said. "Get Torin some more clothes while you're at it. He probably shouldn't go too far in Thianelian clothes or those baggy Griffin castoffs."

"Okay, Mom," Rebecca said. She gave her grandfather a hug and tugged Torin toward the door. "Let's get going before all of the school kids get out and mob the place."

Chapter 11

Rebecca was grateful that the library was such an enormous building. She and Torin arrived in the back where the dumpsters stood like squat army tanks, well away from any foot traffic. As they made their way inside, Rebecca immediately took a deep breath of the familiar air, fresh and slightly bookish. She pointed the way to the computerized locator system and quickly showed Torin how to find the titles he wanted.

Although it was early afternoon, there were still many people in the aisles, including numbers of school kids in the children's section, listening to a librarian reading aloud. Rebecca and Torin found the books they wanted, none of which had been checked out recently, and made their way to the checkout line.

"Why don't we do the automated checkout," Rebecca suggested. "It's faster. Those fluorescent lights make me dizzy. And did you notice that the books in the historical section had a kind of humming in them?"

"Most of the books in here do," Torin replied, patting her arm somewhat absently, as he focused on some commotion at the other end of the checkout line.

"Get out of the way!"

"I want to see them, too!"

"Stop hogging the front!"

A whole group of preschoolers charged through the line, leaving their books on the counter, with their harried teacher and a parent helper scurrying after them. Rebecca had just finished checking out the last book with the automated system when she and Torin were mobbed.

"It is them!" one boy called excitedly.

"Can I see your hands light up?" a little redheaded girl asked Torin.

"Can I come over to your house?" asked another.

"I was a faery once," a little girl informed Rebecca solemnly. "But now my wings are only see-through."

"Children, come back here right now," yelled their teacher, causing one of the librarians to shush her sternly.

"That's enough, back in line," the teacher's parent helper said, trying to redirect some of the nearest children. He soon reached Torin and Rebecca, who were completely encircled by twenty small children.

"I'm terribly sorry, they must have mistaken you for actors or something."

"They're not actors, Dad," his little boy proclaimed scornfully, "they're magic."

"Everything's magic," a schoolmate corrected him. "That's because nobody knows how anything got here really, not even doctors, not even the president. We're magic too."

"Can I go back home?" a little boy asked wistfully.

"Where do you live?" Rebecca said curiously.

"Not that kind of home. I mean, can I go back inside my mom and go back to my real home?"

"Do you remember why you came here?" Rebecca asked kindly, as Torin obligingly showed his spiral palms to several enthralled little kids.

"Not really. I think my mom and dad wanted me to, so I had to do what they said. Can I go back now, like you did?"

"I'm right here," Rebecca reminded him.

"Yeah, but you got to go visit."

Rebecca couldn't argue with that. It struck her as extremely odd that she was standing in the New York Public Library having a chat about Thianely with a child she didn't even know, although he did look familiar. Come to think of it, they all looked as if she'd known them before. It reminded her of a comment her friend Leva had made on Thianely. She'd said that Rebecca probably knew everyone in creation, that because Rebecca had had so many lifetimes, everyone she met was familiar.

Her ponderings were cut short by the teacher's irate voice. "Children, we are leaving the library now, without your books. You've all behaved very badly. I want you to apologize to these people."

"That's it, kids," added the parent helper, "you've bothered this couple enough. Back in line."

The kids waved goodbye to Torin and Rebecca, and after more scolding from their teacher, finally lined up in an orderly fashion and headed for the door, turning back for one last look.

"We're sorry our teacher is so crabby," a chorus of small voices rang out.

"But we're not sorry you're magic," added one small voice. "Bye!"

Torin and Rebecca waited a few moments, until they were outside the library doors, to laugh out loud.

"I felt like the Pied Piper in there," Rebecca said finally. "They all knew who we were."

"And even how my hands could light on fire," Torin said. "I suppose your call to all Guardians included even the youngest."

Rebecca nodded, slumping against the building wall. "Torin, I kind of got sick back there. Not with the kids, but around all of the books. I still feel a little strange."

"Rebecca, there were stacks and stacks of books, like the Great Tree in pages. Perhaps that is why your people use trees to make books, because of the innate wisdom of trees. When I first visited your planet, I became ill from the deaths of so many trees. Now think of all of the energy from all the people who've ever written or read those books. Their reactions, feelings, and experiences are included in those books as well. That is much to endure, Rebecca. I should have warned you to strengthen your shield."

"It's okay. I'm better now. I suppose we could try shopping. We're not likely to meet so many little kids at the mall. At least bookstores have new books with not so much people energy on them."

Torin reached out, pulling Rebecca toward him for a kiss. "It will be easier when you become accustomed to large numbers of your Folk," he assured her. "Your shield can be automatic. Ask that it strengthen as needed."

Rebecca kissed him back. "Let's go."

Rebecca sat down in the mall cafe with a sigh of relief. She'd left Torin in the men's department with a stack of bills in order to replenish his wardrobe. Auran had given her two hundred dollars, which seemed like a lot but probably wouldn't last long. Rebecca had bought herself a new aventurine crystal, a pair of jeans, and some socks, but she felt no interest in buying most of what she saw. Her Thianelian clothes were so much more comfortable. And there were so many things in stores. Things she didn't need or want, things made not to be beautiful or useful, but only to be purchased. She ordered some hot cocoa and smiled at a toddler in a stroller. The child gurgled happily.

That was something that took getting used to, people's responses. Grown men ogled her foolishly, and women kept approaching Torin to ask for his autograph. Many of them had assumed that the two of them were celebrities of some sort. Torin had suggested pulling in their energy fields to be less obtrusive and that helped a bit.

It was so strange to have people notice her this way. The glow that surrounded her and Torin seemed to be interpreted by many as sexual attractiveness. Unlike children, who recognized their souls, most adults attributed their light to physical appearance. It would have been insulting if it weren't somehow pathetic. It was however, quite interesting to see Torin having to deal with so much unwanted attention from the ladies. He had to develop a special shield in order to cope with it. On Thianely, he would have had no need for such protection, and he found the whole experience quite unnerving.

As Rebecca took a sip of hot cocoa, she heard a voice say, "Excuse me." She looked up to see a man, early twenties, with black hair and eyes, staring at her intently. Rebecca inwardly sighed.

"I'm Garen Brown. I can see that you're not in the mood for company, but I wanted to let you know that there are those of us who have vision as well. I know you have many special gifts that need to be developed more fully. I run a psychic training institute, Eyes of Isis, and I'm sure I can help you learn how to control your abilities. Even though you have no idea what you're doing yet, you can learn."

Rebecca wasn't sure whether to be offended or amused. "I think I'll muddle along like I've been doing," she responded. "Thanks anyway."

The man pulled out a chair and sat down. "Listen," he said urgently, as Rebecca looked longingly at the door.

"I can train you to be powerful, to see the future, to know what others are thinking, what secrets they're hiding."

"That sounds pretty rude," Rebecca commented, wondering idly if he could intuit her extreme distaste for his company. Apparently not, as he continued extolling the virtues of his institute. Finally, Rebecca's early childhood training in etiquette gave out. The moment she stood up to go, Torin arrived.

"Here, take my business card," Garen said hastily, not liking the look on Torin's face.

"No thank you," Rebecca repeated, refusing to take his card.

"Leave now," Torin said evenly, a tone in his voice Rebecca had rarely heard. Garen got up slowly, taking a few steps toward the exit. Then he stopped and turned back.

"We know who you are," he hissed, his features shifting to a mask of hate. "You won't be able to do anything here without us knowing. We'll prevent anything you try. We are trained and more powerful than anything you could even imagine. If you don't join us, you'll die." He stomped out.

"Yuck, what a fruitcake," Rebecca said in disgust. "He was a total psycho."

"Worse," Torin said. "Not all the demons and ghouls have left. Humans like that are worse than Bolluxes. At least Bolluxes are merely acting from their true natures; they've never been given a choice. Beings like that one have chosen to use their gifts to manipulate and harm others. He's a dark sorcerer, not only connected with demons, but also aware of that which we intend to accomplish here." He looked around in dismay. "A coffee shop, no less. One never knows where one may encounter such creatures."

"You know what's weird?" Rebecca remarked. "He didn't smell bad, or have an obviously icky energy field. It was deceptive, except that as soon as he opened his mouth, his rotten little soul was apparent."

"Did you look in his eyes?"

"No," Rebecca said in surprise, "I didn't want to."

"Good," Torin replied. "You would have recognized what he was immediately, and defended yourself against him in front of all of these coffee sippers."

"Jeez, I hope not. I don't plan to go around smiting people, even gnarly ones."

Torin shook his head. "It's part of what happens when your shield is up. Any threat to that must leave or be removed."

"Then what about all of those dopey guys, and the women chasing you around?"

"They are merely annoyances, not threats."

"Well, what did you get?' Rebecca asked, gesturing toward his packages.

Torin smiled. "You will see later. Now we have one more stop to make, the grocery store."

By the time they returned home, Rebecca was exhausted from trying to maintain her shield for so long in public. The amount of energy it took was enormous. They stacked the groceries on top of the kitchen table, tossed their shopping bags on the floor, and collapsed for a few moments.

Auran came into the kitchen, took one look at their faces and began putting the groceries away, waving them both back into their seats when they made a motion towards helping.

"You two look like you've been shopping on the day after Thanksgiving. What happened?"

"Everywhere we went kids came up to us and wanted to either come home with us or have Torin fire up his hands. Guys were treating me like I was Marilyn Monroe or something, and Torin kept getting propositioned by strange women. It was crazy."

"You both have a lot of light around you," Auran commented. "It sounds like people were reacting to that in their own odd ways. Did you have any luck being invisible at all?"

Rebecca shook her head. "It was so hard to have the energy to do anything much besides pull in our energy fields. And I think I'm allergic to fluorescent lights. I kept getting dizzy after a while. It's really discouraging to be so sensitive to large numbers of people all thinking too much and worrying about everything. This must be what it's like to come from a farm in the Midwest and move to the City."

"Or come from another planet," Auran reminded her. "How did you like the mall, Torin?"

Torin smiled, pulling a green t-shirt out of one of the shopping bags. He held it up so that they could read the phrase "I Brake for Cabbies!" across the front, directly below a picture of a NY cab.

Auran and Rebecca both clapped their hands as Torin pulled out four other t-shirts of various colors, all with the same logo.

"That's great," Rebecca said, "but what about something with long sleeves, like a jacket? You can't walk around the streets of New York with your palms glowing for warmth."

Torin held up a long black coat with a thick silk lining.

"Wait a minute," Auran protested, "I don't think I gave you enough money to cover that nice a coat. It looks like a designer. My God, look at the tag on this; it's not even on sale! This is a $2000.00 coat."

"The sales woman told me not to worry about the price," Torin said. "She said that they give VIPs free items all of the time. What's a VIP?"

"All right, what else do you have in those bags?" Rebecca demanded, after explaining the definition of VIP to Torin, who could not understand why wealthy famous people who had no need of free gifts were given them when others in need had to go without.

Torin, for the price of $45.38, was the owner of one designer jacket, five t-shirts, three pairs of jeans, four pairs of socks, one green sweatshirt, and an expensive men's watch, which the sales woman had also thrown in for free since "everyone should have a watch."

"Tell me you actually spent some money on yourself, Rebecca," Auran said.

"Well, some," Rebecca admitted. The lady at the crystal shop had given her a discount on the aventurine stone, saying that it really should be marked down. The pair of jeans she'd purchased hadn't been in the computer system properly so she'd only had to pay $1, and the socks were 50% off, even though it hadn't said so on the tag. "But I have most of it left. The only thing we really spent money on was the groceries, but the cashier gave us some free fruit."

"Generosity in New York! Next time I'm going shopping with you two," Auran vowed in awe. "Griffin will never believe this."

Chapter 12

That evening Rebecca and Torin sat on the floor of her bedroom, both meditating before dinner. After clearing her mind completely and entering a state of complete relaxation, Rebecca was attempting to contact Alphumerian in order to access the crystal wisdom again. She needed more information on planting the Great Tree. In the meantime, Torin was contacting their friends on Thianely, informing them about Liliar being his half sister, and catching them up on events.

Rebecca let her breathing lengthen, her heartbeat slow. She watched thoughts moving across her mind for a moment, and then allowed them to dissolve. She pictured the Great Tree in front of her as she'd last seen it, but it kept fading, its huge trunk and blue leafed branches becoming transparent, silvery ghostly images.

"How annoying," Rebecca thought crossly, wondering why it was so difficult for her to visualize the Great Tree. "Perhaps it's like my inability to mindtel long distance any more. I don't have enough control here."

She sighed, and unable to hold the tree steady, she let it go. Immediately, Rebecca found herself back in the interstellar classroom she'd first visited on Thianely. Pausing in the middle of a discourse on vibrational acclimation and attunement, the teacher, a bulgy-eyed Crispung with green algae robes, noted Rebecca's arrival and indicated an empty seat. The room was crowded with all manners of beings sitting on mossy seat pads and listening intently.

"The most common difficulty for most expanded beings," said the Crispung, keeping her multiple eyes on everyone without turning her head, "is incarnating in places of such crude vibratory patterns that they literally lose their integrity. Try to avoid such systems if possible. If, however, you have contracted to be in one of these places, then there are several things you may try in order to acclimate. Some beings become sleepers among "The Great Unawakened," as we refer to dense populations. These sleepers will not lose consciousness, but conveniently hide it until support systems are in place and they awaken again. Many newly birthed beings choose this sort of suspended animation in order to alleviate damage to the psyche. Any questions?"

She swiveled her many eyes, which clung to her forehead and neck like small barnacles.

"To continue, most of the sleepers awaken due to some sort of external trigger built into their lives by their own consciousness. By the time they awaken they are sufficiently familiar with the native vibration to be able to function somewhat, although they will probably notice an increased inability to tolerate large groups of the population. They will probably become fatigued and somewhat repulsed at the thought forms of their fellows. This may in turn lead to isolation, perhaps alienation from others. This however, serves an important function, since one must reconnect to oneness by focusing inwardly. Awakening sleepers tend to need a lot of alone time to further their memories.

There are also those beings that choose to incarnate into dense vibrations and maintain full awareness. They are unaffected by large numbers of the population because they are viewing everything from a state of wholeness, thus nothing is separate from themselves and causes them little discomfort. They tend to have little in common with the ego aspects of lower vibrational beings, and may seem as far removed from them as emptiness is from fullness. Yes, I know there is no distinction in reality, but you must remember that in vibratory patterns of the sort under discussion, there are separations inside separations."

A woolly looking fellow in a front row seat raised his hand. "Why would anyone bother going into such extreme conditions anyway?" he asked curiously. The Crispung surveyed the room slowly, finally pointing an algae-covered digit at Rebecca.

"Ask her," she said, "she's spent more of creation in such places than anyone else in the room."

Rebecca watched as everyone turned to stare at her. She wasn't quite sure what she would say, but hoped that when she opened her mouth something would come. She swallowed once, and then spoke.

"I enjoy it. There is something about going into a particularly thick vibration and remembering all of one's consciousness. Like a child's game called hide and seek, only we are hiding from ourselves. It takes a great deal of trust to know there is always light, even when you can't see it.

Also, some beings do not remember easily, and I enjoy helping others awaken. I've found that the most effective method of doing so is to become one of them. Having compassion for another's struggle is much easier once you have compassion for your own. Finally, any chance I get to sing creation, I thoroughly enjoy. As for the difficulty of maintaining integrity in these environments, that is a challenge. I am still dealing with that one."

The Crispung nodded, remarking, "intention, my dear, intention. Use the elements at your disposal to support you. In places of tensive vibration, you must ask more. Ask the planet to sing her song for you; she is like a rejected child that feels unwanted. Support her, encourage her, or demand from her, because sometimes compassion must be fierce.

Above all, remember to do that which arises from wholeness and love, rather than from some idea of purpose or destiny. Remember the first lesson of creation; set an intention and let it go. If you are determined to hold to your destiny, you are no doubt preventing yourself from living it. Follow that which rings true in the moment. Remember the second lesson of creation; joy in being, joy in doing, joy in all things. Any questions?" There were none, and as the Crispung continued her lecture, Rebecca felt herself fading from the classroom.

She returned to her own room, feeling the carpet under her bottom, the faint sound of the earth beneath her. She reached down through the ground, through many layers of pain and anguish, through the growth of roots and creatures of soil. Humming fiercely, Rebecca called to the earth to sing her song more proudly, more fully. The earth responded with notes of joy, letting the sound move through its layers until Rebecca began to shake slightly in her chair. The sound traveled up her legs, her spine, into her heart and out through the top of her head. She immediately felt better.

"Well done," Torin said, reaching over to stroke the tip of her nose with his finger. He could feel the tip of her nose vibrating slightly with the hum of the earth.

"Now we can work together even better," Rebecca said with satisfaction, patting the ground beside her. "Don't worry, Earth, I know you are still feeling separated in places, but many of us do appreciate everything you have helped sustain here." Again she felt an answering surge of sound from beneath her, causing her to weave back and forth in her sitting position.

"You know, Torin, I probably ought to feel silly talking to the planet, but lately I talk to everything. And most things respond! I was trying to imagine being in school again, learning about biology, for instance. We learned formulas and chemical reactions and all the parts of a plant. But it's so much faster to ask plants what they need. A lot of information taught here seems secondhand rather than direct. And do you know what's funny? Every time I forget really important information, I wind up back in that interstellar classroom, where they just happen to be discussing what I most need to remember. And that in turn reminds me that whatever we need to know is always available if we're paying attention. I was really crabby that I couldn't contact Alphumerian, but once I let go, it turned out that I learned something else."

"It works that way sometimes," Torin said. "Once you relinquish trying to control what you learn, you are more open to receiving what you most need."

"It's too bad our educational system here is so full of unimportant crap," Rebecca declared, thinking about all of the useless information she'd been forced to memorize for too many years.

"Education here provides your people with the kind of information that allows them to cope with Earth society, Rebecca. If your Folk understood plant or animal consciousness, your whole world would be different. Consciousness would be different. I'm sure under those circumstances your Folk would learn as we do on Thianely, from everything around us, rather than in separated forms of education."

At that moment, Auran knocked on the door. She poked in her head to see Rebecca sitting on the floor swaying back and forth like a cobra being charmed.

"Hi, you two. Griff's home, and dinner will be ready soon. Why don't you come set the table?"

Soon they were all seated in the kitchen eating rice and lentils and fruit salad, while Torin described their experience in the library.

"Wait until you see the clothes he came back with," Auran said. Griffin shook his head in disbelief when he heard all of the free items they'd received. He agreed with Torin's plan to invite the closest Thianelians to meet them out at the lake. "I can draw up a map and directions tomorrow morning if you want. Anyone want to hear about my day? It was a doozy."

"Uh, oh," Rebecca said, "what happened?"

"It all started fine," Griffin began, "even if the faeries in the office plants did cause a little distraction. I wasn't quite expecting them to be there for some reason. So the day was fairly normal, until Meg, our secretary, came in right during a meeting I had with a client, and said that someone was insisting on seeing me immediately.

Normally she wouldn't interrupt me like that, but she had such a funny look on her face I thought I should investigate. I excused myself and went out into the reception area. There was this weird little kid swinging around in Meg's office chair. He looked like a tumbleweed of a person, dirt everywhere and hardly any clothes on. Above him I swear there were storm clouds, right over Meg's desk. It looked like it was going to rain all over her computer. Poor Meg looked like she was going to pass out."

Rebecca and Torin looked at each other in dawning horror, while Auran merely looked confused.

"So this kid looks right at me," Griffin continued, "and says, 'you don't look much like a Griffin to me, where's your tail?' I thought at first he was some nut, escaped from a hospital, but then he put Meg up on the ceiling. He just lifted one hand, pointed right at her and up she went, stuck overhead like she was super glued up there. Well, I remembered what you two said and figured the kid was a Bollux or something. As far as I could recall, I hadn't invited him in, so that's what I told him.

He stopped twirling in the chair and said, 'Oh, you *are* a Griffin. You are right, I wasn't invited.' He put Meg back down on the floor and said he'd wait for me outside. Well, I didn't want him wandering around the business district causing mayhem, so I locked him in the bathroom at the office and tacked up an Out of Order sign. Meg went home, probably to have a nervous breakdown.

Anyway, the kid spent the rest of the day flushing the toilets over and over again and making evil faces in the mirrors. I hate to say it, but I brought him home with me. Gilden's got him out in the back yard playing Houdini."

When Torin looked blank, Rebecca explained. "Dad used to tie me up with hemp cords in the living room when I was a kid, and I'd pretend to be this famous escape artist, Houdini, and have to figure out how to untie myself. That's how dad could do some of his work at home; it kept me occupied, sometimes for hours. I loved that game!"

Torin grinned at the idea of Haldane, for it could be no other, immobilized for hours guarded by a unicorn.

"Griffin Bloom, you left a small child outside in the yard in this temperature!" Auran exclaimed.

"I don't think small child adequately describes this kid," Griffin defended himself. "He's like a human-shaped Tasmanian devil, the cartoon kind. He tried to bite Gilden on the leg and only desisted when it looked like he was going to be impaled. Then he wanted to eat one of the pixies for dinner. I thought Houdini was the perfect compromise. When he finally gets out, I thought we could feed him something."

Torin's grin became a roar of laughter. He had to admire Griffin's intuitively appropriate handling of the little Bollux.

"I suppose," Rebecca commented, interrupting Torin's mirth, "that we ought to ask him what on earth, no pun intended, he's doing here."

"I did ask him that," Griffin explained. "Although he'd already given me a spontaneous excuse, something about running away from home before his family chopped him into little bits and ate him on bog toast, whatever that is. He said he was coming to find you two."

"Oh great," Rebecca said, echoing Torin's thoughts exactly. "Things keep getting more complicated. Now we're going to have to baby-sit a wild Bollux child on top of everything else."

"He's only one little boy. Griffin says he looks about six," Auran protested. "How much trouble could he be?"

Rebecca shook her head, certain that her mother hadn't been paying proper attention when she and Torin described the Bolluxes.

"Mom, he's over 10 Thianelian years old, his favorite activity is causing storms, he's allergic to clean water, and he's a Bollux, born and bred. What more do I have to say?"

Before Auran could respond they heard the familiar clip clop of Gilden's hooves on the floor.

"I must again excuse interrupting," Gilden said, proving the adage that unicorns were scrupulously polite, even when dispatching enemies. "The little Bollux is nearly loose from his ropes. I thought to warn you that he complains of a ravenous appetite. Perhaps we could feed him some human food before he attacks the garden Folk outside."

"Oh dear," Auran said, beginning to realize what having a Bollux around might mean.

"We'll get him," Torin volunteered, motioning to Rebecca.

"I'll cook up some pasta or something," Auran offered.

"I'll go upstairs and hide," Griffin said helpfully.

Rebecca and Torin made their way outside just as Haldane, for of course that's who it was, had pulled the last bit of rope from around his body. Catching sight of Torin and Rebecca, he bowed low at the waist, nearly toppling over in the grass. The entire back yard appeared deserted except for Haldane.

"For some reason they all left," Haldane announced. "Are you going to invite me inside?"

"We don't have much choice," Torin replied.

After Haldane had messily devoured four plates of pasta with cheese, declined any vegetables, and tried to swallow his napkin, Torin pulled him unceremoniously into the living room, followed curiously by Griffin, Auran and Rebecca. After tossing down a kitchen towel for him to sit on, Torin plunked Haldane on the sofa.

"What are you doing here? Do any of your relatives know where you are?" Torin asked.

"I told Liliar I wanted to travel to Earth," admitted Haldane, putting one grimy bare foot up on the coffee table. Auran pushed it off, mentally reminding herself to give him a bath before finding him something to wear. Haldane's borrowed finery from the Griffin clan on Thianely seemed to have disappeared. He wore only a tattered loin covering and something like a narrow rag across his middle, neither of which looked all that clean.

"Look, kid, did you actually tell anyone you were coming here or not?" Griffin demanded.

Haldane shrugged. "No."

"Is anyone likely to come after you?" Auran wondered, not too eager to meet any more Bolluxes.

Haldane smiled. "Not after Rebecca killed Royden. They'll probably hope you'll vanish me too. Old Boleria bit a hole through her cheek laughing when she found out how Royden ended."

"I'm sorry about Royden," Rebecca apologized. Haldane glanced at her curiously.

"Are you? Why? He wasn't at all fun, or even kind like Liliar. I'm glad he's dead. Now he can't tease me any more."

Rebecca winced. "Still, it must have been hard to lose a relative," she said consolingly.

"Not at all. No one liked him much. No one cares anyway," Haldane continued. "No one in my family cares about anyone but themselves. That's how Bolluxes are. Liliar and me, we're having our own family. Of course now she's going to have Tehy and his mother with the sharp claws, and someday there'll be offspring. I shall be an uncle and teach them everything I know."

Torin looked vaguely alarmed at the prospect, and not for the first time, contemplated which was more difficult, mating with an outworlder, or aligning with one of the Bollux clan as his friend Tehy had done.

"We have lots of jokes about how Royden turned into a black hole," Haldane explained. "Etestian said if he weren't so selfish, Royden could have sacrificed himself to the Bellorasps to take Liliar's voice away. But that will never happen. Selfishness is in our blood.

Now that Royden and Jierdan are dead, Haldar and Darden and Mosten and Harlane and everyone feel more important. Etestian's only in a bad mood because I helped Liliar, Leva, and Tehy escape. Did you know how they got caught anyway? This part is really clever of Mosten, and he's pretty stupid most of the time. He made a sound trap. It's a kind of black hole that sucks all sound away so Liliar couldn't sing her way out. He learned how to do it from the Bellorasps, but it only works for a short time.

See why we all laughed when Royden turned into a black hole himself? It really was pretty funny. Mosten wanted to roast Tehy over bog flame, and turn Leva into a wall decoration. Then Royden died and I let them go free. I made a sound trap for Mosten and he got stuck in it himself. And I let the bog sprites loose. It was really exciting.

I've always wanted to come to Earth. It wasn't even that hard since I followed Rebecca's energy trail. Bolluxportation doesn't work that great here though so I showed up at Griffin's work place by accident. I can help the Earth, you know. Most Bolluxes don't like the idea of the Great Tree much, but I don't mind it."

Griffin rubbed one hand over his chin. "From what I've seen of your behavior, kid, you're going to be more trouble than help. Remember how many times I told you not to flush the toilet in the bathroom at work?"

"Seventeen," Haldane responded proudly.

"That's not exactly helping the Earth. You wasted water for no reason."

"I had a reason," Haldane said seriously. "The sound of the flushing helped clear out all that terrible electrical noise. Bolluxes are very sensitive to your electricity. It hurts our heads. Royden wore a little black tuner around his ankle to keep from getting electrisickness. I brought some of Liliar's tuning marbles along just in case, but the flushing worked too, even though I hate water. Besides, I'd never flushed a toilet before."

"One way you can help is by listening to what we say and actually doing it," Griffin said. "I understand your sensitivity to electricity, but it may make life tough for you here. For instance, you can't go around turning off lights or flushing toilets whenever you feel like it. You have to ask for permission. I might be able to fix up something to help you cope better. I have some magnets you can wear. In the meantime, will we have to worry about any of your relatives coming after you or not?"

Haldane shook his head. "I'm not worth bothering about. They'll be relieved I'm gone. You see; I showed Liliar how to make sound traps too. No one will be able to catch her again. I came here because I couldn't be anywhere on Thianely without Mosten trying to strangle me. Etestian was really flaming too. His whole body turned red and scabrous. Even though my relatives are all furious, they won't show up here themselves, they'll just send others to do their bog work."

"Somehow that doesn't quite reassure me," Griffin said.

Torin reached over and clasped Haldane kindly, but firmly on the shoulder. "We appreciate your offer to help," he said, "but do not change anything here without being asked. That means no sudden storms, no strange weather patterns, and no sticking humans up on ceilings. This planet is already having enough problems trying to balance. It does not need any more of that sort of help. In other words, if you do not behave yourself, I will help Rebecca send you home."

Haldane considered his predicament for a moment, and then shrugged. "I guess it's better than being ripped into tiny pieces and fed to the bog sprites. Where's my room?"

Torin paled, realizing that he had the only guest room.

"Don't worry, Torin," Griffin said reassuringly. "We would never expect you to share a room with the little gremlin. The walk-in hall closet is bigger than some bedrooms. We'll clean it out so he can have it. There's nothing particularly breakable in there either."

"Now that that's settled," Auran said, standing up and eyeing Haldane in disapproval, "it's bath time."

Haldane shook his head. "Bolluxes are allergic to water. Torin can fire clean me, but don't singe anything!"

Chapter 13

Breakfast the next morning was a meal that they would remember for a long time afterwards. Haldane's manners were Bolluxlike, that is to say, atrocious. Not only did he wolf down his food, but remnants of it sprayed across the table, nearly landing in Torin's oatmeal. Griffin lectured Haldane on earthly table manners, which he grudgingly accepted for the sake of hot cocoa, a beverage he'd never had before. After Haldane had folded his fresh napkin in his lap (he'd eaten the previous one) and finished his cereal, Auran poured him a cup of cocoa. Haldane stuck his nose in the cup to smell the dark liquid, took one lengthy gulp, turned bright yellow, and slid from his chair onto the floor. While he lay there unconscious, Torin ran his hands over him to discern the problem.

"Apparently Bolluxes cannot tolerate anything sweet," he explained, as Auran looked worriedly down at the fallen boy. "It interferes with their natural constitution. I think he will be fine, though. I will lay him in the closet and let him sleep it off." He picked up Haldane and carried him out. When he returned a few minutes later, he was grinning.

"That is the quietest I have ever seen him," he said, sitting back down to finish his toast.

"What are you two up to today?" Auran asked. "Torin, I assume you and Griffin will be designing maps and sending directions to all of those Thianelians on-line. Neither of us is going in to the office. We got a call from Meg this morning; she's taking a few days off herself. I'm planning to make lists of supplies for the trip to the lake. What should we do with Haldane when he wakes up?"

"Bolluxes love destroying things," Rebecca said thoughtfully. "Maybe he could weed the yard, under the direction of Gilden. There's always Houdini if we're desperate."

"Before we get started on the computer," Torin said, "I wanted to speak with you, Griffin and Auran, about money. I understand that here you must work to earn money to live, and both Haldane's and my presence will require you to spend even more of your money. I would like to help provide for necessities, perhaps through working."

"Stop right there, Torin," Griffin protested. "You provided food, shelter, and hospitality to Rebecca while she was on Thianely for a whole year. Don't even worry about money."

111

"I understand," Torin nodded, "but I wanted to experience having to earn the right to survive. Perhaps I will better understand the fear your Folk live with constantly. I have never worried about having enough; on Thianely we all simply ask for what we need. No one would ever go hungry or without shelter, because there are no rules limiting abundance. But if I had arrived here alone, or without any Thianelian contacts, what do you think would have happened?"

"Some dazzled young woman would have taken you home," Auran teased.

"Nothing very good," Griffin said honestly, "but that doesn't mean you have to follow stupid earth laws that we'd be better off without. I'll tell you what, if I ever need your help with anything, I'll ask, although I imagine you'd help before I even got around to the asking part."

"Didn't you once mention that you'd been here before?' Auran asked. "What happened that time?"

"I've been to your world twice before. Both times I was met by another Thianelian, Mialchor Hebral, who has lived here for many years. He lives in a more rural part of New York and we only went to the city once so that he could take me for a taxi ride. We left after only two hours. The first time I came to Earth I became very ill with separation sickness and only stayed for a few days.

The second time Mialchor and I drove to Alaska during one of their summers. We drove for many days to get there, and even though Mialchor had prepared me for its strangeness, I found the people there to be very friendly, and most helpful. The weather was very curious. There was little nighttime and a great deal of sunlight. The mosquito insects did not listen when I asked them to stop biting me, so Mialchor showed me how to raise my vibrational frequency to dispel them. I imagine we will see Mialchor at the lake soon, with the other Thianelians. I suppose even if I had arrived here unannounced, at least other Thianelians would have assisted me.

I stayed on Earth for many weeks, and even managed the trip back to New York with much less discomfort than on the drive to Alaska. Mialchor taught me how to deal with the separation sickness by building energy shields. He's a very kind man."

"Well, let's get going on those e-mails," Griffin suggested. "Before the little monster wakes up."

The rest of the day was spent sending directions to the lake, deciding what to pack for the trip, and monitoring Haldane, who had unfortunately woken up after only two hours. He was determined to take back hot cocoa packets to stupefy his relatives with, thrilled that he'd be able to knock out even Etestian. He spent hours playing marbles with the fauns in the back yard, creating his own rules, of course. The weeding idea had to be aborted when it was discovered that Haldane had no ability to discriminate between plants and weeds. He'd been bitten on the hand by an indignant faery after he'd attempted to pluck out her home by the roots.

Several of the marbles Haldane used, Liliar's creations, emitted tones and flashes of colors when rolled, so the backyard became a symphony of light and sound. Gilden retreated to the living room, fulfilling his promise to keep an eye on the little Bollux by peering out the French doors occasionally, and keeping the fauns from stomping Haldane whenever he changed the rules too often. Meanwhile Rebecca helped Auran with the trip preparations.

That afternoon Rebecca and Torin curled up on the sofa to read some of the books they'd found at the library.

"Hey, listen to this," Rebecca began, quoting from a book called *Lords and Ladies of Elemental Knowledge*, by Olwen Blessed. 'The Lords and Ladies of Earth, Ice, Water, Fire and Air, are not indigenous to the planet Earth, but are visitors from other dimensions, providing a measure of balance throughout the infinite universes.' I know it's true, but it sounds strange coming out of a New York Public Library Book."

Torin, who'd been completely absorbed in his book, *Lore of the Fire Lord*, by Tyor Kehn, glanced over at Rebecca.

"It is a Thianelian author writing such ideas on your world, your Earth. I understand how that could seem odd. Now, here is information that is of specific interest to me. 'In alternate dimensions the Fire Lord is the name given to a being, who, although formless in nature, may choose to incarnate in order to gift his progeny with the following genetically inherited abilities: ability to change form at will, increased ability to work with elemental forces, an awareness of balance in the midst of chaos, a heightened facility for inter-dimensional travel and communication, as well as numerous others.

The Fire Lord has been associated with humankind since their origins, and has acted as a sort of benefactor, thus the myths of

113

Prometheus bringing fire to the earth, or many other culture's fire origin myths.' It goes on to say that the Fire Lord works in concert with the Lords of Air and Ice, and the Ladies of Water, Earth, and Star, also associated with old Gods and Goddesses worshipped by many cultures."

"Star?" Rebecca repeated questioningly. "I don't remember hearing you refer to that one before."

Torin shook his head. "It's the first I've heard of the Star Lady before. How interesting that we had to come here to discover her! I'm going to do further search on the Internet after I finish this book, although there are individual chapters on each Lord and Lady in here. Tell me something," he said thoughtfully. "How long have you known what I am capable of? You have spent more time inside the Great Tree than I have, not to mention all the crystal knowledge you carry."

"I can't say I've known anything precisely, it's more like when I experience things myself, I remember you there with me. Or when circumstances arise, like you being able to laser that Bellorasp before we left Thianely, I'm impressed, but not completely surprised."

"I would certainly appreciate having more forewarning about such abilities," Torin said. "I know I would be more skilled with practice, but it is difficult to practice abilities you do not know you have. My known gifts I have always accepted as a part of myself. Yet the phrase 'and numerous others' makes me curious about the rest of my abilities."

"Having more gifts can only help," Rebecca said practically. "And didn't you tell me once that such skills arose as needed? It sounds like Earth doubt is beginning to creep in. Or maybe it's that having to redo your self-awareness all of the time is kind of jarring. It certainly has been for me."

Torin sighed. "I must also admit that ever since I discovered who my father is, I have longed to meet him face to face, and to ask about my mother."

"I would too, if I'd never met my parents."

Torin cocked his head, listening to something Rebecca could not hear.

"It's Liliar," he explained, smiling. "She had an idea that her youngest brother may have snuck off world and wanted to check to see if we were all right."

114

Rebecca laughed. "She definitely has an idea how much mischief a little Bollux could get into here. Even Mom has more respect for his destructive abilities now. Apparently he got hungry after lunch and ate some of the laundry, with detergent on it. Isn't it odd that sugar makes him sick and toxic chemicals don't?"

"Not really," Torin replied, "he is a Bollux. Wait a minute; Meridwen wants to talk with you. Hold my hand for a moment; it will help you follow the thought connection."

Rebecca grasped Torin's hand and was instantly able to see Meridwen, the leader of the Tree Folk. It was a little like having a conference call, only with visual images as well as auditory input. Rebecca could see the huge forest of trees, diminished now by so many that had fallen during the tremendous earthquake. In a clearing in which the Great Tree, the record keeper of wisdom for all of Thianely, had once stood, Meridwen sat wearily on the ground, her beautiful green face pale with the events of previous weeks. Her long auburn hair hung limply, her dress of blue leaves was worn and dirty. Still, the leader of the Tree Folk managed to look regal despite her exhaustion.

Rebecca noticed that greenery had sprung up in places where the trees had been uprooted. The ground shift damage seemed to have mostly healed, as the cavernous cracks in the soil were no longer discernible. Most of the fallen trees had been carried away to be buried with their Tree Folk, leaving piles of purple and green leaves behind. The area where the Great Tree had once stood, however, remained bare, as nothing would grow there as a sign of respect for its passing. Meridwen greeted Rebecca with a smile of welcome.

"Bless Rhiate you are safe, Rebecca!" she exclaimed. "My greetings to you and your family as well. Their relief at your return must be great. I have heard that you have sent one of the Bollux clan back to the source, and that the littlest one followed you off world. Remember that the young of any Folk can still be taught other ways. We have shifted our roots to protect our own young, though danger still abides all over Thianely.

I wished to speak with you about your planting of the golden root. I thought to give you assistance when it comes time to reestablish the Great Tree on your world. Remember to call on me when you start the planting ritual, Rebecca, and through the power of the crystal necklace you keep, I will come to sing the sowing song of growth and rootling. But you must be ready, for I cannot live long in your world, and crystal travel will not carry me for a greatness of time." She shook her head at Rebecca's offer to teach her to travel by thought.

"It is not for such a one as I to do so. Trees must have roots, and I am as bound to matter as a soul is to spirit. None of the tree people could survive such travel for a long distance as you suggest, for thought is not a sustaining root for us. But crystal call me, and I will come. Farewell, Rebecca, and Rhiate's blessings upon you and Torin."

Torin dropped Rebecca's hand as Meridwen and the Threshold of the Trees slowly faded from her mind. Rebecca opened her eyes to see Torin still intently communicating to Thianely. It annoyed her for a moment that she was unable to follow his conversation without physical contact. She felt like her telepathic phone lines had been unplugged for long distance service.

Finally she got over her pique and tuned into Torin's shield while he concentrated, adding her support. She ran a check over the house to make sure the seals were holding. Everything was fine. Gilden sent her a mind picture of his horn circling in a spiral of white light, inscribing a network of light bars around Haldane, as if he were imprisoned. Three angels patrolled the sky above the roof. Rebecca relaxed, appreciating all of their support, and chuckled at the idea of Haldane playing Houdini with cords of light.

Torin finally opened his eyes. "Grandfather was truly happy to hear from us. All the Fire Folk are well, though everyone fears the Bellorasps. I told him to contact Liliar to learn how to create sound traps. He said the Merfolk would also be interested. Apparently Haldane's choice to help Liliar, Tehy, and Leva has made him something of a hero all over Thianely. Even Tehy's Griffin Folk have grudgingly decided that not all Bolluxes are completely worthless. Tehy did suggest that Haldane not return any time soon; his own clan has put out a morbidity clause against him. The Bolluxes want to kill Haldane and use his death to bargain with the Bellorasps. Liliar must beware."

"I thought that voice thing only worked if the person voluntarily sacrificed themselves to the Bellorasps," Rebecca said. "Haldane's not going to give up his life so they can take Liliar's voice."

"The Bolluxes' belief is that Haldane took Tehy, Liliar, and Leva from them. Therefore, Haldane owes them at least a couple of lives. Since Tehy dispatched Jierdan Bollux, and you took care of Royden, neither of whom sacrificed themselves willingly, they figure they might as well get something out of killing Haldane. It's Bollux logic. Even though they did not genuinely care about Jierdan and Royden, if they can use their deaths for justification in slaying others, they will.

Apparently the Bellorasps are angry enough to overlook the willingness aspect, even though such a misuse of energy is bound to have terrible repercussions for Bellorasps in the long run. Disregarding energy laws is very dangerous, even for such nasty creatures. Perhaps they believe that Thianely is so out of Balance they will not be hit with any consequences; I do not know. My grandfather had a theory that Bellorasps are extremely stupid and inactive because of all of the souls they eat. It would be like having a houseful of bickering relatives that never agreed about anything. But it's a good thing that Haldane got away in time. Although, that means we're stuck with him for a while. I hope we can keep him occupied enough to leave the weather alone."

"Torin," Rebecca asked, "remember when I first came to Thianely, and you told me to ask the stars to shine less brightly if they disturbed my sleep? How is it that everyone can affect the weather so easily, and it doesn't create complete havoc? Why are you so worried about Haldane?"

"First of all," Torin explained, "you may always ask, and the weather, sky, stars, trees, clouds, or what have you, may always decline, especially if it's going to affect the weather on a large scale and cause adverse conditions. Haldane's gift is to create weather systems and storms where none previously existed. The Bolluxes, up to now, have not realized how extensive his ability is, because Liliar had been blocking him until he reached a more reasonable age, (although I am not sure if Bolluxes have such a thing). She is hoping her training with him will hold up, but I think it's doubtful. If he were to unleash his abilities here, in the state of already teetering balance, who knows what chaos would ensue! And as you have probably noticed, he gets bored easily. It is too bad he cannot handle electricity very well. The computer or T.V. would have kept him occupied, at least for a time."

"I doubt it," Rebecca said. "I can't see him sitting still very long for anything unless he's tied up. Oh, I forgot to tell you.

Meridwen wants me to call her by crystal when we go to plant the tree branch; she's going to sing a sowing song."

Torin turned to her incredulously. "Meridwen, come here? Where people build homes of tree limbs and paper of their flesh? The sheer pain of it would destroy her!"

Rebecca frowned. "She said she could not live here long, but that I must call her when we're ready. I don't think the tree will root properly without her."

"Then we will give her some more help." He thought for a moment. "Rebecca, can you talk to the Tree Devas in the trees that grow in your Central Park? Right before you call Meridwen, we may have them provide a welcoming song, and get as many other trees as possible to join in. That will give her a better chance."

Rebecca smiled delightedly. "Why don't we get everything and everyone we possibly can to sing? Trees, plants, rocks, birds. We'll time the singing for Meridwen's arrival, and plant the tree while the park is in tune."

Rebecca yawned, rubbing her eyes. "I can't get used to how much energy everything takes here. Right in the middle of everything I get so tired."

"Nap time?" Torin asked kindly.

"I guess so," Rebecca admitted. "I feel like a little old woman, having to take naps everyday."

"You'll get stronger," Torin assured her. "In the meantime, I could use some rest as well."

Torin headed to the guest room, then thought better of it and followed Rebecca upstairs to her room. "Tomorrow we need to do something about Haldane's clothes," he said, sprawling on her bed. "Remember how children followed us about even when I wasn't dressed strangely?"

Rebecca nodded. "You think it'll be worse with Haldane because he looks so weird already?"

"Yes," he admitted, "I hesitate to take him anywhere at all, even to your lake, dressed the way he is." He paused. "If I am Liliar's half brother, does that mean I am related to Haldane as well?"

"Almost," Rebecca said. "But not enough to panic about." She couldn't help but giggle at the look on his face. "Hey, have you ever used a Jacuzzi? The water isn't clear like on Thianely, but it is relaxing. How about if I run you a bath?"

"I have never been in a Jacuzzi, but I will try it," he agreed, following her into the bathroom. "I liked the bubbles in the hot tub outside," he commented. "Is this the same?"

Rebecca nodded, turning on the tap and letting the water fill up.

"Hey, wait a minute," she said, as Torin began to swing his leg over the side of the tub. "You're supposed to take your clothes off first."

Torin shrugged, tugging off his shoes and socks, then pulling off his t-shirt and tossing it over the sink. Rebecca stared at his bare chest in fascination. He was well muscled, and she realized she'd never seen him before without his shirt. There was a spiral of raised whorls in the center of his chest like those on his palms, and she wondered what they would feel like to touch.

"Would you like some scented bath salts?" she asked absently, still focused on his chest. He watched her for a moment and she suddenly blushed, embarrassed to be caught staring. When he reached down to unzip his blue jeans, she turned even redder.

"Rebecca," he said softly, as she turned away, heading for the door. "One day I will discover whether you turn that color all over. It is fine with me if you look. On Thianely we spend time unclothed as small children, in as natural a state as possible. I understand that most of your Folk equate nudity with mating, but we do not. Can you get used to such teasing from me?"

Rebecca turned around, nodding speechlessly. Torin came over and held her closely. She rested her head on his chest, putting her arms around his waist. He felt strong, warm, and comforting at the same time. The circular pattern on his chest vibrated under her ear, glowing a dull red color.

Torin sighed, gently pushing her away from him. "That's it," he said. "Once my heart center starts to heat, my containment is lost." He gave her a push toward the door.

"Leave now so we do not cause your parents discomfort."

Rebecca headed out to take a nap, wondering if she would be able to fall asleep with Torin naked in her bathtub. However, once her head hit the pillow, she drifted off quite quickly.

Chapter 14

A few days later Auran took Haldane's measurements and left to go shopping, both for clothes and some travel necessities. Griffin cleared out the mini van, while Rebecca and Torin spent time Bollux-sitting. Rebecca taught Haldane the yoga positions she'd learned as a child, and they discovered that he was quite flexible for a Bollux. Not only could he do the lotus position upside down on the ceiling, but he could also stand up with one leg tucked behind his ear. He had just mastered the headstand when Fort and Hazel interrupted them.

"Hello," Fort called out from the hallway as he and Hazel made their way into the living room. "Good morning Sport. Torin, who's this little fellow?"

Haldane immediately righted himself, assumed the crooked tree position and bowed low, nearly toppling over.

"I am Haldane, lately of the Bolluxes, now of the Blooms."

Rebecca and Torin exchanged a glance of dismay. Apparently Haldane assumed that he had been adopted.

"What kind of ridiculous name is that?" Hazel said, tossing her handbag onto the sofa. "And why are you dressed in dirty rags?"

Haldane looked at her sour expression and pursed lips with great interest.

"What manner of a Bollux are you?" he asked curiously.

Hazel put her hands on her hips, eyeing him sternly. "I can see that I will have to teach you some manners, you young scalawag. You come with me."

She reached out to grab Haldane by one ear. He chortled happily, pulling in the opposite direction so strongly that his ear stretched out like an elephant's.

"That's enough of that," Hazel said firmly, tugging him from the room. "You come right into the kitchen with me and I'll teach you how to behave properly."

Rebecca and Torin watched in awe as Hazel dragged Haldane away. Then they both collapsed on the sofa with a mutual sigh.

"Long morning already?" Fort asked. "When Auran called and told us you had company, she didn't go into much detail. I gather that little fellow is from Thianely? I can't say I've ever met someone with Pinocchio ears before. Don't worry; Hazel will set him right. She's great with animals and small children. For some reason they never take her gruff exterior very seriously."

Rebecca smiled. Her grandfather definitely had a different perception of Hazel than most of the people she knew. She remembered being terrified of her grandmother's temper when she was small, and she knew her mother still felt intimidated now and then. She was curious how Haldane and Hazel would get along at the lake in close proximity. Maybe if they were lucky Hazel would make him her project. Rebecca almost felt sorry for the little Bollux.

"Where's Auran, still getting the little monster some clothes?" Griffin asked, wandering into the living room. "Hi there, Fort, glad to see you're looking so well. I'm finished cleaning out the van. Torin and I can load your stuff. I'm ready to start packing the car so we can leave soon. Then we'll have a few days to relax before our alien friends descend upon us.

Did you hear that we had forty-five families respond positively to our e-mails? I figure it's about 130 people altogether. Most of them said they'd bring tents or campers and enough provisions for several days. It turns out that they were in contact with each other anyway. Oh, Torin, some guy named Tyor Kehn e-mailed back and said to be careful because our gathering had been drawing attention from some unsavory characters. He didn't go into detail though."

"Tyor Kehn," Torin repeated. "That's the fellow whose book I'm reading." He exchanged a glance with Rebecca, recalling the unpleasant experience she'd had at the mall with an unsavory character. Rebecca nodded, immediately deciding to call their angel friends for clarification.

While Griffin and Torin left to go load the van, Rebecca smiled at her grandfather. "Fort, how would you like to meet some really interesting friends of mine? I need to talk to them about our trip to the lake."

Fort shrugged. "It's not more of those Bollux fellows is it? That little one smells like the back end of a yak."

Rebecca laughed and shook her head. "No, these are much more pleasant." She tuned her mind to the angels outside the house, wondering why it was so easy to communicate with them on Earth, but so difficult to mind speak with humans.

As Fort waited, glancing idly toward the French doors, he felt a sensation of warmth and well being come over him, much as he had when Rebecca had first laid her hands on him in the wheelchair. The air shimmered before him as thousands of tiny ripples spread out from two center masses of white light. Fort blinked once and the two central figures of white became large winged figures standing beside the sofa, their golden wingspans folded neatly upon their shoulders, wing tips just brushing the ceiling.

Fort swallowed slowly, wondering what the proper etiquette was for meeting angels. His knees shook slightly, both with the grace of their presence and the realization that his Sport, the child he'd known from birth onwards, somehow resembled these creatures of light.

Rebecca turned to him, and grasping his dilemma, made the introductions. "Grandfather, this is Naftaliel," she said, indicating the angel on the right. Naftaliel inclined his head, his long chestnut locks held back by a thin band of gold, and extended one hand through the long sleeves of his robe. Fort reached out and clasped the angel's hand, somewhat surprised to find it warm and solid.

"And this is Mahalim," she continued. The angel on the left nodded gracefully, sending her auburn hair cascading forward. Her forehead circlet was bright white, matching her gown. As she grasped Fort's hand in welcome, it sent a faint electric shock up his arm.

"I am concerned that our visit to the lake will provoke some unwanted attention," Rebecca began. "We and the Thianelians who gather there will be singing aemethra, a song of balance. I ask that angels accompany us for protection, particularly when the Thianelians arrive to sing. I know many of you are already guarding around the house, and I ask that others serve us as well."

Both angels nodded, and Fort was struck again by the idea that his Rebecca should somehow be able to call such help to her without question.

"There are four of us who shall serve this purpose," Naftaliel confirmed. "There are two others in addition to ourselves. We will accompany you even beyond this lake journey, but you will learn more of this later. Well met, Sir," he smiled at Fort, sending waves of grace flowing through him.

Before Fort could respond, Haldane came hurtling into the room, passing through Naftaliel and Mahalim as if they were no more corporeal than air. "Excuse me," he muttered politely, racing to the other end of the room and ducking under the pool table as Hazel came charging after him. She plunged right through the two angels as if they didn't exist, reached under the pool table and grabbed Haldane by the scruff of his loincloth, which unfortunately disintegrated upon handling. When he would have scrambled for freedom, Hazel let out a shout that would have felled a small tree on Thianely.

"Stop right there, you little savage," she yelled. "When I say you're having a bath, I mean it. No more nonsense about being allergic to water. You smell noxious!" And she swept out of the room, herding the disgruntled Bollux before her. He turned to Rebecca as if to plead for help, but she merely waved him on.

The angels bowed in farewell, and flickering out of sight, left Fort somewhat overwhelmed by the experience.

"I don't understand," he muttered to Rebecca. "How could they be solid enough to shake hands, but vaporous enough for walking through?"

"You could see them, so they felt real to you. Haldane doesn't have any problem with something being real and immaterial at the same time, and because they probably weren't real to Grandmother, they didn't exist on any level whatsoever. I bet if you ask her later, she wouldn't even have noticed them."

"So you're saying they exist only at the level in which I'm able to see them."

"I'm saying they exist on all levels, but you only perceive them on the levels you allow yourself to exist."

Fort shook his head. "I'm beginning to understand what Griffin meant. He told me that sometimes when you speak now, he feels like he's in an advanced course in subjects he's never studied."

"But you saw them, heard them, and shook their hands," Rebecca reminded him. "That couldn't have happened if you'd never been there before. Naftaliel doesn't call everyone Sir."

Fort sat down on the sofa with a groan, resting his head in his palms. At that moment, Griffin, having left the last of the loading to Torin, entered the room.

"What's wrong, Fort?" he said. "Did you see a unicorn by any chance?"

Fort shook his head and looked up. "There's that smelly, messy little Bollux here from some other planet with ears that stretch like pulling taffy, but somehow that doesn't bother me. I can walk now where weeks ago I could barely stand, but that makes sense to me, don't know why. It was the angels that did it. I thought only prophets and nut cases saw angels, let alone shook hands with them. You ever see an angel, Griffin?"

"As of last week, I can say that I have seen a whole firmament of them, dancing in the sky like a pantheon of brilliant butterflies and singing like nothing you've ever heard. Hard to describe in words, isn't it?"

Fort looked up at him gratefully. "This big golden fellow, he called me Sir. For a moment, I had this strange recollection of what it was like, having wings and all. Do you think I'm crazy?"

Griffin grinned over at Rebecca and turned to his father in law solemnly. "I'd say it probably means you were an angel before. I have it on good authority, albeit from a unicorn no less, that I myself have been a merman, among other poxy creatures. Mind-blowing isn't it?" He reached over to clap a hand on Fort's shoulder.

"You'll get used to them," Griffin reassured him. "I heard from some fellow out in the garage that we'll be having angelic companions on our little excursion to the lake. The one I talked to, Haliel, had a flaming white sword that looked like he meant business."

"They're all here?" Rebecca asked in surprise.

Griffin nodded. "He said the other three were Naftaliel, their leader, Mahalim, and Mehezriel, and that they'd be with us for quite a long time by Earth measure, whatever that meant. How about that, we're on a first name basis! Anyway, we can leave as soon as Auran gets back. Torin's packing all the stuff you two got ready this morning. Where's the dirty little Bollux and Hazel?"

"I doubt he's that dirty now that Grandmother's got hold of him," Rebecca remarked.

"I almost feel sorry for him," Griffin said dryly. "But at least he won't stink up the car this way."

Moments later a freshly scrubbed Haldane entered the room, followed by Auran and Hazel. He was dressed in new clothes, blue jeans and a green cotton shirt that Auran had purchased for him. His skin, a sickly shade of orange, reflected his extreme discomfort at being clean. Hazel had a look of triumph on her face, the impact of which was somewhat lessened by the queer cobweb-like strands sticking to her hair and clothes. She pushed Haldane down onto the sofa next to Fort, where he sat limply, staring at nothing in particular.

Auran shook her head compassionately. "I don't think Haldane's ever worn clothes before. He really hates bathing too. I found mother stuck to the ceiling in a web sort of thing, while Haldane made the bubble bath explode, but at least we finally got him clean."

Rebecca reached over and ruffled his hair. "Cheer up, Haldane, the lake's beautiful, and we have a power boat or we can paddle around the lake in a canoe. You won't have to take a bath for a few more days."

"You'll love it there," Griffin assured the little Bollux cheerfully, ignoring Haldane's semiconscious state. "There's boating and fishing and solitude; no one lives around the Lake because it's a protected area. Stay alert on the drive, since this is probably the most you'll see of New York."

They all piled into their mini van, an older model Toyota that they saved for long excursions. Griffin and Auran sat up front, Hazel and Fort in the first row of seats, and Torin, Rebecca, and Haldane sat together in the back.

Torin made himself comfortable by the right rear window, putting one arm around Rebecca so that she could lean close from her place in the middle and see out as well. Haldane immediately began playing with the left rear window, moving it up and down with great interest.

Rebecca checked to make sure Haldane was belted in, although he couldn't understand what the purpose of a seat belt was, having never been in a car before. As Griffin he pulled out of the driveway, Haldane began bouncing ferociously up and down in his seat, causing the Toyota to jounce a little.

"Make it go faster," he demanded. Rebecca reached over and grabbed his shoulder.

"Calm down, Haldane," she ordered. "You have to sit still when the car is moving."

"I like this driving," Haldane said happily, staring out the window as they reached 5th avenue. Griffin slowed immediately as they merged into the heavy traffic leading to Central Park. Haldane gawked at the people and cars and tall buildings cluttering the sky. "Cars are better than playing marbles. Wait until Liliar sings me one of these!"

Rebecca looked at him sternly. "First of all, you cannot bring cars to Thianely, they'll pollute the place. Second of all, cars can crash and hurt people."

"If the car runs by sound it won't stink up anyone," Haldane objected, "and crashing would be fun. Listen to all the honks and screech noises your city makes. This is even louder than my mother when she's not getting her way. And look up there, at all the houses with the windows shining way up in the sky. They must have many children. Think what fun it would be to knock them down."

Torin leaned over Rebecca to look Haldane in the eye. "Remember what we spoke of, small Bollux? Any interference in earth matters without being asked by Rebecca or myself, and you return to your family. That means no storms, no toppling buildings, no earthshakes at all, understand?"

Haldane blanched, subsiding back in his seat sullenly. The idea of facing his parents after helping Liliar go free was a dismal prospect.

Rebecca decided not to bother explaining about apartment buildings or offices, as Haldane didn't seem to understand the concept of work anyway. When he'd first arrived at Griffin's office, before he'd stuck the receptionist on the ceiling, he'd thought it was the Bloom's home and had demanded to see Rebecca.

Hazel looked back over her shoulder at Torin and Rebecca cuddling in the back. "God only knows what sort of grandchildren you'll have, Auran."

"Don't worry, Mother, I'm sure they'll be interesting. Still, that will be quite a ways off from now."

"I certainly hope so." Hazel raised her voice to be heard over the sound of the city. "What are you going to do about the FBI investigation? No one will believe any of this. I can't even take your father back to the doctors. They'd want to run tests on him to see how it happened."

Auran shifted uncomfortably in her seat. "We haven't really decided yet, Mother. The FBI agent in charge of Rebecca's case usually checks in once a month to let us know they have no new leads. As long as no one figures out that she's back, we won't have to explain anything."

Fort and Griffin immediately tried to outdo each other in concocting outlandish stories to pacify the FBI. Hazel snorted in disgust and decided to take a nap. Her snores added an interesting counterpoint to the peaceful drive.

The rest of the trip north passed uneventfully. Haldane seemed to be lulled into a sort of stupor by the scenery flashing by the freeway, while Torin and Rebecca amused themselves watching the angels who guarded them flying above and around the sides of the car. Once Auran turned back questioningly. "Rebecca, no one else can see them, can they?"

When Rebecca shrugged, Auran said, "Maybe a few lucky people will see them flying by. Do you think they're helping our speed? We seem to be making very good time. I suppose we could have shown up like we did at the Statue of Liberty, but don't you like this way too? It's definitely the scenic route. Driving can be so relaxing." She hummed along to the radio while Griffin drove on. At last they reached the turnoff for the lake.

Rebecca shook Haldane gently to get his attention. "Come on, Haldane, we're nearly there. It's only a few more minutes to the cabin."

Haldane stretched his arms and legs, knocking Rebecca with his elbow. They were driving a narrow paved road lined with trees and bushes with not a building in sight. Once in a while they passed a sign for boat launches, but Griffin stuck to the main road until they passed a little clearing on the left. He turned down a dirt driveway into a secluded stretch of road, merely two tire tracks in a path of weeds. They rounded a small bend, and the driveway ended in front of a brown cabin, so overgrown by trees and bushes that it seemed to be alive. Griffin stopped the car and turned off the engine.

"You wanted to work, Torin," he called. "Well, there's plenty to be done here clearing the trees and foliage."

Rebecca eyed the cabin in shock. "Dad, haven't you guys been here since I left? It's all wild."

"We couldn't until you returned," Griffin answered simply.

Auran unbuckled her seatbelt and stepped out of the car.

"Haldane, go ahead and carry in your clothes and your satchel, it's in the back. Torin, you can help with the food and some of the sleeping bags. Mother, you and Dad can follow us in and unpack. Rebecca, bring in the ice chest and the blankets. Griff, how about unlocking the doors for us? I'll get the food bags, and with everyone helping it'll take no time at all."

Chapter 15

It had been so long since the cabin had been used that everything needed a good dusting. Auran and Rebecca swept the cobwebs and dust from the five bedrooms, which were located at the back. Although Haldane had suggested clearing the rooms out with a gust of wind, they hurriedly declined his offer.

The cabin was very spacious. The front door opened up into a combination living room and kitchen, and the hallway led to the bathroom and the bedrooms. The place was only carpeted in the living room section, with bare wood floors throughout the rest of the place. There were cots in each room, and the facilities were charmingly rustic. In other words, as Rebecca explained to Torin later, there was running water and a flush toilet, but only a camp stove.

Torin looked down at his hands and shrugged. "I have two hands here to boil water, and yours as well. That's four burners."

"How could I forget?"

Hazel and Auran prepared an early lunch. Hazel and Fort took a long walk afterwards, promising to be back for dinner. While Rebecca sat meditating on crystal wisdom, Haldane went outside to chase squirrels and Torin offered to help Griffin clear some of the plants and brush away from the cabin.

"Some of this stuff is so dry, it's a fire hazard," Griffin explained, handing Torin a pair of work gloves. "Let's move this dead stuff out of here and we'll load it into bags and take it to the dumpster."

Torin watched Griffin for a moment, as he began to haul the grass, leaves, dead branches, and stems away from the cabin. As Griffin paused to wipe leaf dust from his face, Torin stepped closer, slowly turning in a circle while sweeping his arms from side to side.

"Branches move and shift your clinging, round the cabin so closely ringing, trees do bend and move and sway, help clear this debris away."

Griffin gaped as the grass and dead leaf material started to roll away from the walls of the cabin and stack themselves in neat piles. The trees whose branches had crowded the structure twisted slowly and, roots and all, inched away from the cabin as well, until they were a good fifteen feet away. The ground where they'd grown appeared freshly plowed, but as Griffin stood shaking his head, it smoothed together into completely level ground. Soon there was a good clean swath of earth around the cabin.

After they'd bagged the debris, Griffin took off his work gloves. "I'd say you just earned a few days worth of lodging and meals there." He suddenly grinned at Torin. "Some day I'm going to have to go to your Thianely. I like the way you get things done. Doesn't look like you have to do much in the way of physical labor."

Torin returned Griffin's work gloves. "I am more accustomed to asking plants to move than imposing my will upon them. Though, I do not think the trees in the city would have responded so readily. When separation is present, asking does not always work, but I am glad I could help. I still do not think I understand how it feels to have to earn the right to live, but perhaps it is beyond my understanding."

"Be glad for that," Griffin said simply. "The way you say it, the whole concept sounds ridiculous. Now where did that little Bollux fellow get to?"

After some hunting, Torin found Haldane up a tree, still chasing squirrels. Luckily for the squirrels, they'd successfully scampered out of Haldane's reach. Unfortunately, Haldane did not understand that earth trees do not necessarily obey Bolluxes, and the tree had refused to capture any squirrels for him. Haldane was in the middle of angrily twisting the tree's limbs when Torin grabbed him.

"Do not ever," roared Torin, expanding out to his full size energetically, "torment a living creature again!" He pushed Haldane's ear to the tree trunk and held him there. "Hear the sound of its suffering, and know the pain it feels."

For the first time in his life, Haldane actually listened to the agony of another being. He gasped. Gray tears oozed down his face like viscous ash, dropping off his chin and eating holes in the dirt at his feet.

He stared up at Torin speechlessly as sap from the tree dripped onto Haldane's gold colored hair, staining it brown.

"Make it stop," he gasped. "Make it stop that terrible noise."

Torin shook his head sternly. "I cannot stop it, but you may. Sing it the song of healing. It will only work if you truly mean it. From here." And he tapped Haldane in the heart of his chest. Haldane gulped. Bolluxes did not ever apologize for their actions, let alone make amends. He looked up into Torin's angry face, listened to the mournful sound of the tree and nodded miserably.

"I know how; I saw Liliar do it." He pushed back a lock of hair that had fallen into his face, inadvertently smearing sap down the side of his cheek. Then he took a deep breath, and laying one hand on the tree's trunk, he sang:

> "From Rhiate all are born,
> From Telches are we made
> All humans, beasts, fowl, and fin
> Are one within, are one within
>
> From Rhiate all are born,
> From Telches are we made,
> All trees, plants, rootlings, kin
> Are one within, are one within
> From limb to leaf, all feel your grief,
> For we are one within, yes, we are one within."

Haldane patted the tree. "I am sorry for your suffering, and that I caused it. Let the pain of my actions fall from you."

The tree shifted slightly in the ground; its leaves began to flutter as it murmured a reply. A kindly breeze enveloped them, though there was no wind. Haldane stood transfixed with his hand still on the tree.

"It thanked me!" he cried. "It thanked me and nothing bad happened. I felt it!" He began to dance around the tree, as its leaves fluttered faster and the trunk swayed in time.

Griffin, who'd observed the whole incident, clapped Torin on the back. "I'd say there was hope for the little gremlin yet."

That afternoon Griffin suggested that they take the boat out of the boathouse, which was behind the cabin further back in the clearing, and go down to one of the boat launches for a cruise around the lake. Hazel and Fort weren't interested, while Auran, who'd gone on a cleaning frenzy, decided to remain at the cabin. Rebecca and Torin wanted to try out the canoe, so Griffin volunteered to take Haldane for a spin in the motorboat.

"Here," he said, throwing life jackets at the three of them. "You probably won't need these, but humor me."

Haldane looked at the vest dubiously.

"I never go in water," he protested. "We Bolluxes bathe in bog weed dust. If I don't go in the water I won't need one of these."

Griffin stared right into Haldane's slanted brown eyes. "No vest, no ride."

He backed the car up to the boathouse, attached the boat trailer to the back, and pulled forward. Haldane climbed into the front seat wearing the life jacket.

"Rebecca, you two can grab the canoe and take the shortcut down to the lake. We'll see you on the water." Griffin slowly pulled out of the driveway back to the paved Lakeview Drive, while Rebecca showed Torin the place where the canoe and paddles were kept.

"There aren't many people who have access to boating around here," she said, untying the oars from their wall perch and dropping them into the canoe. She tossed the life jackets in after them. "And for now it looks like we have almost the whole lake to ourselves. Gee, it would be much easier if we didn't have to lug it there." She began to pull the front of the canoe out the open door, while Torin pushed from the back.

"Why don't we guide it, but let the air support most of its weight," he suggested. Rebecca agreed happily.

"Yes, we'll just hoist it by the carry handles. I'll get the air to hold it up. Too bad people don't remember how to do this, think how much back strain could be prevented."

They grabbed a handle at either end and let the air cushion the weight. At first Rebecca had trouble maintaining her end, until Torin reminded her to allow the air to lift it, rather than try to force it. From the cabin it was a brief walk down to the lake trail and the water. They followed the trail, a soggy mess of grass and mud. Their sneakers made squelching, sucking noises, prompting them to let the canoe hang in midair while they removed their shoes.

Finally they reached the opening to a little sandbar, and let the canoe down. Torin stood quietly in awe, feeling the bare ground beneath his feet. The lake was much larger than he had imagined, though Rebecca had informed him earlier that it was 29 miles long, but only a few miles wide. From where they stood the sun glinted off the water in dark green ripples. The banks were lined with small sandy beaches and further back, a dense forested area. Near by were several piers, and far away in the distance they could see a few boats tied up in the water. Where they stood there were no people to be seen, only an occasional bird standing in the sun or fishing from off the rocks that jutted out from the bank.

While Rebecca sat down on a large rock, Torin dropped to the ground and allowed the sand to run through his fingers. Its brown roughness was very different from Thianely's white and purple beaches. He sniffed the air. It smelled of fish and trees, water and stone. He glanced up, pointing out to the water.

"Rebecca, look."

Gliding toward them along the top of the lake was a long snake, its coils sparkling under the sun. Its body undulated back and forth as if it were weaving a water tapestry.

"It's a water snake, Torin," Rebecca said. "We usually avoid them, but I don't think it will attack us or anything."

Torin watched in fascination as the snake neared the edge of the lake. Rebecca found herself climbing down from her rock perch and backing up slightly as the creature reached the bank. It writhed up the path, stopped directly in front of them, and flicked its head left and right as if trying to decide which one of them to speak to. Finally it reared up its head, hissing loudly.

"Torin, you ought to back up slowly so that it doesn't strike you. Maybe it's crazy or something. I've never seen one act like this."

Instead, Torin bent down and brought his face close to the snake's flickering tongue. He listened for a moment, nodding thoughtfully to himself as the snake dropped back down. They both watched it make a speedy return to the water.

"What was that all about?" Rebecca asked in frustration. Her ability to mindtel must be seriously obstructed if she couldn't even tell whether the snake was a threat or not.

"It warns that others gather, besides those Thianelians whom we have asked here. It is as Tyor Kehn said. The beings that approach are very dark, like earth Bolluxes. We must call on those who live beneath the lake for their assistance, as well as those creatures that dwell nearby. When the rest of the Thianelians arrive, they will provide defense too, but we have a responsibility to the lake's inhabitants to help keep them safe."

"Bad company," Rebecca muttered. "Just what we need to sing aemethra, although even discordant sounds are part of the fullness of sound creation. I tell you, Torin, I'm sick of feeling so fuzzy-brained all of the time. I had no idea what that snake was intending. It's ironic that the idea of defying, or rather asking to circumvent physical laws, used to freak me out, but compared to mind communication, it seems almost simple. And yet I have no trouble hearing angels at all."

"I noticed your fear has grown, Rebecca. It is a natural result of the separation of mind here. Let me try something. Here at the lake there is less interference, no traffic, and few people, less electricity. Open your mind; let some of your defenses go, and see how you feel. I will hold a fire shield around you awhile."

Rebecca nodded, realizing she was afraid to let go completely, in case her headaches returned. Torin increased the thickness of the fire shield until it was so dense she could barely make out his form through the flickering flames. Slowly she let down her mind shields, one layer at a time, until she could again hear Torin's voice in her mind.

"That's it. Now focus on the tone of my mind, so that you can distinguish it from anyone else's. Expand your inner hearing to include the beings that live in the trees, the ground, and even under the water."

Rebecca first concentrated on the clarity of Torin's mind, a familiar beacon of comfort, and gradually relaxed, allowing her perception to encompass the entire lake area. She could hear the worrying of the wind, though the day appeared calm. Tiny sounds reached her inner ear, the wriggling of worms burrowing deeper into the earth, the unease of the trees. Even the birds and fish felt anxious, dreading something, but not knowing what. It was a strange contrast to the warmth of the sun on her face, the fragrance of the air.

Then she felt it, a dark mass of rage and fear, the arrogance of power stunted and twisted, moving toward them like a cyclone of hate. It was still many days away, but the effect on her mind was pure dread. Barely registering the thoughts of her parents, grandparents, and Haldane, she withdrew immediately, drawing her shields back over her mind like a small child cowering under her blankets.

Rebecca turned to Torin incredulously. "Don't tell me you've been feeling that for days! It's enough to make a person hide inside their head and never come out."

Torin dropped the fire shield and clasped her hands in his. "Rebecca, I too have had certain shields up; I merely have fewer than you do. You grew up here, and are even more susceptible to separation than I am. I am curious about the fear you experience so deeply. Have you noticed that as many of your physical abilities increase, for example, your accuracy in using fire elements, shifting form, allowing air to support you, and so on, your fear of not being able to protect yourself also increases?"

Rebecca leaned over to rest her head on Torin's chest. He wrapped his arms around her to hold her. Finally she raised her head and looked into his eyes. "When you put it like that, it makes absolutely no sense."

"Yes it does, Rebecca," Torin protested. "That is exactly how separation works. You may hold two or more completely conflicting thoughts or emotions or states of being simultaneously. Imagine being strong of mind, but having a disease in your body, as your grandfather did, or being strong of body, but full of emotional refuse, as your grandmother does. You have overcome your fear of disobeying the physical laws of your planet, but are unable to both protect your mind and keep it open at once. You need practice in this, as I do in learning to travel thought. And when it comes to the angels, you need have no barrier against them because they have no egos, and do no harm. Also you trust them completely."

"It still sucks," she said miserably. "I can't believe I have come so far and still have difficulty with things that should be easy for me. Oops, I know, I'm judging myself again. Tell you what, let's get this canoe in the water."

They spent the next couple of hours paddling about. Torin, who'd never used oars before, proved to be both coordinated and tireless. While they took turns rowing, Rebecca practiced dropping several of her mind shields at a time, both to develop expertise in secure openness, and to inform the lake's inhabitants of the incoming danger. Several small fish swam up to the canoe to receive suggestions for protection. Torin indicated that they needn't worry, the Thianelians would be responsible for the lake creatures' well being, but the fish insisted that they help also. Birds from nearby nests joined in as well, as did snake and bug, squirrel and rabbit. There was a similar response from the trees. Once Torin and Rebecca had spoken to a small cluster of maples, word was immediately passed by underground root system and trees all around the lake moved closer together in preparation for defense. Even after Torin assured them that the menace would not occur for several days, they still shifted in readiness.

With Rebecca's help, Torin set up an all-elemental shield of defense, completely encircling the lake in a 10-mile radius. Within seconds, each inhabitant joined in as Rebecca sat in the canoe, gently rocking back and forth in the waves, marveling at the energetic strength of fish and tree, bird and insect. With her mind clear and perceptions expanded, she could determine the subtle differences between energies, the humming vibration of insects, the full pulsing presence of the trees, and the soaring movement of birds.

Suddenly she heard the faint droning of an engine and looked over to see Griffin and Haldane approaching in the motorboat. Haldane stood balanced on his head in the yoga position Rebecca had taught him, while Griffin tried to hold onto him with one hand and steer with the other.

"Hey there, you two," Griffin called out as the boat neared the canoe. "I assume you're responsible for that weird halo thing up in the sky there."

He pointed to the vibrantly colored shield encompassing the lake. Rebecca, who'd been more focused on experiencing the shield rather than seeing it, gave out a gasp of pleasure. Though it would be invisible to most, the shield, rippling with waves of energy, held particles of silvery metallic sparkles, pastel hues, and bright primary colors somehow mixed together and distinct at once. It reminded Rebecca of a scribble picture she'd done in kindergarten when she'd received a new box of 64 crayons and she'd used every one.

Meanwhile, Torin replied, "We have had a great deal of help, and at least it provides some protection until the rest of our visitors arrive. It will also act as a beacon for those Thianelians who travel here."

Griffin said wryly, "I could use some time to relax. On that note, I'm taking the little monster back to the cabin. I'm worn out. I let him drive and you know what he did? He took the damn boat off the water. We were airborne way too long. I've yelled at him so much my throat is sore."

Haldane shrugged from his upside down position, causing his life jacket to settle down around his face.

"I wanted to go faster," he said loudly, speaking around the thickness of the vest. "Bolluxes don't like water, even traveling on it."

"I'd offer you a ride, Torin," Griffin continued, "but I think it will have to wait until another day. Can you two make it back on your own steam, or do you want a tow?"

"We can handle it, Dad," Rebecca said. "I thought we'd stay out a little longer before we head back, but we'll be in before too long."

As the sound of the motorboat faded in the distance, Torin and Rebecca drifted for a while. Torin tucked the oars beside him and leaned back against the seat, Rebecca curling up beside him. They watched as the sun began to sink, sending pink and magenta rays streaming across the sky. For a time they floated in silence, watching the water lap against the sides of the canoe, the sunset echo along the rim of the waves.

Rebecca trailed her hand in the cool water. "Torin, how are you feeling about meeting all of the Thianelians here? Tyor Kehn, at least, may have some further information for you about your father. It must be strange to still be wondering about your parents after so long."

Torin said nothing; merely stroked his fingers along the edge of her other hand, clasping it gently. She could feel the raised whorls in his palm heating slightly from the contact. Torin sighed, and encircling her in his arms more closely, rested his chin on her head.

"I do wonder," he finally admitted. "I am curious and longing to know both my father and my mother, who they truly are, how they met, where they exist now. I had surrendered to not knowing, Rebecca. When the Great Tree would not tell me, I realized I was not to know, perhaps for this whole lifetime. Though I was frustrated as a child, one cannot argue with the Great Tree. Now though, I find I do not fully know myself, or the parts of my nature I received from my parents. It is strange."

Rebecca ran her fingers over his palm, feeling the tingling warmth in her fingertips. "I've come here every summer from the time I was very little. This is the same canoe that I first learned to paddle, the same lake where I learned to swim. Mom and Dad and me, here, every year. And the sky is the same blue it's always been, unless I look closely and see the energy of creation rushing by in each moment, or watch the angels guarding us, or the faces of the trees smiling. Are we human because we have forgotten our other forms, or are we more human because we remember them?"

"Does it matter how we describe ourselves?" Torin asked. "Even these forms will pass away, and we will change again, no matter what happens in this life. The Rebecca and Torin we once were and are now and all of the lives we've ever lived keep changing. You are daughter and sister, friend and mate and all the roles you've ever played, and all of them together are no more real than the name you call yourself this time. And every bit of it is part of real, but not all of it. Even the words of the Old Tongue cannot help me, because we are moving from experience in thought, to something else entirely." He reached out a hand to touch her face, and his green eyes glowed so brightly he looked like he himself was aflame.

As he looked into her brilliant eyes, tears began to course down his cheeks. He felt the wetness on his skin and said in amazement, "I had not thought to weep as you do. I am no longer contained by my own self-perception at all. I do not know myself." He shuddered. Rebecca held him, as he grieved for the Torin of Thianely whom he had once been. Finally he fell asleep, completely exhausted.

Rebecca rowed back to shore, marveling at the deepening colors of the sky, the sound of oars pulling through the water. Birds called to her, giving her added encouragement, and once every few canoe lengths fish would poke their heads out of the water to monitor her progress. Torin awakened right as she was pulling the canoe up onto the sand.

He sat up and climbed out of the canoe, assisting her to drag it the rest of the way out of the water. "Rebecca, I have seldom been so weary in my life. Could you please carry me and this canoe by thought? I can not stand much longer."

Rebecca put one arm around his shoulders and held the canoe strap in her other hand. In a moment they were standing in front of the boathouse.

"Torin, you go on in and lay down. I can manage."

He nodded and left without another word, walking to the cabin with shaky steps. Rebecca hung up the oars and life jackets, and lifted the canoe into the boathouse. It shook slightly, floated up high overhead, and then crashed back onto its rack. At that point Rebecca realized how tired she was from rowing, and headed back to the cabin.

She looked in on Torin and found him sleeping deeply in his cot. The space around him seemed charged, multicolored lights streaming off of him in waves. She closed the door quietly, heading into the living room to lie back on the couch. Auran, well pleased with her afternoon tidying up, sat reading in an armchair.

"Hello, Rebecca," she said, setting her book down. "Where's Torin?" She leaned forward, peering at Rebecca intently.

"Re, have you looked at yourself in the mirror today? You look different again. There's even more light coming out of the top of your head, spilling down over your shoulders like a fountain. Your eyes, well, they look..." She paused. "I don't have words for it, but go see what I mean. The whole room looks brighter."

Rebecca got up and went into the bathroom to examine herself in the mirror. Her eyes were blue and shining, nearly transparent. The top of her head looked very much like Torin's had as he lay on his cot, surrounded by streams of light. As she stared into her own eyes her face began to shift into the faces of all she'd ever been, both human and non human. She smiled, liking the fact that all she was could be seen in her eyes. It was curiously comforting; any time she became lost in the drama of humanity, she could get a reality check by looking at herself in the mirror.

"You're right, Mom," she said, heading back into the living room. Auran was over in the kitchen area trying to prepare something for dinner, but couldn't seem to get the camp stove lit.

"Just in time, Rebecca, can you light this for me? Or maybe you could heat it up with your hands. By the way, where is everyone?"

Rebecca held her hand over the burner and sent out a huge gust of flame. At the same time Auran turned up the gas. The whole stove lit up, shooting flames high in the air.

"Ow!" Auran cried, jumping back as the heat singed her hand. Rebecca quickly sent a cooling vapor over the fire to douse it.

"I'm sorry, Mom," she said, shaking her head over the twisted, melted stove. "I guess I'm too tired to have much control. Why don't you let me cool off that burn for you?"

Auran obediently showed her the second-degree burn on her left hand. Rebecca gently waved her palm over it and the burning sensation subsided. Auran watched as the blister slowly sank back into her skin.

"You know, Rebecca, if someone had ever told me that I'd be seeing instantaneous healing I wouldn't have believed it, but it seems so normal around you. I wonder sometimes what would happen if everyone could do that. Doctors would go out of business, hospitals, health care. Our whole system would collapse. It would completely revolutionize everything."

"Yeah, but I don't think most people are ready for that," Rebecca commented.

Auran examined the damaged stove ruefully. "Looks like we'll have to cook directly by palm. I guess Torin can help too. Where is he, anyway?"

"He's asleep," Rebecca replied. "But Dad and Haldane should be here already. And where are Hazel and Fort?"

"Mother forgot her favorite coffee." Auran explained. "They took off to the supermarket to get a few things she couldn't live without. I know it's thirty minutes away, but Pop is so happy he can drive I don't think he minded that much."

Rebecca shook her head in disbelief. "Sometimes I'm amazed how patient he is. It's cute how he thinks Hazel is such a sweetie under her crusty exterior."

Auran smiled. "It would help if the crust wasn't so thick. But I have had some good times with her, and remember how she brought you soup when you were so sick?"

"I know, Mom," Rebecca said. "Can I be grateful you didn't inherit her crabby gene though?"

"As am I," Auran chuckled. "I wonder where Griff and Haldane went. I haven't seen them since early this afternoon. Did you see them out on the lake?"

Rebecca nodded. "They left a couple of hours ago. Do you want me to scan the lake area for them? I've been practicing being more open without getting headaches."

"Could you? Then we can start dinner."

Rebecca cleared her mind of any extraneous thoughts, dissolved several of her shields, and expanded her perception. Moments later she saw Haldane and Griffin walking along Lakeview Drive.

"Don't worry, Mom," she reassured Auran, "they're headed this way. Maybe they went on a walk or something."

"By the way," Auran said, as she motioned for Rebecca to start warming the soup by hand. "I noticed the angels are still hanging out over the roof. Do we have a permanent escort?"

"They're our assigned guardians for now," Rebecca informed her, "and also help me send messages from time to time."

They both turned as Griffin and Haldane walked through the door. Haldane was soaking wet and scowling, while Griffin looked as if he were trying hard not to laugh.

"He pushed me in," Haldane said indignantly, making a wet puddle on the cabin floor. Auran hustled him off to the bathroom to change. Griffin grinned widely.

"You should have seen him, Rebecca. After we docked the boat I took him to our favorite fishing spot. He insisted that he could catch fish better by demanding they come out of the water. All he did was create massive waves that nearly knocked out the pier. I told him to stop it, but he wouldn't listen. So, sploosh! In he went. If he were a regular kid I never would have tossed him in like that, but I figured the waves wouldn't want to be in his lungs long enough to drown him. I fished him out and you know what? He was outraged that the lake had the temerity to saturate his clothes. He thinks he ought to be waterproof and that the fish are rude and ignorant for not listening to him."

Rebecca chuckled, remembering that on Thianely the water of life she'd bathed in hadn't even dampened her.

"Rebecca," Griffin said curiously, as he noticed the brightness around her, "what happened to you, anyway? You look radioactive."

"Dad! Don't worry; I'm just a little more incandescent than usual. I'm not exactly sure why, except that I've been practicing staying more open. Torin looks all sparkly too, but he's having a little nap."

Griffin rolled his eyes. "I swear one of these days you'll be so bright, I'll have to wear sunglasses. Where's Hazel the Harpy and Fort? And what's for dinner?"

Rebecca pointed to what remained of the stove. "Off getting supplies, and don't you think you ought to be careful what you call her? It looks like we're having soup and hamburgers and salad, but I overheated the stove a little. I think we're going to have to do it the hot palm method."

Griffin reached over and laid his hand on the top of her head. "Looks like we need a new camp stove. What did you do, see how hot your hands could get? Did you know there are little wiggly colored things coming out of your hair? They actually feel warm through my palm. I bet we could close all the windows at night and you'd keep the place well-lit." He looked up as Torin entered the room, still yawning.

140

"Torin, you're purple," Griffin remarked. "I mean, your skin isn't purple, but all around you is. What have you two been up to? Most people go for a little row on the lake and come back slightly sunburned. You two look like you ate the sun instead."

Torin made his way over to the couch. "I do not know how to explain it exactly, but I think I am mixing up. Not fire or water or earth or air, but all of it at once, without separation."

"You're integrating," Rebecca said, and watched the flickers of colors around him expand out to the corners of the room. He sank down next to her gratefully. "Whatever I'm doing, it is very energy consuming. I am still weak."

"Maybe it's from lack of food," suggested Auran, as she strolled into the room and began opening cupboards purposefully.

They cooked hamburgers and veggie burgers on a grill heated by hand. Torin and Rebecca were both erratic when it came to heating the food. Heat streamed from them much too quickly and intensely at first, and they both had to concentrate fiercely to keep from burning anything. The soup was hot, the burgers slightly charred, and the salad tossed by the time Hazel and Fort returned. That night, both Torin and Rebecca went to bed early, but Haldane stayed up late with Griffin, Auran, Fort and Hazel. He used his natural abilities in deception to beat them all soundly at poker.

Chapter 16

The next few days they all spent on the water, picnicking by the lake, and for Rebecca and Torin, relaxing their mind shields. Haldane spent hours outside, imitating birds and squirrels, while Hazel and Fort went for numerous walks. Haldane was declared poker champion, until Rebecca and Torin joined in the nightly games. First Torin caught the little Bollux attempting to snoop through his mind. Then Rebecca felt a nudge against her own shields.

Apparently, by making himself at home in everyone's energy fields, Haldane had been able to easily discover what cards his opponents held. Although the concept of fair play was completely new for him, Haldane learned quickly after subsequent attempts at cheating resulted in him being docked points. After numerous losses, he finally accepted the 'no mind peeking' rule.

In the meantime, the four older adults learned to keep their minds protected so that even Haldane's most invasive attempts were met with failure. Fort called it 'keeping a stiff upper brain,' a phrase which seemed to stick. Rebecca was especially impressed with Hazel's cooperation in such matters, until she realized that most of her grandmother's willingness to mentally discipline Haldane resulted from her dislike of losing at cards.

Auran and Griffin alternated Bolluxsitting duties with Torin and Rebecca, although most mornings Haldane followed Hazel around like a frenetic puppy. Haldane explained that being with her reminded him of his Bollux home, a comment Hazel took as a compliment.

One morning, Rebecca awoke uneasy, vaguely panicked, as if wrapped in thick blanket of dread. Her heart pounded. She lay in bed, trying to figure out what felt so oppressive, so intensely frightening. She couldn't remember any particular dreams. Testing her mental boundaries, she realized that despite her intact defenses, the dark energy she'd perceived earlier had gathered imminently closer. It felt noxious. It even had a kind of smell, musty, dank, rotten.

Ignoring the urge to pull the covers over her head and spend the day cowering in her cot, she sat up, breathing deeply in an effort to calm down. Before her heart rate had even begun to subside, an angel with brilliant white wings appeared. He wore a beautiful emerald robe that reminded her of the Renaissance paintings in her art book. As the warmth and glow of the angel's presence comforted her, Rebecca thought to herself how lucky she was to be able to perceive such magnificence.

"You are welcome," the angel said, although his voice was more mental than physical. "I am Haliel. Be at peace, child of Earth."

Rebecca smiled. It would be awfully difficult to disobey an angel, particularly when his presence had already provided the calm. She felt better already, although she could still perceive the extreme nastiness of whatever was incoming. She could also detect the traveling group of Thianelians, however, whose energy was a welcome respite from the darkness of the others.

Haliel nodded as if she had voiced her thoughts aloud. "Those who have forgotten themselves are on the move, and your discomfort increases with their proximity. Expand your focus and experience the assistance of those from Torin's world who arrive later this day. Remember, you are not required to face this danger alone. This darkness is not of your making; it is a choice made by others. Do not take on the responsibility for having created it here. This world can be confusing for those of clarity, particularly when they lose themselves in the reflection of others' shadows. You faced your shadow on Thianely, do you remember? All the fear and darkness in your own soul became transformed to light and humor, and this awareness exists in you always.

Do not take on the burden of others' suffering, or their forgetting themselves; the time for that has passed. Each being must choose whether to awaken or not, and bear the responsibility for it in their own soul. The deepest nature of healing springs from willingness and faith, and you may only encourage another being along such a path. You cannot make them choose it. What do you fear most, Child of Earth? That the darkness they bear will swallow you up, or that you will be unable to help them?"

Rebecca stared at Haliel for a moment. "Do you know," she said calmly, "I find the thing most comforting about angels is their ability to converse without ego. No BS at all, they just get right to the point. I actually do feel responsible, and until I returned here I didn't realize quite how much.

At first on Thianely I was overwhelmed at the idea that I was so much more capable than I ever imagined. Now I'm upset at the idea that it might not matter. I feel how much anguish and fear and hatred exists here, and watching others suffer, even if it is a conscious choice for them, makes me sick. I know there are many who've simply forgotten that there is any other way to live, or perhaps have never experienced any other way of life, but those who deliberately choose to hate, that disturbs me. Here I am, complaining to an angel, but don't you find it odd that humans choose to be nasty so often when being kind doesn't seem all that difficult?"

"I have never been in human form," Haliel replied. "I have no capacity to judge, as judgment does not exist in this form. However, I am able to make distinctions. I find from my observations of humanity that living in a sensory-based form compounds the difficulties of making choices that support one's highest nature. What you call ego, for instance, filters all of the sensory input in very complex ways.

Most angels who have experienced human form lose the clarity of their innermost beings for a time; it is a very curious phenomenon. Even those who study diligently to become human find the transition to be a lesson in humility. I think this is referred to in certain religions as "the fall," a judgmental description of the incarnation process. We, however, do not perceive the angelic realm as being more exalted than yours, merely a different learning experience. It takes great courage and faith to incarnate as human, particularly in such challenging times."

"I think 'challenging times' covers most of human history," Rebecca said, absently rubbing her eyes. She yawned widely, covering her mouth as Haliel observed her with interest.

He stepped closer and sat beside her on the edge of the cot. As he did so, the edge of one wing passed through Rebecca, causing a sensation of pure joy to flood her body. She sighed blissfully, noticing that it was extremely difficult to be uneasy while in the presence of an angel.

"Which forms have you found the most difficult?" Haliel asked. "You have more experience in form than any being I have met besides your mate. And which form was the most enjoyable, if you have these distinctions? Of course, your opinion will be colored by your human memory of those other lives, but I do value your current response."

Rebecca burst out laughing. Here they were, about to be descended upon by a whole bunch of residents from another planet, not to mention the earth equivalent of demonic Bolluxes, and an angel was interviewing her about her favorite lifetimes. She could imagine an intergalactic talk-show host querying guests on human trivia. Or a call-in show called "Ask an Angel." She shook her head in bemusement, pausing for a moment before answering.

"At this point, I would have to say that being in any third dimensional form can be tricky. It is kind of dense and slower than, say, fifth dimensional space. I remember being an angel had its own rules, though, like not being allowed to interfere with free will, or not often having permission to affect third dimensional space. It is odd being so fluid in one dimension and so ineffective in another at the same time. I become frustrated here when I cannot communicate by thought or control physical reality very well. What about you? Where will you incarnate next?"

"I am studying to be human," Haliel said. "I thank you for your openness in sharing your thoughts with me; it will be of immeasurable value when I do incarnate."

"Any time," Rebecca replied. "I appreciate your help too. By the way, good luck with becoming human."

Haliel bowed and floated out the door at the same moment that Auran knocked. "Excuse me," she said, as Haliel stepped right through her, giving her a tremendous jolt of light. As tingling began in her feet, immediately racing up and down her spine, Auran shook slightly, grasping the doorjamb for support.

"How about that! Being walked through by an angel is like a mini lightning strike," she thought aloud, still somewhat wobbly. "I wonder if that happens often, angels moving through us. Perhaps that's what causes instant inspiration." She pushed open the door at Rebecca's "Come in."

"Rebecca, how did you sleep? Torin still has those wavy light lines streaming off of him, but he seems much more rested." She peered at Rebecca curiously. "You know, sweetie, you and Torin look alike somehow, only your lights are more rainbow colored. His are iridescent."

Rebecca looked down at her hand. "I slept great, but I woke up a little distracted. I see what you mean. I'm all lit up. Isn't it funny that we have conversations about what colors our auras are now? I remember you told me once that all that new age stuff made you gag."

"It's the new agey stuff I can't stand," Auran admitted. "I like the old age stuff fine. And it's people like Magdalen Raventree Goddessblossom that really bug me. Even her name makes me want to vomit. She twirled some crystals in front of your Dad and I after you disappeared and told us that we had kidnapped someone's child in a previous life so now we had to bear the consequences. Your father picked her up by her purple robes and practically tossed her out the door. Her condolence call supposedly was going to cost $300.00 even though we hadn't asked for anything. My client Helen Davenport sent her over to help. Some help she was. Yuck."

"Sorry, Mom. But wouldn't it be interesting to see what her response would be to where I really had been? It's too bad you couldn't call her up and tell her."

"I'll just have to imagine the look on her face," Auran replied with a smile. "Now up you get and have some breakfast. We're preparing a feast today since most of the Thianelians will be arriving in the next few hours. Your grandmother has us all organized by jobs. Griffin and Torin are going to go down to the beginning of Lakeview Drive to greet our guests, while the rest of us slave away in the kitchen."

They finished breakfast quickly. Hazel, who had been looking forward to cooking great quantities of food, put Rebecca, Auran, Fort, and Haldane to work boiling potatoes for potato salad, slicing vegetables for soup, and skewering meat and vegetables for kabobs. After Haldane tried to juggle several sharp knives directly above Hazel's head, he was relieved of slicing duty and made to peel potatoes. He quite enjoyed the job, remarking that the nubby potatoes bore a striking resemblance to his brother Darden's toes, and he took great pleasure in plopping them into boiling water. As the morning progressed, mounds of delicious food piled up on the kitchen table, in the small refrigerator and on the counters. By the time the first Thianelians began to arrive, the food was ready.

The first vehicle to pull up beside the cabin was a midsize blue-green van. Out of it stepped a striking couple, a tall fellow with brown curly hair, gray eyes, and extremely large feet, and a lovely golden-haired woman, with clear green eyes in a youthful face. They were both dressed casually in jeans and cotton shirts. Fort looked vaguely disappointed that they looked so normal. Although Torin had few obviously alien features, Fort had been secretly hoping for something a little more dramatic.

As Auran and Rebecca stepped forward to greet them, both visitors bowed, a formal gesture, but one that somehow fit the occasion.

"I am Tyor Kehn," the tall fellow said, his resonant voice carrying all the way to the door, where Hazel stood waiting impatiently to serve the food.

"I am Thessly Kehn, his mate," the petite woman added. Her voice reminded Rebecca of an Indian chime anklet she'd gotten when her parents had traveled abroad. It was very melodious, soothing and mirthful at the same time.

Auran introduced herself, letting Rebecca and the others do the same. Again, it appeared that Rebecca had needed no introduction, for both of the Thianelians had already heard of her. Hazel was actually cordial with them both, while Fort appeared more curious than anything. Haldane made a credible return bow to the two, who were definitely surprised to find a Bollux among them.

"I'm not as bad as some of my kin," Haldane said confidingly to Tyor, as they made themselves comfortable in the living room. "I can sing the healing song to trees after I rip their bark or twist their limbs, and I'm only allowed to do storms when asked." He stared at Thessly for a moment.

"I know who you are," he said. "You're..." Thessly reached over and clasped her palm firmly over his mouth.

"Some things are not meant for you to tell," she said, her musical voice losing its lilt for a moment.

"Oh all right," Haldane said grudgingly. "It's one more thing on my list of not allowed."

As they filled their plates with food, more Thianelians arrived. Most of them knew each other, though some lived far enough away that they rarely met. Haldane made friends with two Thianelian boys his age, Dax and Solen, though they had been warned about Bolluxes and took some convincing before they would play with him. Other small children gave him a wide berth, preferring to play with relatives or friends.

Around late afternoon, the last stragglers had arrived. Torin and Griffin made their way back to the cabin to find it thronged with visitors. Within a fifty-meter radius were a whole camp of tents, small motor homes, and campers. Thianelians lounged on cots set up outside, roasted food over fires lit in nearby fire pits, or barbecued

147

over outdoor grills. Hazel was in her element, passing large quantities of food around, making sure every family had all that they needed.

Griffin shook his head in amazement. "It's like a whole city sprang up in a day."

Torin could feel himself relax in a way he hadn't been able to previously. He might have been off world, but the company of Thianelians made him feel at home. He'd already met several Fire Folk, not to mention Folk of other clans he remembered meeting as a small child. He was especially gratified to spot his old friend Mialchor Hebral, his mentor when he'd visited earth before. Mialchor had married Malima Ortian, a Thianelian woman who'd arrived on earth fairly recently, and they appeared very content.

Torin quickly realized that he hadn't eaten anything since breakfast, and headed over to find something filling. There were many visitors clustered around the kitchen table. He found Griffin leaning on one counter, digging into a huge plate of salad and barbecued vegetables.

"Your stomach growling too?" Griffin asked companionably as Torin filled a plate for himself. Two Thianelians who'd finished eating made room for them at the table.

They ate hungrily, each consuming two plates full before sitting back replete. "One thing I'll say for Hazel; she sure can cook," Griffin commented.

Torin smiled. It was hard to hear over the many voices conversing in the kitchen and living room. He stood up, ready to look for Rebecca, when she appeared at his elbow.

"Hi there," she said happily, reaching up to kiss him. Torin's lips tasted like potato salad and barbecue sauce. She waved over at Griffin, and then pulled Torin from the kitchen, weaving him in and out of numerous Thianelian conversations.

"I have a little surprise for you," she said, tugging him down the hallway toward her bedroom.

Torin immediately quelled his first instinctual response, which had begun to heat his heart spiral. A house full of guests was no time to be considering mating. Besides, Rebecca looked as if the surprise had astounded her as well. She was fairly humming with anticipation. She knocked on her own bedroom door, and before he could fully register the oddity of that, she'd given him a little push into the room and shut the door. He turned to see that she had left, leaving him alone with a couple of Thianelians, a tall brown-haired fellow he'd met at the entrance to Lakeshore Drive. He'd been very pleased to discover that the man was Tyor Kehn, the author of the book he'd been reading. Tyor had been driving a mini van at the head of a line of vehicles, and Torin hadn't had time to chat. The other Thianelian, a small woman with golden hair, he'd never seen before.

"I'm Thessly Kehn. I was asleep in the back," she explained, responding to his thoughts effortlessly.

"We met at the entrance," the tall man said, placing his palm out to hold it against Torin's. His hand spiral began to heat up, confirming that here was another of the Fire Folk.

"I am grateful that you are both here." Torin said simply. "Tyor, your book has been of immeasurable help. I wanted to ask you some more about the Fire Lord if you could spare some time soon."

"Certainly," Tyor replied. "However, now is not the time. Perhaps in the next few days if you have not already learned what you need to know."

Torin watched in puzzlement as Tyor bowed, smiled, and left the room.

"Come sit beside me for a moment," Thessly said, patting Rebecca's somewhat lumpy cot. "I have a story to tell you, if you have not already guessed."

When Torin sat, still looking at her in confusion, she sighed. "It is often said that we cannot often see that which affects us most closely, so I will tell you. I lived on Thianely up until four seasons past my mentoring journey."

Torin nodded encouragingly, thinking for a moment of his own mentoring journey, the walkabout that all those coming of age were required to take. It was not only a growth experience for young Thianelians, but also an important method for the dissemination of information worldwide.

"After my final visit to the Great Tree, I was told that in four seasons time I would be living off world, under rather strange circumstances. Those of my relatives living on Thianely would not know of my journey, nor even if I were still alive or not. I would disappear, be presumed killed. Four seasons after mentoring, I was to return to the Great Tree, although such callings are rare. And on that final visit, though I feared my future, I agreed to it. All the Lords and Ladies of the Elements greeted me, and there I received the essence of the Fire Lord into my womb. I was then transported off world, where I met Tyor. He became my true mate, nurtured me until I was brought to childbed here on earth. When my child was three months old, the Lord of Fire, his father, returned to take him from me to be raised on Thianely."

She paused then, for hot tears were trickling down Torin's cheeks as he shook uncontrollably. She turned, pulling him close, while he sobbed, holding onto her tightly.

"Ah, my son, born of both Earth and Thianely, I hated to let you go, knowing your father would leave you in that pit of ash. My own family did not know my fate, for all Thianelians here are forbidden to speak of me, lest those who seek to harm you would do so through me. We are linked, we two. But now that you are to come into full awareness of your nature, the truth may be known. And my own father Imanayon has raised you well. Did he not tell you of his daughter Thessly of the Fire Folk, who disappeared so long ago?"

Torin sat back, shaking his head as though to clear it. "Imanayon is truly my grandfather then. He will be so happy to hear of you at last! He mentions you but rarely, as it causes him much grief. So many answers to questions I have long asked. I understand why the Great Tree would not inform me of my birth! It would only have endangered me. Yet somehow the Bolluxes have come to know."

Thessly nodded. "The Ice Lord Skelric chose to share this knowledge, for his own purpose. He aligns with the Bolluxes as long as they are of use to him. He thought to have them destroy you so that he would not be confronted with you at the height of your power. And no, I cannot tell you all of your abilities, only your sire may do that, though Tyor has made a study of such things. But now you may understand how it is that one of the Fire Folk may shed tears," and she lifted a finger to catch a droplet from his cheek, "as well as mate with a woman of Earth. For even Thianelians who have chosen to live on this planet may not mate with those of Earth unless they themselves are Earth born."

"My own mother," Torin said wonderingly. "Rebecca told me she had a little surprise. I would call this one immeasurable. Though I know I should have recognized you immediately, for we look much the same, I had never thought you existed at all. To be the Fire Lord's son was shock enough, but to meet my mother, after so much longing, is beyond imagining."

"I am really here, and we meet at last. I have never been able to have other children, Torin, so you are my only son. I am well pleased to have borne you. Tyor had a share in the raising of you as well, and felt your loss as keenly as I did. I hope you will welcome him as another father."

She leaned over to kiss his forehead. "I will leave you now. I am sure you must need some time to think, and feel and remember. We will talk again soon. From now onwards, we will not be out of contact."

She opened her mind to him fully, and Torin could feel the power, the grace, the integrity of this woman, his mother. He recognized the similarity in the tenor of their minds, a certain shared resonance, reminiscent of the connection he shared with his half sister Liliar. He let the breadth and scope of her soul experience wash over him, recognizing another Guardian. He admired her strength of purpose, her ability to let him go despite the anguish she had felt giving up her only child.

He sat back quietly as she left the room, feeling his world shift. He was complete. When Rebecca came in and lay down beside him, he wrapped his arms around her fiercely, incredibly grateful for this particular incarnation, these beings who loved him so deeply, the ability to appreciate it all.

"Your mom is way cool," Rebecca whispered into his ear. "She's beautiful, like you. She and my mom were instant friends. She's kind, but really firm at the same time. Haldane actually behaves himself around her. And Tyor's great. How about that, you show up on Earth and get a couple of extra parents! Even though I can still feel this wall of oppression, a kind of dark creepy energy coming, I'm so happy for you I feel like I could explode."

"Do not do that, it is too messy. But thank you," he added, turning to gaze down at her. "I appreciate your joy for me. I am most grateful for you." He shifted, leaning down for a quick kiss. Sweeping back her hair with one hand, he continued placing kisses down the side of her neck. The skin of her neck was so soft, her long hair tousled and silky, her scent arousing. The depth of his feelings had provoked his usual physical response in proximity to Rebecca. His chest grew hot, nearly scorching the cotton of his shirt. Without her consciously intending to, Rebecca's hand was drawn there, tracing the raised spiral ridges. Torin responded immediately, finding Rebecca's mouth with

151

his own, and completely forgetting to hold himself back. They were lost, all restraint swept away in the urgency of their coming together.

Rebecca slipped her hands under his shirt, stroking the muscles of his chest and arms, but it wasn't enough. Torin pulled his t-shirt off, tossing it aside. He tugged Rebecca's blouse off over her head, sliding his hands over the smooth skin of her back, tugging impatiently at the clasp of her bra. He pulled her under him, tangling her legs with his as a tidal wave of energy drew them inexorably together. Torin paused, looking down at Rebecca's glowing face, her incredibly open eyes. Torin's eyes were so luminous, so bright a green as Rebecca looked up at him that she wondered how she'd managed to wait so long.

Torin smiled ruefully, realizing at that moment that a small cot in a house full of Thianelians was no place to love his mate for the first time. He bent over, giving Rebecca a soft kiss on the tip of her nose, and shook his head.

"The closer we get, the harder it is to stop," he sighed. "You are not helping, my lovely mate. You are so uninhibited in your response I would have kept going if I had not heard my mother caution us. I forgot to shield my mind because I was so out of it with wanting. I imagine anyone with any openness at all knew exactly what we were doing."

Rebecca's blush began at her cheeks and moved all the way down her chest as Torin watched in fascination. Realizing that staring at her breasts wasn't helping any, not to mention the fact that he hadn't moved away from her at all, he rolled off to one side.

Rebecca sat up, turning slightly aside to put on her shirt, still flushed. Torin ran one palm over her cheek, bringing her back to face him as she looked down, trying not to stare at his flat stomach and muscular chest.

"It is not shameful, to want so much," he said simply. He reached for his shirt, enjoying the look in her eyes as she watched him dress.

"Rebecca, Torin, we're going to have music out here, you two," Griffin called, tapping on the door impatiently. "Come on out."

Rebecca stood up on shaky legs, still reeling from the waves of Torinicity she'd experienced. He stood as well, grasping her by the hand to steady her slightly as they made their way to the door. Once outside, Griffin eyed them askance, noting their flushed faces, but Torin looked at him calmly, shaking his head. Mollified, Griffin led them out into the living room, where a whole band of Thianelians was setting up instruments. Most of the audience had gathered outside, listening to the musicians tuning their instruments as the sunset sent streaks of color shooting across the sky. The rainbow hues in the lake's protective shield added a beautiful addition to the pageant of the setting sun.

At first it was hard for Rebecca to sit quietly and listen to the music with her body still trembling in reaction. But finally, the harmony of flutes and drums, guitars and voices soothed her. Outside, the Thianelians moved even closer to hear the music and join in the songs. Although the tunes were familiar, Rebecca could not recall hearing them before. Everyone seemed to know the words though, even her parents. Torin, noting her bemused expression, leaned close to whisper in her ear.

"These are songs every Thianelian child hears from birth. They are being sung in the old Tongue, which has rekindled your memory as well. Do you remember now?"

Mostly Rebecca felt shivers as Torin's breath brushed across the sensitive skin of her ear, but she nodded. Needing a distraction, she joined in the singing, hearing the deep resonance of Torin's voice as he sang beside her. The Thianelians had a large repertoire of material, from lullabies and mellow folk songs to more boisterous ones. Rebecca particularly liked one of the Thianelian ballads, written by a fellow named Afden Orlek.

The Purple Earth of Home

I have two arms, two legs, and eyes,
But where I'm from would be some surprise,
I miss that purple earth,
That purple earth, that purple earth of home!

Here folks kill trees to use their skin,
Build their homes, house their kin,
Slaughter animals to feed their girth,
Forget themselves right after birth.
How I miss that purple earth,
That purple earth, that purple earth of home!

153

Here progress means pollute the skies,
Poison water, legal lies.
Some folks don't eat, others suffer pain
You might have thirst, but don't drink the rain!
Yes, I miss that purple earth,
That purple earth, that purple earth of home!

Folks don't ask the weather,
They often tell the time,
Force is necessary and they even organize crime.

They must control their breeding,
Overpopulation is a threat
And what they ought to learn from,
They'd rather just forget.
Oh, I miss that purple earth,
That purple earth, that purple earth of home.

I know we all are human,
But these Folks don't seem to get
From where I'm looking at them,
They don't act human yet.
Maybe a reminder will help them on their way,
Or maybe they can travel to where I'm from some day,
And see my purple earth,
My purple earth, my purple earth, my home.

After the last song, most of the Thianelians headed off to bed. Rebecca and Torin made a move toward the outside door, when Thessly stopped them.

"Being alone outside under the beauty of skynight will not assist you in maintaining your containment," she suggested gently, while Rebecca felt her face turn its usual rosy hue. "I would borrow my son for a while," she continued. "Tyor rests now, but I napped earlier and have more to say."

Rebecca nodded speechlessly and would have turned away in sheer embarrassment, if Thessly hadn't put a hand on her arm to detain her. "What is this shame you feel, my daughter?" she asked curiously. "Surely you do not regret my son as your mate?"

"No," Rebecca mumbled, wishing she could sink underground for a moment like she'd done on Thianely. As Thessly waited for her to respond, Torin reached over to clasp Rebecca's hand reassuringly.

"I guess I'm not used to talking about mating, with adults or actually much of anyone. I mean, I knew kids at school who were messing around, but this is so much more than that. I feel completely out of control."

"That is as it should be," Thessly said approvingly. "Meeting one's true mate in intimacy is an intensely natural force, not to be feared or controlled. Being contained, however, particularly among Earth Folk, is essential. Such containment takes practice, but also grounding. As it is now, you are both still enjoying the effects of your last encounter. Your grounding is shaky at best. You will need time apart to regain your center. And your shields so that you do not broadcast your longing to all of creation."

"Okay," Rebecca agreed, blushing again. "That makes sense. It seems like no big deal when you talk about it, but I always seem to turn red, even after all of that body training I had on Thianely."

"Many abilities manifest differently here than they do there," Thessly said compassionately. "Besides, it is a very pretty color, that red."

"I like it," Torin said, grinning.

Rebecca made a face at him, and then headed back to her room. Once inside, she sprawled on her cot, yawning widely. She wondered vaguely what Torin was up to, but fell asleep as she was trying to decide whether to get up and brush her teeth or not.

Chapter 17

"Watch this," Rebecca heard Torin say the next morning as she stretched and slowly awakened. Torin's wide green eyes were only three inches away. He kissed Rebecca's nose, then tugged her up to a sitting position.

Rebecca yawned, rubbing the last sleep out of her eyes, as Torin stood across the room, hands by his side, concentrating fiercely. Soon his skin glowed a fiery red. Maroon and blue lights undulated across his body, reminding Rebecca of particularly flamboyant fireworks. Flickering intensely, Torin shot into flame like the golden light of a taper, sending sparks across the room. Before Rebecca could even worry about burning bedclothes, he had descended into a river of fire, cascading across the floor.

Somehow, the wood finish remained unscathed without even a singe. Torin had dissolved into fire so thoroughly that even the vague outline of his humanity had disappeared. The fire coalesced into a thin blue line, then traveled up the metal leg of Rebecca's cot, where it pooled around her body. A moment later, Torin was curled up around her like a particularly self-satisfied cat.

"Nice floor show," Rebecca commented. "I guess Thessly showed you a few things."

"She reminded me of several of my father's abilities I did not know, or at least I did not know the extent of them," Torin confirmed. "There is even a containment exercise I have learned. You notice I am lying in close proximity to you and my heart spiral did not ignite. It will take much more contact to unbalance me now."

Rebecca shook her head at him. "I could take that statement more than one way, and from the look on your face, I think I know just which way you meant."

Torin responded by grabbing her close and tickling her mercilessly. Obviously, he still needed to practice the containment exercise, because in a few short minutes his heart spiral glowed perceptibly.

Rebecca nudged him aside. "Okay, that's it, you goof, I'm getting up. It's got to be at least eight o'clock by now. Did you see anyone else up?"

"Actually, I changed to fire and flowed under your door so I would be undetected," Torin explained. "I have difficulty hearing much aside from my own crackling when I fire change, so I did not hear anyone else. After breakfast I would like to take you to meet Mialchor Hebral and his mate Malima. They have been asking to speak with you. Also Tyor and Thessly have called a meeting after the noon repast to discuss not only singing aemethra, but also the dark clan who will arrive. And we have been asked to update them all on the latest events transpiring on Thianely. Long distance teling between planets has become difficult for most lately."

"I'll say," Rebecca grumbled, still annoyed that her teling abilities were so stymied. "I'll get dressed while you grab us some breakfast. Scoot, Torin, and let me get dressed by myself."

After eating a couple of bagels toasted by hand, Rebecca and Torin set out to locate Mialchor and his mate. They found Haldane outside with Dax and Solen, playing marbles nearby the lake path. Liliar's marbles moved with a will of their own, confounding the two Thianelians and causing Haldane much satisfaction. He looked happier than Rebecca had ever seen him, and she realized it was probably the first time he'd ever had friends, particularly ones his own age.

Many Thianelians were already out and strolling about, chatting or eating breakfast. On the lake path they passed Hazel and Fort explaining to one Thianelian, a homeopathic doctor, about Fort's amazing recovery. They spied Thessly, Tyor, Griffin, and Auran all out on the lake in the boat.

"Looks like they're all getting along well," Rebecca noted. "By the way, how do you Thianelians show up on earth and manage to get jobs and stuff? I mean, what about social security numbers and birth certificates?"

Torin shrugged. "You can ask Mialchor about that. I know he is very skilled at the details of living on earth. When I first arrived here, I had no identification at all, but I stayed for only a few weeks. Long time Thianelians receive proper documents. I do know that even long visiting Thianelians are very careful to use their talents in small amounts, particularly in the medical fields. Otherwise many people would be regularly experiencing what your folk consider miracles. It would not be safe for them to be so exposed."

"When was the last time you talked to Liliar or Leva or Tehy?" Rebecca asked somewhat absently, enjoying the sun on her face as they walked along.

Torin grinned. "This morning actually. I was going to surprise you at the meeting, but since you asked, Leva has fixed the Time Gate! Thianelians are no longer experiencing so many lifetimes simultaneously, and the Bolluxes are extremely busy fending off Kerithan's Griffin Folk. Tehy said that his Folk have helped defend the Earthen Folk successfully."

"That's a relief!" Rebecca commented. "I've been worried, especially since I feel so cut off from long distance teling. How are the Tree Folk doing?"

"Meridwen said that the Tree Folk are still recovering from the earthshakes, but have had no new Bellorasp attacks against them. The Griffin Folk and Merfolk have done wonders as well. They assisted the Earthen Folk in creating underground channels to divert clear streams into the Bellorasps' territory. Apparently the Bellorasps do not enjoy swimming; two of the Merfolk channels flooded a Bellorasp breeding cave."

"I guess Bellorasps and Bolluxes have a distaste for water in common, then," Rebecca said.

"Liliar said they have also had messages from the neighboring planets of Hevald and Torildian," Torin continued. "In response to Liliar's song the Folks on those two planets have planned a sing as well. Timing between planets is still very different, but Leva said it will not matter that much. It is more important that the sound moves on all planets, rather than it having to be simultaneous. She can actually adjust the timing through the Gate itself. Anyway, that is very positive news. Hevald and Torildian have also reported, however, some dark mass of energy approaching as the singing becomes more organized. Liliar was a little confused about that since the long distance teling is still patchy."

Rebecca made a face. "I wonder if their black blob is related to the one we've been feeling lately."

Torin shook his head. "I do not know, but I am sure we will find out soon. And I told Grandfather about my mother. He is so relieved and grateful she is alive! He has missed her terribly. We had a long talk. He and the Fire Folk are well, too."

"I'm so happy for you, Torin," Rebecca said, clasping his hand and swinging it in delight. "You found your mom, your grandfather has his daughter back, the Fire Lord is your father, Tyor is your other dad, and Liliar is your half-sister. You seem to have a lot of relatives."

Torin smiled, and drew her close. "I am very blessed," he said gratefully, kissing her lips gently. He pulled her by the hand to resume their walk, but they'd only taken a few steps when he stopped abruptly.

"Here they are," Torin announced, "Mialchor and Malima."

They'd stopped by a large rocky outcropping. Perched atop one of the rocks was a stocky dark-haired gentleman that looked to be in his mid thirties. Next to him sat his mate, Malima, a slender brunette. The two raised their palms in greeting before they climbed down.

Torin made the introductions, but as usual, both Mialchor and Malima had already heard of Rebecca. Rebecca felt awkward that she only knew what Torin had told her of them, but once they started talking she realized it didn't matter.

"Let's go walking about the lake until it's time for the gathering," Mialchor suggested. "It's a fine morning, and I miss tree speech. Where we live there are trees, in upstate New York, but many of them have not communicated in years. It's a very slow process getting them to talk. These trees seem ignited somehow, more vital. I expect you two had something to do with that."

"They wanted to help welcome everyone," Torin explained, "as well as defend their territory from the darkness."

Malima caught Rebecca by the hand to walk beside her. The path was really only wide enough for two abreast. Torin and Mialchor started exchanging memories of the last time they'd met, while Malima talked about her own earth experiences.

"I came but two of your years ago," she told Rebecca confidingly. "When I first arrived I contacted Mialchor for my papers and recognized him as my mate. It's been very strange being a Thianelian on your earth. Having him with me has been a great blessing, as you must know with Torin here." Her topaz eyes glistened for a moment. "We would like to have a child, but merely asking as I would do at home does not work. There is no physical reason preventing it, but a child has not come."

Rebecca paused for a moment, causing Malima to halt beside her. She quickly accessed the specific information she needed in the crystal wisdom. "Your child will be arriving sooner than you think, Malima. He or she has been very busy elsewhere, and has indeed heard you calling. It's just a case of timing, that's all."

"Oh thank you, it's very kind of you to check in for me. I know Mialchor will be pleased as well. Now tell me, how has it been for you to return to earth, so lately come from Thianely?"

They spent the next hour walking the lake path and talking. Rebecca realized it was the first time she'd gotten to talk to someone else besides Torin who could understand her discomfort being on Earth.

"I'm much better now," she said as Malima listened intently, "but at first I kept getting sick. I still can't mind tel worth beans, and as for long distance teling, only in my dreams."

Malima laughed.

"Some things become easier the longer you reside here," she said. "And others become even more difficult. It is a challenge to live among folk who know so little of their deepest selves. I dream of Thianely sometimes, and it comforts me greatly."

The four started back, arriving at the cabin in time to assist in lunch preparations. As they ate outside facing the lake, groups of Thianelians drifted back from walks and boating adventures. Not long after the noon meal Tyor called for quiet to begin the meeting. He explained the recent events on Thianely as Liliar had apprised Torin of them, briefly reminded everyone that their part in assisting the Earth would be of inestimable value, and then indicated to Rebecca that it was her turn.

"As you know," Rebecca began, "Leva of the Tree and Earthen Folk has been able to repair the Time Gate, at least in several dimensions. We have been asked to sing aemethra here, to coincide with the singing on Thianely, Hevald and Torildian. Only then will time be sung completely, and the rifts heal. I know you are also aware of the dark mass of energy that comes to prevent or interfere with our singing. There are those beings, both in physical form and merely energetic, that would have the earth's separation spread to other planets, creating further imbalance, which is why I propose we do it now, today. Though most of you know of the aemethra wedding knot, to sing aemethra is another proposition, one you may be unfamiliar with. What I suggest is that I begin the energy pattern of the sing, and everyone join me as they're ready."

Tyor, along with many of the other Thianelians, looked at Rebecca in surprise. "Now, this moment, you wish to sing?"

Rebecca nodded. "When I checked in with the crystal wisdom recently, I received information that confirms that we must act now."

Several of the older children were sent to locate the younger kids, for every voice was needed. Meanwhile, most of the Thianelians rose to standing, for singing would be easier erect. Because the Earth's atmosphere acted as a kind of suppression blanket, the Thianelians would have to project their voices as far as possible.

Rebecca considered for a moment that on Thianely singers had sat on the ground, for the purple earth had acted as a kind of amplifier. But when Liliar had contacted Hevald and Torildian, Thianely's neighboring planets, she had stood for hours, sending her voice ringing through the spaces between.

As they all waited for the youngest to arrive, Torin reached over to clasp Rebecca's hand. "This is news to me," he commented. "I thought we might have more preparation."

"There isn't time to wait," Rebecca replied. "It came to me very quickly, that we must sing now. I have the template for it within me, so I will start and let others accompany me as they may. I think you will know when you hear me. It's a very old song, of weaving creation when the worlds were new."

And without any more explanation, Rebecca opened her mouth, took a deep breath, and began to sing the first notes. Within a matter of moments, all the Thianelians, from youngest babes to oldest adult, had joined in. Though most of them could not detect any particular words or discern meaning in a cognitive sense, all of them recognized the sound, much as a child finds familiar the heartbeat of its mother. Sound waves merged, swelled, hurtled from them, descending swiftly through the center of the earth, rising above their heads and meeting the rainbows of colors doming the lake.

Entwining, winding, weaving musical voices poured through the lake, inside each tree, stone, building, expanded beyond the sky, traveling within the entire country, below ocean depths, throughout each continent, finding kindred singers as the sound moved in other countries, where visiting Thianelians and reminded earthlings paused to listen, to feel, and occasionally to accompany.

Rebecca could feel them all, for the sound brought her in contact with the threads of each awakened life, each conscious being, not only human, but plant, rock, tree, animal, all part of one great song. She experienced, below her feet, a surge of sentience, the awakening of the earth itself, like a creature uncoiling itself from a long slumber and gradually stretching itself awake.

Finally, after time lengthened minutes into hours, Rebecca exhaled completely, allowing the final notes to stream from her throat effortlessly. The rest of the Thianelians followed and suddenly all was still, silent in the cessation of breath, when even nature pauses to savor, to revere creation. Quietly, all of the Thianelians, even the youngest, sat down on the ground wherever they'd stood, too moved to speak.

Torin, still holding Rebecca's hand, tugged her to follow him as they made their way down to the bank of the lake. One moment they stood motionless at the water's edge, the next they were on the opposite bank, gazing at the Thianelians from across the wide expanse. When Rebecca looked at Torin questioningly, he merely pointed to the water before them.

In the center of the lake large bubbles formed, swirled, popped on the surface, signs of incredible churning below. Something moved in the depths. Torin's hold on Rebecca's hand tightened as they watched.

Rising from the lake directly in front of them was a tall woman formed entirely of water vapor. Her sparkling hair consisted of thousands of tiny bubbles, each catching the sun and glinting rainbows across her smooth features. Her eyes were the blue green of sky and water mixed, her lips pink as inner shell. Though her pale green form was garbed in vines, algae and the scales and bones of fish, the effect was beautiful rather than frightening. She floated above the water, her finned feet barely gliding along the waves. She was perhaps fourteen feet high, majestic, compelling. Releasing Rebecca's hand, Torin knelt in the sand, his head nearly touching the earth. Rebecca stood still, merely staring, unable to move, while the woman laughed like ripples on the lake, in widening spirals that reached beyond hearing.

When she spoke, her voice drifted over them, creating a breeze that caressed the trees.

"Must I kneel also, son of my brother? Respect is not a body position, but a state of being. And you, my Water Maid, are you startled at my presence, though your song called us, called us all? I am Lady of all Oceans, all forms of the element you call water, as he who fathered you, my nephew, is Lord of Fire. Come, will you not speak with me, your kin, Meruane?"

162

Torin rose to his feet in one smooth movement and bowed. "Greetings Lady Meruane, it is an honor to meet with you in form as well as in spirit."

The Lady smiled, beckoning Torin forward with one webbed hand.

"Come to me here, and I will remind you of that which was forgotten so long ago."

Torin stepped into the water, clothes and all, and walked out to where the Lady floated. The water lapped against his chest, swaying him slightly in the currents.

As the Lady reached out one fluid hand, and gracefully swept it over the top of Torin's head, he felt his legs twist, shifting beneath him. His clothing dissolved completely. Suddenly he no longer stood in the water, but balanced atop it with a well-developed tail fin. He felt the sides of his neck open and close, his gills calling out with joy at the feel of the water against them. Diving deeply, he enjoyed the coolness against his new skin, and recalled his lifetimes under the seas on many worlds. As small fish swam up to greet him, he heard their ancient waves of water speech, and he rose up, shaking water from his head like a playful seal. Glancing over at Rebecca with the lidded eyes and brawny arms of a merman, he lounged contentedly while the lake held him in its watery arms, and his fishy brethren darted around him in excitement.

"I am in the water life remembered," he murmured finally.

The Lady nodded, and as she blinked once, Torin's legs reemerged, his clothes reformed, and his eyes returned to their normal shape. He stood in the water, feet on the bottom of the lake once again, and splashed back onto the shore.

The Lady turned to Rebecca, making a gesture of approval towards the opposite bank where the Thianelians waited. "Well sung, this aemethra has been. The effects have already begun here as well as on Thianely, though our brother, The Ice Lord Skelric, heeds us not. Working against his intention will slow our efforts, as our powers may only assist those who serve Balance, not inhibit all those who choose destruction. We, the Lords and Ladies, who sang this earth so long ago, may not balance you; only you may do this yourselves. We too, are bound by laws that limit our intervention. Your call is but a beginning, not the ending.

Now meet those whom you have called forth. My brothers and sisters and I have been Guardians here from in the beginning, when Mother Rhiate and Father Telches gave this universe the gift of life, when Niaphani and Heric made their presences known, and when humans first came to be. Here are Lords Torienmar and Dariel, Ladies Emera and Blaisel."

As she spoke, the ground beneath Rebecca transformed into glass and she could see fathoms down. The earth was clearer than the clearest lake. From out the molten core came a red skinned man of fire, his hair aflame and eyes crow black. At his arrival, Torin said faintly, "Father."

The Fire Lord, Torienmar, looked to Torin for a moment out of dark coal eyes, and smiled a smile of great warmth, but he turned to Rebecca, and leaning over her from his huge height, he placed two hot hands upon her shoulders. His thoughts were loud as raging flames, searing her mind with their force.

"Daughter, I give you that which you need most. Let the fire of your soul speed you on your way, and the flame of your passion deny nothing."

Rebecca closed her eyes, and it seemed to her that only those burning hands held her upright. The fire sank into her cells through the core of herself, until she no longer felt separate from the penetrating heat.

The Lord of Fire stepped away, saying only, "Do not forget that the fire of destruction also creates."

He swiftly moved to Torin, and picking him up as if he were a small child, the Fire Lord embraced him fully, until Rebecca could no longer see him in the heat of his father's love. As Rebecca watched, the huge fiery man, still clasping his son, sank down into the hot clear core of the earth.

For a time there was stillness, until out of the sky flew a man with white, multicolored wings, lightning bright wings of all dimensions, and a cool white body. His hair, long ivory strands of pale silk, framed a face so chiseled in its beauty that he looked like a living sculpture. Large silver eyes with pale lids, a regal nose, and a firm-lipped mouth dominated his face.

Rebecca had the impression that every word the Lord of Air spoke and every action he took, would be exactly, precisely appropriate. No more, no less. In Dariel's certainty, in his authority, there was great power as well as flexibility. He embodied a kind of unparalleled creativity and he exuded organized freedom, limitlessness with boundaries.

Where Dariel landed the air freshened, as if it were the first air at the beginning of the world. Rebecca took in several lungfuls, breathing in and out continuously, feeling as if she was bringing the whole world inside herself until she felt somewhat lightheaded. At a nod from Dariel, she breathed the sweet air in even more deeply, causing her shoulder blades to undulate behind her, rippling in and out in a steady rhythm. All at once large wings emerged, tearing through the back of her blouse as if the cloth were paper. They stretched wide, golden spans ten feet tall, and settled open behind her, giving her an incredible sense of balance. Then the huge winged man blew his cooling breath over Torin, who had returned from his father's domain and sat, with Torienmar standing behind him, at the Air Lord's feet.

The Air Lord chuckled in gusts that formed small twisters and hurricanes. Tiny tornadoes clustered about his head before spiraling off harmlessly into the sky. As he flapped his wings slowly, sending a warm current of air cascading over Torin, his slanted silver eyes sparkled with humor.

"Here, my nephew, I return to you the wings of flight that you had severed from your memory. Fly far and freely."

Torin breathed in the fragrance of the rich air, feeling it fill his lungs with strength. His shoulder blades began to twitch and writhe as his own wings unfolded from the constriction in his back, unfurling with incredible grace.

"Ahh," Torin exhaled, letting the expansion of his wings pull him upright. He extended his wings fully, great spans of lavender gold, and remembered his lives of flight, eons of traveling air currents, riding the winds. Rebecca stood before him, her own golden wings completely extended. The look they shared was powerful in its understanding, in its relief from the narrow constrictions that had kept them earthbound.

"Our brother Skelric, Lord of Ice, will not join us," The Air Lord said somewhat soberly. "But we will serve as well as we may. Listen, our sister arises."

And they heard it, the sigh of another Lady, who rose to join her siblings from the sifting sand before them. Her face was kind, though shaded with time, colored in all the browns of earth and soil, sediments and silt. Her hair wove about her face with threads of growing nature, in long tendrils of flowering plants. Her wide brown body, entwined with leaves and moss, curved sinuously like the trunk of a tree forced to grow around some obstacle. She reached out her root hands to gather Rebecca and Torin against her bosom, while their wings shrank back against their shoulders. Emera, The Lady of Earth, crooned to them in compassion for all the sorrows of creation. They cried then, for the pain of forgetting, the loss of separation, for hatred, and despair, until they were completely drenched in earthly tears, weary in body and heart.

Finally, she rocked them both on her bountiful lap, smiling kindly. "The greatest gift I have to give you is your own grief, for the measure of all joy can only be found in the depths of your sorrow. Do not be afraid to feel, though it tears your heart in two."

As Emera held them close, they heard the sound of bells, ringing and toning a cadence of comfort. They looked up from the solid warmth of her earthy lap to see a tiny sliver of a woman descending from the sky. Her form was garbed in night, a dark oasis lit by thousands of twinkling stars that shown brightly against the backdrop of her body. Her hair flowed from her shoulders in a fountain of galaxies, forming and reforming in trails of stardust. Her face was too light to focus upon, as if a neighboring sun shone through her skin. Rebecca and Torin both lowered their eyes, not from lack of self worth, but because the sheer magnificence of her radiance was too intense for human eyes.

They heard her approach from the lilting music of her walk, and felt the lightness of her arms as she lifted them from her sister's heavier embrace. Soft touches brushed against their eyes, creating tiny veils to shield them, shadows against the sun. When they looked up they could see the kind wisdom of the Star Lady's face, the incredible depths of her eyes, twinkling with universal warmth.

"Here you are in human form, the glow of your starness shining through your eyes, the gift of light bestowed on all that exists. Do you remember?"

The Star Lady, Blaisel, held up one palm, and in the spirals there they glimpsed their own experiences in star form, the explosive nature of creation itself, the breadth and depth of the universe. Rebecca felt as if she were hurtling through space, surrounded by emptiness, momentarily lit by stars and planets, and speeding through

166

galaxies of incredible majesty. When she had lost all sense of individuality, she suddenly landed back in her own body with a thump. Inside herself, she fell deeply into her physical nature. She could perceive the interconnectedness of each cell, organ, structure, body system, so parallel in complexity to the universe that she gasped in awareness.

"How could I have forgotten?" she wondered.

"Nothing once known is ever truly forgotten," The Star Lady said. "If you know that starness glows in everything, you will see the light in all that exists. Each of you must let the light of creation lead you home. Good fortune to you both, and all whom you touch, in word, in thought, in deed. Let the daystar, your sun, and the night stars give you solace when you lose perspective. There is always an element of nature to guide you. Pay attention in each moment and you will know yourselves again. Thank you for your song, and the courage it takes to come together in such a place of separation. May we meet again in some other time and space."

The Star Lady bowed to them both, stepping back to stand with her siblings. The Lady of the Water emerged onto the sand and all five Lords and Ladies linked hands. In less than an eye blink, Torin and Rebecca found themselves back on the opposite bank, standing next to Thessly and Tyor, Griffin and Auran, as well as the rest of the Thianelians. They stood silently, watching as the Lords and Ladies of Thianely, called by them all to earth, danced together the dance of all elements, a binding integration of aemethra. Above them the sky swirled, fire and air, water, earth, and star all merged together into one.

Chapter 18

For Rebecca the next two days passed in a kind of altered state. Colors were brighter, details sharper, the energy field encircling each human, tree, or rock much more distinct. The air smelled wondrously fresh around the lake, with a purity she hadn't experienced except in the presence of Lord Dariel, or on Thianely. Like Rebecca, most of the Thianelians felt a need for silence, going about their tasks as if they were performing sacred rituals. None had words for what they'd seen, for though most of them had heard of the Lords and Ladies of Thianely, few had ever met them before. Even the children were awed. Haldane and his new friends kept their play confined to quietly running along the paths or skipping stones across the lake.

"I feel like I'm on a major drug trip," Griffin confided to Auran one morning. "I swear I can taste each molecule of food as it enters my mouth. And you have colored lights all up and down your body that keep stretching and shrinking when you move."

Auran nodded dreamily. "Griff, have you seen how my mother's been acting lately? I caught her pouring the syrup on the pancakes over and over again, as if she were mesmerized by the sound and the color. She said the syrup sounded like a symphony sliding down. She's so spaced out, she's almost nice, while Dad's been going out in the motor boat by himself to chat with the fish."

"Rebecca's become nearly transparent," Griffin commented. "I wonder if she'll get so light she'll float away. And Torin hasn't let her out of his sight for a minute."

Of all of them, Torin was the only one who'd become more solid, earthier. Meeting his father had grounded him in a way he'd never been before, and though Rebecca asked, he would not confide in her about what had happened between them in the fiery center of the earth.

"I'll tell you when it's time," he promised, and she had to be content with that. But ever since the Lords and Ladies had arrived, Torin made sure he was within touching distance of Rebecca.

"Does it have something to do with the dark beings who are coming?" she asked him, when he stood watch outside one of the outhouses she used during a walk. Torin only shrugged. With Griffin's permission he'd taken to sleeping on the floor of her room, and for the first time on earth, he was able to completely hold his containment in her presence. He spent hours each day working on increasing the strength of his fire shielding. And several times Rebecca was convinced he was sending invisible pulsing flames far distances, as if fighting something so far away she was unaware of it.

As the days passed, the sense of timelessness and spaciness dissipated. Gradually, the Thianelians began to respond to the sense of oppression, of darkness moving toward them at the lake. The littlest ones began to moan in their sleep, and Torin shook Rebecca awake several times when she cried out during the night. Hazel took a broom with her wherever she went, and even the weather changed. The sky grew ominous, cloudy, with rain pelting the landscape except above the lake where the rainbow dome held fast. Slowly, despite the efforts of several weather-wise Thianelians, the darkness encroached more and more hour-by-hour.

On the morning of the fourth day after the singing, Rebecca awoke to a dusky sky, nearly the color of twilight. The sun shone fiercely red through the gray haze, the way it looked in the city during the smoggiest days, and the air smelled dank, as if something was rotting under the floorboards.

She dressed quickly, waking Torin, who'd spent most of the night on guard. He fire-cleansed them both, and following her outside, joined many Thianelians who stood peering up at the sky. The rainbow dome had gone, completely dissolving into the dark gray sky with its angry sun. The wind had picked up, tossing leaves from trees; swirling small eddies of dirt into the air. Fort stepped up to Rebecca, gently clasping her shoulder.

"The fish are all hiding today," he said in concern. "Whatever's coming, it's coming soon. Where are all those Lords and Ladies, now that the song's been sung? How could it be so light, so bright one day, and the next look like this?"

"How could we have airplanes and cures for illnesses and incredible art and still be fighting each other so furiously all over the globe?" Rebecca said. "Because humans have such a range of greatness and ghastliness, I guess."

Nearly everyone had already awoken and they breakfasted as best they could in the eerie daylight. As had been previously agreed upon, Hazel and Fort had taken most of the children indoors for safety, out of the foul weather. Auran and Griffin stood in the large circle the Thianelians had formed nearby the cabin. Before them Tyor and

169

Thessly led a smaller group, those with the ability and the authority to defend. Torin stood fast by Rebecca's side in a small unit of their own, in front of both circles.

As they waited, the first of the dark beings appeared across the lake, black images against the gray fog. Their arrival was accompanied by a terrible combination of odors, reminiscent of rotting garbage, backed-up sewers, decaying bodies. To Rebecca it smelled like every fault known to humanity had emptied itself upon the lake.

Beyond the edges of their vision they could discern a huge congregation of creatures lurching, hopping, creeping toward them, each one twisted, distorted. One horrific creature strode across the lake, the water barely reaching its enormous belly. It trudged toward them, leaving the water in its wake dark and thick as molasses, advancing slowly until they could see it was a female. Her garment, made of dead fish sewn together in rows, glistened wetly as she walked, the tails slapping her skin in a kind of macabre rhythm. She stopped at the lake edge and stood glaring at them. They could see her grotesque face, with one dark eye rolled slightly to the left, the other bulging out of its socket. The white of each eye was streaked yellow and red, as if she was afflicted with some dread disease. Her hair, twined with spider-like creatures, hung limply over her forehead and twitched occasionally in the breeze of her own foul breath. Her long bulbous nose was tipped up in a snout, and the sour stench of rotting seaweed clung to her slimy arms.

As the terrible Goblin Queen turned, gesturing to her companions to advance, dark imps with long monkey arms skittered and scampered over the lake as if it were solid ground, leaving oily spots on the water. Inky birds darted overhead, their leathery wings sweeping them swiftly across the lake. Each stood on the back of one of its brethren, talons embedded in the thick flesh of the one beneath like savage totem poles in flight.

Lumbering creatures, their opaque eyes filled with malice, stumbled through the lake, heavy hands dangling like maces from their wrists. Tall skeletal beings wielded fingernails sharp as razor blades that pierced their own palms when they curled them into fists. Bobbing their heads up and down in rhythm with their undulating bodies, creatures with serpentine smiles hissed furiously, spitting venom so acidic it dissolved anything in its path.

For Rebecca the most repellent of all were the human beings numbered among the grisly crew. Though they looked remarkably normal at a brief glance, a second look belied that conclusion. Masses of sluggish shapes hung and clung to their necks and shoulders. The suctioning bodies adhered tightly, but several at a time would disengage with a sucking sound and leap through the air to another host. What had first appeared to be a woman's huge mop of hair was actually a group of the writhing creatures attached and feeding from her scalp.

The entire company of creatures ventured no further ashore than the edge of the lake, scarcely twenty feet from where the Thianelians stood. Most of the Thianelians held their noses, trying not to retch from the overwhelming stench.

Haldane, unlike the rest of the children, had been allowed to stay outside. He sniffed nostalgically, thinking of the bog pits at home on Thianely. Torin too, was reminded of the Bolluxes' home ground, though not with the same reverence as Haldane. Torin thought longingly of the crystalline dew that had saved him and his friend Tehy before. The magical vapors had coated their lungs and allowed them to endure their stay in the Bollux enclave.

The grim lead figure, the Goblin Queen, splashed onto shore, gesturing menacingly at Rebecca and ignoring the rest of the Thianelians completely. She bared her sharp teeth, drooling as her thick purple tongue hung below her bottom lip. In a motion more quick than anyone would have expected from the sluggish creature, she spit a black oily glob directly at Rebecca. Torin immediately became fire, elongating his form into a human blowtorch and igniting the dark glob, sending it splashing harmlessly into the lake. As Tyor and Thessly raised their hands to deal with the rest of the threatening creatures, Rebecca called out, "Wait!"

With Torin still flaming close beside her, Rebecca stepped forward. Stopping well out of spitting range of the acid tongued serpents, she opened her mouth and began to speak in the strange dialect of the Goblin Queen. Later Griffin would describe the sound as a cross between gargling and choking to death, but the enormous goblin woman listened intently, occasionally scratching her armpit. She finally shook her head furiously, yelling something indecipherable by most of the Thianelians, few of whom spoke the goblin language,

171

then stomped her hairy foot into the ground, creating a crater in the soil beneath.

"I call upon you in the name of your soul and the essence which has no name," Rebecca said sternly in the goblin tongue, ignoring the repellent queen's outbreak of temper.

"Either you agree to cease interfering, and assist us in our tasks here on this planet, or you will be removed, you and all your subjects. For this planet has asked and we have answered. You may no longer stay here and behave thus. If you wish to remain, you must help, if not, you will be sent back to the place from which you came. Each of these beings must make this choice, as have we all. You have from now until the time it takes to birth a goblin babe to give me your answer."

Rebecca stepped back, giving the Goblin Queen and her cohorts time to decide, while most of the Thianelians watched warily. The creatures before them appeared to be in terrible humor, as they spit and hissed and roared even more loudly than before. The Goblin Queen was especially perturbed, hurtling epithets at Rebecca like, "You are no true goblin, you soft-skinned, weak-limbed, human-faced creature," and "May you never taste the dark flesh of despair again," none of which would particularly disturb anyone but another goblin.

"Looks like she said something to really piss them off," Griffin muttered to Auran, trying not to worry as his teenaged daughter faced down a whole population of horror movie creatures.

"They haven't attacked though," Auran reassured him, "and it appears that Rebecca has some sort of authority over them. Look."

Although a fact known to few, Rebecca was aware that goblin children were birthed very quickly, nearly as fast as a lightning strike. It wasn't long before most of the horrid crew had decided. The Goblin Queen grimaced horribly, and turned to watch as most of her clansmen simply vanished.

"Where'd they all go?" Haldane asked loudly, one of the only Thianelians in the crowd who understood goblin, it being related to an early dialect of Bollux speech.

"Back to the source," Rebecca replied. "According to the spiritual law of place, once it has been invoked they have to assist the highest will or leave. The planet has asked for clearing and well, you can see that a lot of them left."

It seemed to the gathered Thianelians that the air became instantly clear, the stench dissipated, and the sun began to shine golden again. The Goblin Queen sat down on the bank of the lake in disgust, kicking her misshapen toes in the water. She gestured morosely at her remaining subjects, who circled about, not quite sure what was expected of them, and occasionally cuffed one of them if they came too close.

"I'm not sure what just happened," Griffin said, as the groups of Thianelians began to disband, realizing that the danger was over. "Did they all choose death over helping?"

"They did," Torin confirmed, shaking his head in admiration at the way Rebecca had handled the situation. "Rebecca invoked the spiritual law of place, which states that the highest will in any location supersedes the lesser, and the universe did the rest. It is much like your police officers that uphold the courts of law, only at a much higher level. Most of the creatures chose to go back to the source to be reborn anew rather than have to change their ways now. Goblins are brought up to be as lazy as possible."

Griffin shook his head as several Thianelians came up to thank Rebecca for her efforts. "So any one of us could have done this if we'd known the law?"

Torin smiled. "Not quite any one. Some souls have more experience being in authority and others recognize this. Everyone knows Rebecca on some level; therefore her authority in this matter is unquestioned. You notice that none of those beings even attempted to fight their way out of the situation. Even the queen's first strike was mostly a show of strength. If you or I had confronted them, they may not have been so docile. Besides, I did not absorb several crystals full of knowledge, nor do I speak goblin."

After much consultation, it was agreed that the Goblin Queen's new duties would take place around the area of the lake. First she would use a special scent gland in the back of her knees to attract other goblinesque beings from within a thousand mile radius, both those attached to human hosts, and those that existed independently. Then the Goblin Queen would give the creatures the same choice Rebecca had given her, to help, or to leave. She would also protect any beings that chose to stay. In effect, the Goblin Queen would become a guardian of the lake, the very place she had come to attack.

She went grudgingly about her new role, complaining bitterly at having to work. Her usual reign had consisted of stealing the best food from her subjects and attacking them or whoever crossed her path, interspersed with hours of lazing about, which Griffin said was just like any head of a large organization. She was somewhat mollified when several of the trees donated fallen leaves and old bark to clothe her in less odorous garments. Fort quietly buried her dead fish dress under a large rock, while Haldane showed several of the remaining goblin subjects where to find some tasty bugs and worms for later meals. The goblins soon dug mud holes for their homes in the banks of the lake and went to sleep. Finally off duty, Torin went to take a short nap, leaving Rebecca alone for the first time in days.

"That was a very efficient use of authority," Thessly commented to Rebecca some time later. The Thianelian children were all racing about boisterously, releasing pent up energy from being indoors, and Rebecca could barely hear her.

Thessly tugged Rebecca along the lake path until they were out of child range.

"I said it was a marvelously efficient use of authority, Rebecca. Very little effort required on our part, particularly since Torin has practiced his new abilities. It was a nice idea to let universal authority do the rest of the work, although you did have to communicate in that dreadful language. How is your throat feeling after that?"

"A bit sore," Rebecca admitted. "Human vocal cords really aren't built for some of those sounds, but beings usually listen better if you speak to them in their own language. And the Old Tongue is almost too universal for them to respond to; it was better to speak as if I were also a goblin queen, even if the words did rasp my throat."

"Come along, I have just the thing for you," Thessly said kindly. "It will soothe any soreness you still feel. I also have some information for you. Now that the danger is past, and the songs are sung, most of us will be heading back to our homes soon. I know we'll be visiting you often, but some things need to be said now."

Thessly took Rebecca over to her campsite and poured some red liquid from a small vial into a cup. Rebecca took a sip and was immediately relieved to feel the rawness in her throat subside. The juice tasted of an unusual blend of fruits she was unable to identify, and Rebecca was not surprised when Thessly informed her that it was Thianelian in origin.

"Sit here," Thessly said, sitting down on an inflatable mattress and patting a space next to her. "I wanted to talk to you about your communication abilities, Rebecca. Torin said you had been practicing opening your mind shields with varying degrees of success. I wanted to remind you that like the law of place you invoked, the law of intention also states that the higher intention supersedes the lesser. Therefore if your intention for staying open is of greater purpose than experiencing oppression, it will no longer cause you pain."

Rebecca burst out laughing, realizing in that moment that her intention to stay open had met resistance and rather than moving to a higher intention, she had crumpled, creating obstacles for herself. It struck her as completely humorous that she had been her own headache. At that moment Rebecca felt a wave of joy sweep across her face and down her body. The image of energy shields disintegrating made her chuckle aloud as her mind cleared.

Thessly nodded approvingly. "There is one more intention that may help you plant that tree," she suggested.

Rebecca smiled. "Between my mind and the Great Tree there is no separation. Let the purpose and highest intention in planting this wise old tree remove any obstructions created by lesser intentions..."

The next thing Rebecca heard was the sound of someone calling her name from what sounded like very far away. She opened her eyes to see Thessly peering down at her with great interest.

Thessly gave her a hand to sit up, because for some reason Rebecca didn't seem to have very good control over her limbs.

"That's the first time I've watched anyone turn into a tree and back again," Thessly commented, "and that was after you became a series of large crystals. Do you know, I think you must be related to Alphumerian by blood. Otherwise, you wouldn't be the present Essence Being of the Great Tree."

Rebecca stared at her in shock for a moment, until the meaning of the words fully penetrated her brain and she realized the truth of them. She sat resting her chin on her knees as she contemplated what that might mean. Would she live beneath the Great Tree once it had grown large again, as Alphumerian had done on Thianely? No, that didn't seem right. The old way had died with Alphumerian. But now it made sense to her that she held the crystal knowledge of the Great Tree inside her until it could be planted once again.

What an honor to be of such a lineage as Alphumerian! Once, the responsibility would have seemed overwhelming, but now she realized she was merely a custodian of knowledge that had been sustained in Great Trees from the beginning of time. No wonder so many cultures esteemed trees as symbols of knowing! Mythologies had sprung up around a simple truth, for the wisdom of trees had never been lost. What great mentors all trees were, for humans and otherworlders alike.

Her ponderings were interrupted by a shout and a tumble of arms and legs, as Dax and Solen appeared dragging a reluctant Haldane with them. Rebecca was impressed with their ability to keep Haldane restrained, as he was making quite an effort to bite their hands and kick whatever body parts were within range of his feet.

"Rebecca, make him stop," Solen demanded, his once cheerful face twisted in rage.

"Tell him never to do it again," Dax added angrily, "or I will hold him down and step on him in the lake."

For the first time since Rebecca known him, Haldane looked genuinely puzzled.

"What did he do exactly?" Rebecca asked, as Thessly watched the proceedings attentively.

"He went inside our minds and tried to change us," Solen explained in disgust. "And he didn't only try to change our minds, but even how our bodies work!"

Rebecca looked at Haldane calmly. "What was the reason for that?' she asked. "Were you playing cards or something?"

Haldane shook his head miserably. "I was doing what you did with the goblins. You made them behave so I thought that even if I'm not allowed to change the weather outside here, I could change the weather inside people, maybe make them happier. I'm supposed to be helping, you know."

Rebecca nodded, then gestured to Dax and Solen to let Haldane go, which they grudgingly did. She pointed to a spot next to her and they all sat down, waiting for her response.

"Haldane, what I did was not exactly the same as what you tried to do," Rebecca began.

"I'll say," Solen commented sourly, still annoyed that Haldane had been poking around inside his head.

"I didn't make the goblins do anything," Rebecca continued. "I merely reminded them that they could choose whether to go or stay. Reminding beings that they have choice, or free will, is not the same as using your own will to make people into what you think they should be.

Each being has free will, in what to think, feel, and how to behave. If they violate spiritual law in some fashion, the universe holds their soul accountable and they must bear the consequences. Even how they choose to do that is a choice. Some beings leave and return to the source, some take another form, others grow in awareness immediately, others reincarnate many times in similar patterns in order to gain understanding. You can remind others that they are always free to choose in the moment, but you cannot coerce them.

If you instantly made everyone on earth happy by force, they would not learn lessons of sorrow and anger and other emotions, not to mention the experience of understanding the development of will itself. Your intention to make them feel better might even result in interfering with their soul growth. Besides, how did you two feel, Dax and Solen, when Haldane was trying to make you happy?"

"It was disgusting!" Solen burst out angrily. "I could feel him judging me inside my head, like there was something wrong with me that needed to be fixed. I've been sad because my grandmother died, but I didn't want it to go away. I loved my grandmother, and I'm not ready to feel happy yet, because I miss her."

"He tried to take my scar away," Dax said, "the one I got when I fell off the ladder and broke my arm. I like that scar. The girls at school think it's really cool. And it's creepy having someone roaming around inside your head without your permission. It made me want to barf."

"You can be of great assistance, Haldane," Rebecca assured him, "but you need to make sure people want your help first, and remember that they always have a choice. And you are not allowed in someone else's mind, body, or energy field without their permission. Got it?"

Haldane snorted. "There are so many rules the way you live. Bolluxes don't worry about laws or rules at all, except the one that says you can eat whoever comes in your house if you want. The hall of Bolluxes is one of the only places we can all be at the same time without fighting, but even then we do sometimes. I don't want to worry about laws like you do, Rebecca, because then I'd have to think too much."

Dax reached over and socked Haldane on the arm. "Stupid, you never think at all. You didn't listen to anything she said. You can't go around ignoring the rules if you want people to play with you."

"I never gave you permission to punch me," Haldane said, raising one eyebrow. "And I have the choice to think or not, because I have as much free will as you do, so leave me alone, stupid yourself. And you don't know what it's like, always playing with the weather and then not being allowed to. I thought playing with people's internal weather was a good idea until you two got all mad at me. Now you think of something fun to do without stepping on some laws by accident."

"I have an idea," Solen said. "Come on."

The three jumped to their feet and took off down the lake path without a backwards glance. Thessly and Rebecca grinned at each other in mutual understanding. Haldane's self-awareness was certainly expanding, even if he used most of it to defend irresponsibility.

Chapter 19

Over the next few days the Thianelians slowly packed up their belongings in preparation for leaving. Phone numbers and addresses were exchanged, along with the offer for Rebecca's family and Torin to visit any time they wished. Thessly and Tyor promised to keep in touch by phone and e-mail. It was comforting for Rebecca to know that there were so many understanding folk living nearby, or at least within driving distance. And it was much easier for Auran and Griffin to contemplate the future with friends that not only accepted their growing awareness, but also encouraged and appreciated them.

"It'll be strange going back," commented Griffin one morning between mouthfuls of some particularly tasty pancakes. "I haven't even called the office since we've been gone."

"Talk about another reality," Auran agreed.

Finally it was time to leave, and as the campers and mini vans drove away, Rebecca felt like she was saying goodbye to friends she'd known forever. It was especially hard to watch Mialchor, Malima, Tyor, and Thessly depart, although they did plan to visit fairly soon. Haldane looked frankly miserable to part with Dax and Solen, whose parents had agreed that they could visit Haldane at Griffin and Auran's, but weren't too excited about Haldane heading in their direction. Once all of their guests had left, Griffin and Auran made a last check of the cabin to make sure they hadn't forgotten anything, while everyone else piled into the car.

As soon as they were all buckled in and ready to go, Rebecca patted Torin's shoulder and pointed toward the window. All four angels who had escorted them to the lake had materialized to escort them home. Haldane stuck out his tongue at the nearest angel, who merely smiled in return.

In front of them, Hazel gasped aloud. "Matthew, would you look at that! There are angels around us; I count four altogether. The span of their wings is enormous. And look at the light around them, Griffin, Auran, look!"

"Aren't they awesome, Mom?" Auran asked, pleased that for the first time her mother could actually perceive their winged guides, not to mention the fact that she'd actually called her by her real name.

"Wait a minute," Hazel said. "Do you mean to tell me that you could all see them before now? None of you even seem surprised."

179

Fort admitted somewhat sheepishly to his previous encounters, and luckily Hazel was too busy staring out at the angels to stay offended for long.

Griffin began the drive back on Highway 87 and, as with most journeys, the return seemed to go faster than the trip there. They were about thirty minutes into the drive when Rebecca and Torin both yelled, "Pull over!" At the same moment all four angels flew to the front of the van and stretched their wings protectively across the windshield. For Griffin it was as if a thick, transparent membrane had suddenly appeared, forcing the van over to the side of the freeway.

"What was that for?" he asked, but barely had he spoken before they heard it, the sound of screeching tires and metal hitting metal, glass breaking, successive impacts of cars hitting cars. Up ahead of them, several hundred yards away, a driver of a small car had tried to pass a large truck and careened into another vehicle head on. The truck driver, trying to avoid the two cars that wound up in his lane, pulled sharply to the right and was in turn hit from behind by another vehicle. All told, seven cars had been unable to stop in time, completely blocking the freeway. Several drivers, seeing Griffin pulling over abruptly, had followed suit, thereby avoiding the crash as well.

"Whew," Griffin said, turning around to make sure everyone was okay. Haldane and Hazel, who'd both fallen asleep, hadn't even woken up. Fort nodded, along with Rebecca and Torin.

"That was close," Auran sighed. "Do you think we can do anything to help?"

Within a few moments nearby drivers had laid out flares to warn approaching traffic, while someone else dialed 911 on his car phone. Rebecca and Torin made their way to the center of the accident where several people milled around, complaining of sore necks, though luckily all had been wearing seat belts. Torin calmed them with his presence and got them all to sit down. Meanwhile, one woman remained trapped in the crushed driver's seat of her car. Rebecca reached through the shattered window to comfort her, and placing her hand on the woman, who looked to be in her thirties, felt the extent of her injuries.

The woman, who said her name was Lucy, stared straight ahead, unable to turn her head. Considering the fact that she couldn't move at all, she was surprisingly calm.

"You can tell, can't you?" Lucy said haltingly. "That car hit my side and I can't feel anything at all, except where you're touching me. It's like your hand is the only feeling I still have left. Even my heartbeat is slowing down, like it's stopping soon. And breathing is getting harder and harder. But I'm not as scared as I thought I would be."

"I'll stay with you," Rebecca promised, knowing that the injuries were too extensive to heal before the woman's heart gave out. So Rebecca stood there reaching through the broken window, holding the woman's shoulder companionably. Lucy smiled, feeling a comforting warmth, and told Rebecca about her life, her work as a teacher, her family. She asked Rebecca to tell her about herself, and for the first time since her parents and grandparents, Rebecca described her adventures to another person. Lucy's eyes grew wide as she listened quietly. "Thank you," she said simply, as the sounds of ambulances and emergency vehicles came closer.

"Look at that!" Lucy gasped, as one by one the four angels materialized around her battered vehicle. "They're so beautiful."

As she stared in awe, her heart stopped. Rebecca waited a moment, then slowly pulled her arm back from the side window and watched as Lucy uncurled herself from her body and skipped out of the damaged vehicle like a child released from school. She paused briefly, turning to smile at Rebecca, and then quickly faded from sight. Rebecca stepped back from the vehicle just as emergency personnel arrived, removing the door and trying in vain to resuscitate Lucy.

Rebecca made her way slowly back to the van where Auran and Fort had just climbed back into their seats. Torin had recently returned from calming many of the victims, most of whom were being transported to the nearest hospital for observation. Griffin, who'd been directing traffic until the police arrived, sat down in the driver's seat and shook his head.

"If you two hadn't said anything, and if our flying friends hadn't pulled us over in time..."

"What is it, Rebecca?" Auran asked, noticing the look on her face.

Rebecca described Lucy, how she'd stayed with her while she died, and how strange it was to be so sad and so okay at the same time.

"There was too much damage and it wasn't going to heal," she explained. "I felt so sad for her as a person, not getting to live the rest

181

of her life, and how much her friends and family will miss her, yet she seemed so happy and free when she left. It's the contrast between the little human details and the big universal picture that really got me."

Torin put his arm around her and pulled her closer. "It must be difficult to be a healer and not be able to do anything about her injuries. The angels knew about the accident in advance and were not allowed to prevent it. Other than warning us, they could not alter events. But you gave her comfort, and the angels said that they visited her before she left so she would not be frightened. It was a good way to travel to her next adventure."

"How terribly sad," Auran said. "Yet it also sounds very peaceful. I'm glad she didn't feel any pain. Perhaps we could contact her family and let them know that she didn't suffer. While you were all busy, Fort and I handed out blankets, coffee, and snacks. Mostly we were on the outskirts of things. You two have been through so much already. I wish you would have a respite to truly relax for a while, and I'll say a little prayer for Lucy, that she rests easy."

They waited for twenty more minutes until the police opened one lane of traffic and they could continue on. Hazel and Haldane slept through the whole thing, sirens and all. While Fort sat quietly thinking how lucky he was that Rebecca's abilities had worked so well for him, Rebecca rested her head on Torin's chest and let herself feel the grief of Lucy's death. Auran handed back a box of Kleenex, and Rebecca went through quite a few before she stopped dampening the front of Torin's shirt.

The rest of the trip home was uneventful. As soon as they arrived, the four angels guarding the car flew off to join the other angels still monitoring the house. Fort and Hazel didn't feel like making the drive to their own home and decided to spend the night. After unpacking, Auran and Griffin went to check on the visitors in the back yard, while Haldane, fully rested, tried to engage Torin and Rebecca in hide and seek games. They declined, so Hazel, still convinced she could teach Haldane manners, began playacting formal occasions. Fort went outside to lie in the hammock for a while.

It was strange to be back in the noisy, frenetic activity of the city after the relative calm of the lake. Rebecca and Torin sat in the beanbag chair in Rebecca's room, not talking at all, just recovering from the stress of the accident, and all the previous events.

"Since we last sat here," Torin remarked, twirling a lock of Rebecca's hair between his fingers, "I learned to row a boat, remembered my fins and wings, met my father and my mother and my other father as well, in addition to the rest of the Thianelians and the Lords and Ladies. You fended off the Goblin Clan and assisted someone in dying. What is the word, yes, vacation; I think it would be good to have one."

"That's what most people go to the lake for," Rebecca said wearily.

"I think Mom's right. I think it would be great to have a few days where nothing much happens at all."

Over the next few days, Rebecca and Torin did as little as possible. Hazel and Fort took Haldane home with them in hopes of continuing his life skills training, while Auran and Griffin went back to work.

"I don't mind admitting I'm having a bit of culture shock," Griffin mentioned one evening as they all sat down to dinner. Rebecca and Torin had taken over household tasks like shopping, cooking, and cleaning, which kept them somewhat busy.

"I'm sitting there talking to a client about blueprints, and the faeries in the flowerpots are sliding down the flower stems and giggling. It's a little disconcerting."

"It has been a bit distracting, Auran agreed. "But I've been having a burst of creativity. Combining Thianelian elements of design with more earth-oriented ones has been exciting work and I really love the result. I'll show you some sketches later, Torin, since you draw as well. What have you two been up to?"

"The basics," Rebecca admitted. "Cleaning and food shopping, laundry and cooking. Now I know how housewives feel. Torin's been keeping a picture journal of all we've been through, and I've been rereading my favorite kids books and trying to think of nothing in particular. We took a couple of walks, but we traveled thought a few streets away first so that no one would see us leave from here."

"Sometimes housework can help organize one's mind," Auran said.

"This free time has given me the opportunity to think about the future more," Rebecca commented. "I wonder how I'll ever fit in again. I really miss Thianely. I mean, what sort of job would I get here? The Thianelians amaze me in their abilities to integrate themselves here. I don't think that carrying large amounts of universal information around in one's brain is the best thing to put on a job application."

Griffin stared at her. "After all the things you two have done you're worrying about job applications? I don't think society has a job that would fit you, sweetie, so you may have to create your own."

"I wouldn't worry about that sort of thing too much, Rebecca," Auran said. "Things are changing so fast, who knows what will happen, and aren't you supposed to plant that tree soon?"

"Oh, about that, Mom, I woke up this morning and realized that we have to plant the tree on the fall equinox. Torin and I will scout out the right spot in Central Park tomorrow. I can tell the singing we started is affecting things already. The earth is truly ready for the Great Tree now. There's a kind of expansiveness, a readiness that wasn't as apparent before. I wasn't quite sure what to expect, but it appears that rather than instantly creating balance, singing aemethra has influenced the earth like the Lords and Ladies described. The opportunity for clarity and awareness is more available to those who choose it, but it really is their decision.

And the gap between those who choose balance and those who do not will become even more noticeable. It's kind of like two extremes, and we're offering an option to create more harmony between them. And from what Torin says, Thianely, Hevald, and Torildian are also responding to the song. Things might become a little rough, though, as beings make their decisions to balance or not."

"Are there going to be mass numbers of people deciding to leave or something?" Griffin speculated. "Kind of like those creepy goblin creatures that disappeared?"

Rebecca shrugged. "I'm not sure that it will be that mysterious, Dad. But there will be lots of people who decide not to stay. Also, some may help better when they're not in human form."

Auran looked sorrowfully down at her plate. "I guess whatever will happen will happen," she said. "But I still find it heart wrenching when people die. Even after that incident with Lucy, and knowing she was all right afterwards, I felt so distressed."

"Me too, Mom," Rebecca sympathized. "Just because someone is fine on a soul level, doesn't mean it's still not incredibly sad on a human one. On a lighter note, we might have a few extra guests staying with us soon. Tehy, Liliar, and Leva will be arriving here before the equinox."

"What is that, two weeks away?" Griffin figured aloud. "I suppose we could rig up something by then, maybe some tents in the back yard, but it might be a bit crowded with so many mythical creatures sharing the space. I guess there's always the living room floor."

"It will only take a few days, Dad," Rebecca assured him. "No one will be able to stay very long."

"Just be careful in Central Park, you two," Auran admonished. "Remember what happened the last time you were in public. You don't want to attract too much of the wrong type of attention in the park."

"I can't wait to show Torin all of the weirdoes that hang out there," Rebecca said, chuckling when she realized she could be included in that category herself.

The next morning, Torin and Rebecca sat slumped next to each other on a bench in Central Park. They were in the part of the park known as the Ramble, a wooded area frequented by many birds, and today, luckily not too many people.

"It wouldn't have been so bad if those kids hadn't followed us around everywhere trying to get you to fire up your hands." Rebecca said. "And that little girl who wanted you to incinerate her 'really mean' nanny was a little bit much.

Torin shook his head in disbelief. "Despite our best cloaking efforts, it was even more intense than the library and the mall. The children are certainly remembering themselves quickly, but I did not expect them to blurt out the first thing they thought of when they saw us. When that little boy that used to be your dolphin companion called out, 'Remember when you used to be a mermaid and I used to be a dolphin?', his parents were totally alarmed. And the way children kept climbing up our pant legs, as if we were Tree Folk. Their initial joy at seeing us and their misery over not coming with us disturbed me. I wanted to take them all back to Thianely, until I reminded myself that they incarnated here for a reason. Still, we can rely on most children assisting us; they seem so eager to do so."

Rebecca nodded. "Children here are basically underestimated. It's no wonder they don't understand about respecting our space when they don't get respected themselves. It's also hard to have self respect when you don't know what you're capable of and rarely get the chance to find out."

She looked around for a moment. "Torin, I know you're tired, but let's look around Central Park some more. We still haven't found the right spot for the tree."

"That sounds fine to me. I could use some more time in greenery and this part of the park has fewer of your folk."

"And since we've already walked so far," Rebecca said, glancing around to make sure no one was watching. "Let's travel to other parts of the Park the quick way. I've thought of a place that might be perfect."

She paused for a moment, and then disappeared, with Torin following her thought trail a few seconds later. Torin opened his eyes to find himself on top of a large hill, as Rebecca stood surveying the view approvingly.

"Well, what do you think?" she asked, throwing her arms wide as if to embrace the grassy hill and the series of paths around its base.

Torin turned about, noting the beauty of the view and the openness of the area around the hill. "Your people would certainly see the Great Tree if we plant it here." He closed his eyes and felt the ground through his feet.

"We'll definitely need Meridwen. The ground is home to many trees and flowers from all over your world, but even with aemethra sung it must be prepared for a tree from our planet." He gazed up at the sky for a moment. "The birds would be very welcoming, and I think perhaps the tree will draw unusual varieties of them here. What is this place?"

"It's called The Great Hill," she said. "It's not as popular as the Mall or the Reservoir, and I thought about the Conservatory Garden, but it's so well-designed and organized, the tree would be out of place. Besides, here it can put its roots down deep and wide."

They lay down on the hill, staring up at the late afternoon sky, sinking into the ground and letting the earth support them. They asked the trees in the park to help welcome Meridwen when she arrived, and they all were honored to do so, but suggested that Rebecca and Torin speak to other beings that guarded the park.

"For there are many who would be willing to assist," one old maple informed them, "and will come if you call."

"We'll be back in a few days and sing to other beings for their assistance," Rebecca promised.

Suddenly she chuckled aloud. "Torin, I've thought of a job for Haldane that is so appropriate! I mean, it would be awkward to plant the golden root in the middle of a crowd of people, so we've got to ask Haldane for a storm. Only enough of one to get people out of the park until we're finished. What do you think?"

"I think he will be very proud to help, though making sure he does not go to extremes may be difficult."

"We'll have him practice," Rebecca replied. "He'll do it if we ask. You know, I think Grandmother is actually teaching him some manners."

"Her method of teaching is strange to me," Torin commented. "As are most of the educational systems here. We teach by doing, or by our myths. Remember I mentioned one long ago when you first arrived on Thianely. The greedy giant story?"

Rebecca sat up. "Can you tell it now?"

"This is one of my favorite stories that Grandfather told me," began Torin, settling back more comfortably. "It is a creation myth of the Mountain Troll Folk, though not the same sort as the troll you met. These trolls live on mountains, and don't become them. Most trolls on Thianely are quite small and very shy, and it's a compliment to have a place be 'troll-friendly.' One of these days they'll probably show up in your parents' yarden.

Anyway, long ago there lived a very bold universal giant named Ryfo. As giants go he had a very large appetite, and was known to consume many quantities of stars and planets and even galaxies for his meals. This became annoying to the creators of worlds, because after they'd spent all that effort in celestial designing, he'd simply wolf down everything in a gulp or two. Then he'd skip gaily off to find his next meal.

It didn't take long for the creators to band together and banish Ryfo from the universe entirely. The problem though, was that he was a difficult fellow to catch. The universe was large enough to hide even so big a fellow as Ryfo, and finally, the creators had had enough and hired a star-tracker to catch him and send him away. Giants, however, are also notoriously tricky, and can talk anyone out of anything. One tracker after another located Ryfo only to be outwitted and eaten by the giant, whose intellect was as large as his appetite.

187

At last, the creators asked every constellation in the universe to give it a try evicting him, but none would attempt it except a small constellation by the name of Trollgar. The reward for banishing Ryfo was great, but the possible consequence was to become his next meal. Still, the valiant star cluster in the Milky Way Galaxy decided to make the attempt.

The constellation huddled for a conference and then began a siren song that would tempt any hungry giant.

> "Come have some
> Sirius stew, or Andromeda pie,
> Orion's belt on a bed of sky,
> Spiral galaxies with black hole sauce,
> Fresh quasar salad, lightly tossed.
> A nova sandwich for a cosmic blast,
> A slice of blue moon for a tasty repast,
> Horse head nebulae arranged on a plate,
> Sunspot appetizers to tempt your palate.
> Have a sip of Venus, for an acid chaser
> Or a bite of Mars, (tastes like planet eraser),
> Please try it, the flavors, the textures, the crunch,
> Come feast the Milky Way at the universe brunch."

And the echoing chorus sang, " A slice of moon, a cup of stars, a sip of Venus, a bite of Mars."

Of course, Ryfo could hear the sound of the menu broadcast throughout the universe, because of the resonant speaker system set up for Music of the Spheres concerts. He traveled as quickly as only a hungry giant can and had just reached the Milky Way galaxy when the small constellation Trollgar hailed him loudly.

"Too busy to talk now," Ryfo replied, grabbing a small handful of stars. He'd almost stuck them into his cavernous mouth, when Trollgar began to sing a cautionary song about the cost of one of his meals. Ryfo stopped in dismay.

"You mean if I eat these stars, I have to spend creation working. Working? Giants don't work. And you'd have to catch me first anyway."

He threw the stars down disgustedly, eyeing the tiny constellation with displeasure. "Now you've ruined my appetite talking about work. What happens if I eat and leave?" he demanded. "I've done it before."

Trollgar twinkled at him sternly and whispered a warning. "If you nibble without asking, creators will pile on much tasking. If you take and eat in spite, your mouth will taste creation's blight."

Ryfo, however, being much larger and stronger than the constellation, disregarded the advice and had just taken a little nibble from one moon, causing a crater to appear, when he tossed it back into orbit in horror. For every meal eaten without asking, Ryfo would taste terrible, wretched, and disgusting flavors whenever he took a mouthful. And since he'd been stealing meals for millennium, he had many foul mouthfuls to go.

Ryfo was so angry at the constellation for ruining his meals with its song, that he dashed the stars to pieces with one great fist. The pieces of Trollgar's stars fell to the ground in many of the planets of the Milky Way and became the Troll Clans. Because of his greedy behavior and bad temper, Ryfo was made to work, as the little constellation had warned, and was put in charge of the gravitational forces for many galaxies. To this day, the mighty giant works hard to support the galaxy that he would once have eaten for lunch. And trolls are considered to be good luck, since the creators blessed them for their universal service. That's why it is said to be great good fortune to rub their bellies. And of course, it is only lucky if one has permission first."

Rebecca laughed, "I think you ought to tell Haldane this story. Maybe it will help with his table manners."

Torin grinned. "Actually, it is one of those tales told to children to remind them to ask before eating and think before acting. Much of our schooling takes place through storytelling. We all help the little ones learn, mostly in day-to-day living. We have no separate place for schooling, like folk do here. And of course, much knowledge was transmitted through the Great Tree."

"It's strange thinking I'll never finish high school here," Rebecca mused. "I almost wish I could take you for a day to see what it's like, but I wouldn't be able to stand it any more. I wonder what all my friends would think."

"Do you miss them?"

Rebecca rested her chin in her hand and thought for a moment. "Sometimes. I miss who I used to be with them, but it was already getting strange between us before I left for Thianely. I don't know; everything is so much more complicated here. I miss the pink sky on Thianely, the trees that sing to their leaf babies at night, and the water that speaks of creatures and clear flowing, and everyone there."

They lay quietly until the sun began to set and the air grew chill.

"Come here," Torin said, tugging her to her feet. He led her through thought to the backyard of her home. Gilden was dozing by the fence, and the only creatures stirring were the evening primrose fairies. The small lights of their wings made lacy patterns above the flowerbeds. Torin and Rebecca lay back in the hammock and looked at the sunset, holding hands.

"The texture of the sky here is so different," Torin said. "Thianely cannot be seen by most eyes, yet there are thousands upon thousands of dimensional worlds, spread out above us now. How lucky we are to know this, and to experience as much as we do, still only a tiny part of the vastness of everything.

Your knowing is much greater than most, but it is still such a tiny knowing, let it be not so great a burden to you. We have a saying on Thianely that living is for opening the heart, exercising the mind, and celebrating the body."

He squeezed her hand gently. "So let us love as much as we can, enjoy each moment, and experience all as fully as we may. That is as much as anyone can ask. And if we have to tolerate difficult people and a distressed planet, at least we have something to compare it all to, which is again more than many of your people have."

"I feel like I should have this place figured out, after everything else I've been able to do," Rebecca said in frustration. "I can travel thought, and yet I can barely handle a few hours of being in public. And I was able to handle being open at the lake."

Torin smiled. "That sounded out of tune. You are comparing your strengths to your weaknesses, as if they were of equal weight. What is the most difficult thing you have ever done?"

"Accepted that I am not who I thought I was," she answered.

"Perhaps you are not accepting who you are in this moment."

Rebecca chucked. "Okay, you got me."

"As for me," Torin said, "I am accepting that I find earth energy consuming, being stared at by women who do not know me appalling, and being clung to by those very needy children sorrowing.

I do not expect myself to feel at my best yet, Rebecca, or even understand all of this planet's effects, but I can still have compassion for my own suffering, particularly in the face of so many others'. I know that in some ways we cannot be as close here as on Thianely. I do not like this, but I understand it. There is much grief here that has not been fully expressed by either this planet or your people. I do not fault you for feeling it yourself. I do not cry as easily as you do, but I still feel it here." He tapped his chest, and Rebecca could see, in the dark, the glowing of his heart through his t-shirt.

They lay comfortably in silence. Finally Rebecca began to tell him of the Christian creation myth of the Garden of Eden and the snake and Adam and Eve. He listened intently until she had finished, and shook his head in amazement.

"You have the same kind of story as the trolls do," he said. "Only your people took the fruit without asking the tree. They ate of the knowledge of separation and had to leave the place of wholeness. Just as the giant has to work off his stolen suppers, your people must heal their way to wholeness even in the knowledge of separation. I wonder if it was a tasty apple. And do men really think it was the fault of the woman? That must cause grave suffering. Blame is so straight a path to separation."

Rebecca leaned right over and kissed him soundly. "Too bad you couldn't convince others of that. There are many other creation myths here too, from many different cultures. My parents have a book about them you might like to read."

They spent the rest of the evening keeping Auran and Griffin distracted from the fact that Hazel had unceremoniously dropped Haldane off right before dinner and he had promptly eaten everything in the refrigerator. They ordered a couple of pizzas and sent Haldane to his closet room in disgrace, except that he didn't really understand the concept. He seemed to think that they should all have been grateful that he'd eaten the leftovers before they could even become leftovers. Luckily the food put him to sleep early, although they could hear him making strange growling noises down the hallway, a kind of Bollux snore.

191

Chapter 20

Several days later Rebecca and Torin returned to Central Park with Haldane in tow. They materialized in a small grove of trees at the base of the Great Hill, glancing around cautiously to make sure no one had seen them. Across the lawn was a large family picnicking, but they were too busy eating to pay much attention to anyone else.

"Okay, Haldane, remember what we said," Rebecca reminded him as they climbed to the top of the Great Hill. "We want only a little storm now, a few thunderclaps, a bolt of lightning, not much rain. Enough to keep the area clear, but not enough to drown anyone. And not extending further than a few miles or so in all directions."

Haldane nodded importantly, kicking off the tennis shoes Auran had bought for him. He stood barefoot in the grass, wiggling his toes happily. He'd never been able to abide socks; they made his feet itch terribly. The grass was definitely a funny color, all green and sickly looking. He didn't see one purple blade anywhere. But the view was nice, and creating a storm was an added bonus. When Torin pointed out the area they planned to plant the tree, admonishing him not to disturb the ground, Haldane stuck one finger in his bellybutton and began to puff through his cheeks. To Rebecca he looked like a little kid trying to blow up a balloon.

Overhead, white clouds suddenly formed in the empty sky, turning green, then brown, then bright pink.

"Storm clouds here are purplish gray, Haldane," Rebecca informed him. "Anything else is kind of unnatural."

Haldane scowled, sucking the breath into his cheeks and exhaling in a huge burst of sound. The clouds turned dark purple, clumped up into a funnel shaped mass, then spun down toward them.

"Stop!" Torin shouted.

Haldane stopped, raising his eyebrows questioningly.

"Here's the thing, Haldane," Rebecca said kindly. "On Thianely you told the sky to storm, and in Bollux country the sky above you liked to be wild and blow all of that bog stench about. But here you're going to have to ask. The earth isn't that used to Bolluxes changing the weather. People have messed with everything else, but haven't quite figured out how to do that yet. Also, you almost got us sucked up into a tornado. I know you don't like water coming from the sky, but here that's normal. So think clouds, thunder, a little rain..."

192

Down on the lawn the family they'd seen earlier began to pack up their picnic rather hurriedly, leaving in a matter of moments.

"Well at least now we don't have to worry about an audience," Torin muttered.

"It's hard to try to get wet," Haldane explained. "It's like trying to kill yourself or something. I liked the big tunnel thingy, but I won't do another one right now if you don't want one. I know, I'll put a little rain shield over me first."

Rebecca looked over at Torin, who shrugged. Within moments, Haldane had created some deep gray clouds and the first sprinkling of rain. As it came down it hit Haldane's invisible shield and ran down to puddle in the grass. Suddenly a single bolt of lightning shot into the ground several feet in front of them, raising the hair on their arms and setting the grass ablaze.

"Whoopee bog fire!" Haldane yelled, and began to dance around on the scorched grass like the demented child he was. "Shall I do another one?"

"No!" Torin and Rebecca cried together as they stomped out the flaming grass.

"I think we should call it a day," Rebecca suggested, eyeing the circular singe mark the lightning bolt had left. Curiously, it was just the right diameter for the size of the hole she'd calculated necessary for the great tree root.

"Don't I have good aim?" Haldane said proudly. "Now we'll know right where to dig."

"Come on, Bog Boy," Torin said. "Time to get home."

"You two go on, I'm going to stay and prepare the ground a little. I'll see you later." Rebecca smiled as Torin grasped Haldane firmly by the hand. Torin's ability to travel thought had increased to the point where he barely caused a ripple. She only hoped Haldane's weather control would improve with practice.

Rebecca sat in the center of the circle scorch and let her hands sink into the grass. She reached down into the depths of the welcoming earth, humming a little tune.

> Crystal wisdom soon returning
> To root and stem, to grass, to ground
> Let the earth behold its splendor,
> And embrace this tree profound.

When golden apples bloom on branches
We will taste this fruit of peace
Full of knowledge and of wisdom,
Faith restored and sorrow eased.
Come now, all of Nature's Children,
Yield to oneness, heart and mind
Help us welcome wisdom's birthplace
Within us all compassion find.

Rebecca heard the earth sigh in relief. Within the circle where she sat the air glowed silver and green. Up from the ground crawled bugs and worms, and all along the grass ants congregated in little groups. Butterflies by the hundreds converged on the spot, and so too did bees and birds, who'd left their flowers and nests to wing high above Rebecca's head. The sound of birds singing and bees buzzing and the humming of insects filled the air. Rebecca laughed with joy, remembering Imanayon's garden on Thianely, the colors, scents, and tones of beauty.

"Soon," she murmured. "Soon it will be time. From now until then, in this sacred circle, I ask the four winds for guidance, the four directions for wisdom, and the four elements for purity. May all those beings who reside here be blessed, and those who visit here, be refreshed."

Rebecca took from her pocket a small marble that Liliar had sung for her on Thianely. Placing it before her on the grass, she watched as it rolled back and forth, emitting a song of such beauty that the birds and bees and insects stopped their music to listen.

"I call to thee, the ancient ones who dwell between dimensions here, come back to this earth. Those who dwell in flower and bush, in tree and leaf and rock and stream, in green growing spaces everywhere, be welcome here. The Great Tree will be rerooted and so will you all. Come now, come to me, and let me tell you more of this."

She could see them then, some materializing out of the air, others shyly making their way from nearby trees and bushes and flowers. Faeries, gnomes, elves and dryads moved towards the hill, first a small group and then more until they numbered in the hundreds, all making their way from miles of park land, converging upon one sacred spot.

Three unicorns, pure white with golden horns, stepped up the hill, their manes aglow. Several naiads, still damp from their stream dwellings, glided over the grass, while fauns and satyrs played their pipes in joyous celebration. Last of all came a very old centaur. He moved through the throng gracefully, the others stepping aside for him. His long hair was nearly white, his face deeply lined, his arms, though muscular, were somewhat thin. His worn hooves looked like he'd seen many battles. He bowed to Rebecca as she stood to greet them all.

"That you are here means it is nearly time, my friend," the old centaur said. His voice was resonant, still strong, though his great age seemed to weigh heavily upon him.

"We who have held the bridges between this realm and the next grow weary of the wait," he continued. "And though the finer dimensions provide safety for our kind, we do miss this solidness of form, this bold earth. The Tree comes soon then, Roathina?"

Rebecca nodded. "It will be rooted in ten days time, Martas, at the time when the sun is directly overhead."

"We will return then, to provide assistance. The wild boy from the other world will provide the weather?'

"He will. And the Dryad Queen from Thianely, Meridwen, will sing the planting song."

Martas smiled. "It is a brave task for a tree lady of Thianely to journey here. Please tell her that she may refresh herself in any tree home in this park, if it will help."

"Thank you, " Rebecca responded, and dispensing with the formality of greeting that was part of Centaur etiquette, she threw her arms around him and gave him the hug of one warrior to another.

Martas returned her embrace, giving her a gentle pat on the back, which nearly felled her.

"Not so brawny as you once were, Roathina," the old centaur commented. "How is it to have but two legs to balance upon?"

"No stranger than having no tail, or wings, or hooves. Human form has its own joys." She laughed as Martas snorted in disbelief, stamping one forefoot in emphasis.

"Where is your mate, Kyros?" he asked. "Minding the wild one?"

"Haldane needs a lot of minding. We take turns," Rebecca explained.

195

Martas pawed the ground with his hooves, and three creatures only four feet tall pushed through the crowd in response to his summons.

Rebecca gazed at them with delight. Their thick red hair, tied back in small leather bands, nearly touched the ground. Their wide brown eyes were kind but firm, set above large protruding noses and full lipped mouths that looked used to smiling. They wore clothes of bright colors with boots that tilted up at the toes. Tails were held coiled about their forearms in a polite gesture of respect. Two were obviously male, though they and the female all wore gold rings in their ears.

They grinned when they saw Rebecca, inclining their pointy chins.

"Troll kind are well versed in parenting even the most obstreperous creatures," Martas reminded Rebecca. "They are pleased to assist you in child minding duties."

"Thank you so much," Rebecca cried. She felt better just seeing the trolls, so the idea of them returning home with her gave her a feeling of enormous relief.

"We will be here to welcome the Great Tree in ten days time," Martas said. "Farewell, my friend Roathina, until then."

He gave a loud cry, and all of the creatures turned away, beginning their retreat down the hill, with Martas following them out of sight.

Rebecca was left with the three trolls, who stood smiling up at her amiably.

"I am Berla Dunts," said the lady troll, curtsying deeply.

"I am Pierts Wentoly," the older of the two males said, tugging at his earring.

"And I am Ren Dornl," the younger male said shyly.

"My troll name is Sohar Anala," Rebecca introduced herself.

Pierts raised his eyebrows in surprise. "A star troll you are, one of the old ones. We're forest trolls, though some of our relatives have taken to cave dwelling like the dwarf folk. Is it true you can speak to the ancient mountain trolls?"

Rebecca nodded, remembering Gomfrey Risco on Thianely, an enormous mountain troll whose head reached so high into the sky she'd barely seen his face even when he sat down.

"Will you tell us stories of Thianely?" Ren asked eagerly. "I've never traveled beyond the earthen dimensions myself."

"I have lots of stories, and so does my mate Kyros, called Torin, in this life. Why don't we head on home now? We'd be very grateful if you could take Haldane in hand. He can be a bit much."

"Don't you worry about that," Berla assured her. "We've fostered goblings before, and even a fal-gnebling. We're used to difficult creatures, and we love all children, no matter what manners of beings they are."

Rebecca smiled to herself, wondering if manners and Haldane should even be part of the same sentence. "Well, hold each other's hands, please, and if you, Berla, and you, Pierts, each take hold of mine, we'll be there in no time."

At the Bloom household Pierts, Ren, and Berla were immediately made at home in the back yard, the other inhabitants greeting them like old friends. In order to give Haldane practice with the weather, the trolls put him to work making small fog shacks on the lawn. The little structures were so dense they provided some much needed privacy, particularly for a couple of gnomes who'd recently celebrated their wedding. While Haldane was thus occupied, Torin and Rebecca sat in the living room, calling to their friends on Thianely.

"I still can't reach them very well," Rebecca admitted, after trying by herself for a few minutes.

"Here, let me help," Torin offered, taking her hands in his and concentrating on blending his will with hers.

In seconds, Rebecca could see the tall trees of Thianely, and Meridwen of the Treefolk, standing in a circle of her kin, her willowy form swaying gracefully back and forth as they all sang an old tree-calming song. The tree folk were singing on the very ground that used to hold the Great Tree, now a bare circle of purple earth surrounded by leaf strewn ground.

Meridwen, sensing Rebecca and Torin's presence, left off singing and turned about, clapping her hands to halt the singers.

"Ah," she said, her blue-green eyes alight, "it is nearly time to plant the golden root. How are your preparations developing there on earthen soil?"

"It goes well, Lady Of the Trees," Rebecca said, and repeated what the Centaur Martas had offered.

"Tell the Centaur Elder I appreciate the hospitality and will most willingly spend time with the Tree Folk there," Meridwen replied. "But I do not think I may stay beyond a few hours of your time at most, even with all the nourishment my healers may provide. I am strongly tied to my own tree and folk and dare not tarry too far. Your crystal necklace will call me there to the planet of your birth, and send me back when it is time that I must return to Thianely. Tehy and Liliar are traveling by Time Gate, so that you are not over taxed bringing them by thought. Rebecca, it will take a great deal of energy to plant the tree and return the great crystal wisdom to the Earth. You must rest and build up your strength. Torin, your grandfather sends his greetings. Farewell for now. We must finish our song to the trees, as they are uneasy about my traveling so far away."

Meridwen bowed, then turned back to her folk as they took up singing right where they had left off. Rebecca found that the sound of their voices soothed her as well, and she returned to her parents' living room with a sense of inner peace.

Torin leaned over, kissing her firmly as she opened her eyes. "We have much to do," he said, "before the planting. And what you must do most, is rest."

"Thank goodness for baby-sitting trolls," Rebecca said. "Haldane thinks they're great fun, and they manage him much better than the rest of us have. Even Hazel wore out finally."

"Your grandfather told me by telephone that he's been taking Hazel on walks of many miles each day," Torin informed her. "I think she has less energy to discipline Haldane lately, but her mood is much kinder."

"Too tired to be crabby," Rebecca grinned. "I bet Dad wished he thought of that a long time ago."

Neither of them had seen much of Griffin and Auran in the past few days. Griffin had a project he needed to complete, while Auran had a difficult client who kept changing her mind about the style of her new apartment. They'd been arriving home late and leaving early, giving Torin and Rebecca a lot of time to themselves and Haldane. Having the trolls take over keeping Haldane out of mayhem was more relaxing than anything else Rebecca could imagine.

Haldane had poked his head into her bathroom one morning without even knocking, and could not understand why she would be annoyed. Privacy was not something Bolluxes understood in general, although in specific they often tried to kill each other when they were in too close proximity. Torin had suggested half seriously that if she wanted him to stay out of her room in future Rebecca could always threaten to kill him, but she decided to lock the door with a mind lock instead.

"I am looking forward to seeing Tehy and Leva and Liliar," Torin said. "I wonder how it will be for them here, so far from Thianely, especially Leva. I can't imagine how she will handle the way trees are treated here. Though Tehy has always been very curious about earth and asked me many questions after I was last here. If they can handle it, I would like to show them the city. What places do you think would be appropriate?"

Rebecca eyed him skeptically. "You want to take a Tree maiden, a Bollux and a Griffin out on the town?"

"It could not be more difficult than Haldane," Torin pointed out. "And I know we will have to be careful about Leva and the trees in the city. I promise I won't show her any money."

"Books, billboards, buildings, paper," Rebecca reminded him, shuddering at the idea of having to explain the use of dead trees on earth, not to mention the killing of them, to a tree dweller.

Torin winced. "When I first arrived, I could not imagine such disrespect to living beings. Now, sadly, it has become more usual. You are right; it would be better to take them only to the park. Leva may not last here much longer than Meridwen, even though she is half Earthen folk."

"I'll be sure and not ever mention Christmas to her," Rebecca promised, regretting the many live Christmas trees they'd bought over the years.

"Perhaps one taxi ride," mused Torin, picturing Tehy in a seat belt careening through New York.

"Should I cut a hole in one of my dad's pairs of pants?" Rebecca laughed, since most earth clothing was not fashioned to accommodate tails. "I can't imagine Tehy actually wearing clothes though."

"He rarely wears much," Torin admitted.

"Why don't we do something fun now?" Rebecca suggested. "Let's go to the movies. You've never seen one, and I really don't want to do anything profound for the rest of the day. We can always leave if it gets to be too much."

Torin's favorite part of the movie experience, abbreviated though it was, was eating the popcorn. The images he saw projected before him were disturbing, made even more so by their enormity.

199

After three small children tried to climb into their laps during the previews, he and Rebecca quickly made their escape. They stood outside the theater, holding hands and just catching their breaths.

"How did they recognize us in the dark?" Rebecca wondered, since they'd arrived after the lights had dimmed.

"Children operate by their senses instead of earth reasoning," Torin suggested. "Maybe we felt familiar to them, though their parents certainly worried a great deal. There seems to be much fear here about keeping one's gaze always upon one's child. It must be exhausting. At home there are always others to monitor each child, as they belong to everyone in the Folk. Mind teling means communication is never lost."

"That's what we have cell phones for," Rebecca said. "It's funny how we have so much technology to replace what we've forgotten how to do naturally, and we think it's quite an accomplishment."

Chapter 21

Rebecca and Torin spent the next week running errands and chatting with the trolls and other faerie creatures in the back yard. They learned a great deal of troll lore from Berla and Pierts, including great child rearing techniques like stabilizing, which basically meant freezing a child in place until he calmed down. Haldane actually enjoyed being frozen; he said his brain grew as quiet as the breaths his mother took between shrieks.

The trolls also loved to cook, which meant Rebecca and Torin were relieved of most of their kitchen duties. The food was tasty, plentiful, and well received. Ren, fascinated with the T.V. and computer, spent many long hours trying to understand how they worked, inadvertently blowing a few circuits while he experimented. Torin filled his third sketchbook with drawings of Rebecca in repose, the unusual creatures in the back yard, and myriad impressions of New York.

One morning Berla made an over abundance of barley pancakes with maple syrup so everyone in the back yard was invited to a flapjack feast. Haldane played horseshoes with the leftovers, tossing them on the unicorn's horns or frisbeeing them across the lawn to a couple of fauns. Meanwhile, Torin and Rebecca sprawled on a blanket in the chill autumn air, eating blueberries and enjoying the impromptu concert several satyrs were conducting.

"May anyone join in?" came a deep voice. Rebecca and Torin turned to see Tehy, all six feet of him, striding toward them with Liliar by his side. His furry torso was bare above his loincloth, his tail coiled upon one arm and his shaggy hair looked in need of a trim. He stepped firmly, both hooves digging into the grass for balance. Large wings folded neatly on his back gave him the appearance of a half human horse angel. Liliar, his mate, her long auburn hair flowing behind her, wore a simple rose gown and slippers. She looked at ease, as if she traveled between worlds regularly.

"Welcome," Torin said, tugging a surprised Rebecca to her feet. It was somewhat staggering to see her friends in her world. She knew Thianely was real, she had been there herself, and Torin and Haldane were a constant reminder. Yet somehow seeing Tehy and Liliar standing in her backyard on earth made the other world more immediate. She hurried over and embraced Liliar while Tehy and Torin greeted each other.

"We traveled through the Gate of Time," Tehy explained. "Leva sent us. The Time Gate is difficult to calibrate between worlds as yet, and we landed in a closet in your house. It was such a small space I broke the door when we arrived. A troll named Ren found us and sent us out to you here."

"Don't worry about it," Rebecca assured him. "That's just Haldane's room. We can fix the door no problem. Where is Leva?"

"She will join us at the time of the planting" Liliar replied. "She does not feel safe too far from our world or her tree."

"How are you feeling here?" Rebecca asked them once they'd all sat down upon the grass.

Tehy examined the green blades curiously, as if the grass was an exotic plant he'd never seen before, which it was at least in terms of its color.

"I feel very unsettled," he admitted slowly. "I take a breath and the air is not friendly to my chest. My feet do not feel the ground's support, but its instability. The song of this place is like a broken melody, each note different than the rest, and few sung together."

Liliar nodded. "I also feel a lack of harmony here. Many sounds, all disparate, tiny places of song trying to hold together under cacophonous noise. But I carry the sounds of all nature inside me; I breathe harmony inside and out, it is my own nature as a songstress, so I do not experience the imbalance as strongly as Tehy does. Also he is part Air Folk, so the cleanliness of air is life to him. If we remain close to trees while we are here, they will help us feel more at home.

And I can hear the beginnings, the stirrings of cleansing on this planet, the places of sound that wish to expand truly, others of malady moving away. Rebecca, I can tell that you have sung the clearing song here, as well as aemethra. And, Tehy, the Lords and Ladies have been here! I can feel them, supporting the changes. Tehy, if you reach deeply into the ground, then reach high, into the air where Lord Dariel has been, you will breathe more freely."

Rebecca looked at her friend in amazement. "You got all that just from sound?"

"Oh yes," Liliar nodded, her auburn hair tumbling about her shoulders. "And it was so beautiful, the Lords and Ladies bringing their resonance to this place. They gave you everything you needed to plant the golden root properly. And Torin, you have our father's song upon you. As well as, your mother, she's here! Tehy, Torin's mother has been on this world waiting for him, for the right time, and we will some day meet her. She is my relative too, since we are kin."

"Slow down, Liliar," Tehy said gruffly. "I'm still trying to catch the wind of Lord Dariel's clear air. Ah, that's better. Now I can feel the clear drifts through the clouds of bog air. Ah, I can breathe. Still more of an effort though. For some reason, I'm very weary." And Tehy lay down his head on Liliar's lap and promptly went to sleep.

"I think I'm more used to this sort of environment since I grew up in the Bollux enclave," Liliar said, narrowly ducking a large pancake that Haldane had sailed in her direction. She watched as Haldane did a series of eight forward rolls towards her in the grass, leaping to his feet triumphantly.

"Greetings to you, Liliar," Haldane said politely, as Berla and Pierts looked on in approval, "and to the sleepyhead on your lap. I live in a closet and eat earth food and saw goblins. I'm going to make a storm to keep humans away when it's time to plant the Great Tree. And I lost three of your marbles in a poker game and I have two friends named Dax and Solen who are the same age as me, well not really because I'm a Bollux, but they like me! I live with a Griffin too, only he's Rebecca's father and he has no tail. Did you know Rebecca's grandmother is almost a Bollux herself? Oh, is everyone still mad at me?"

Haldane was so excited he leaned over, stood on his head with his feet sticking up in the air, and let his ears flop out to the side so that he could hear better.

Liliar laughed. "I don't think I've ever seen you so happy, Haldane. Earth must agree with you."

"No one really agrees with me, they mostly tolerate me. I do like it here, even though everything is colored wrong."

"When Tehy wakes up we can take you back inside and show you around properly," Rebecca offered. "Tehy can sleep in the guest room with Torin and you can sleep in my room. We have a couple of folding cots you can use."

"Why would you not sleep with Torin and I with Tehy?" Liliar asked curiously.

Rebecca sighed, while Torin grinned.

"You explain it, Torin," Rebecca nudged him with her elbow. "I'm going to call Mom and Dad and let them know company has arrived. See you soon."

After Rebecca headed into the house, Haldane ran off to resume playing with the trolls. Liliar watched him fondly.

"It appears earth has been good for him; he looks lighter somehow. How are you, my brother?"

"I'm well, sister," Torin said teasingly. "I never thought I would be calling a Bollux kin."

"I think the Great Tree showed wisdom in not informing us earlier," Liliar commented. "The rest of my family would not be so welcoming."

"They have already attempted to kill me," Torin admitted, "when I was but a baby. My mother, Thessly, told me much of my birth and also about our father, The Fire Lord. Meeting them was beyond anything, Liliar, and I have a gift for you from our father. Hold out your palm."

Obediently putting her hand out palm up, Liliar waited expectantly as Torin created a fireball in his own palm and placed it carefully in hers.

"I can hold fire," Liliar cried in surprise, as the small ball of red-blue fire rotated in her palm.

"Put it in your mouth," Torin instructed.

When Liliar eyed him skeptically, Torin nodded. "Go ahead, it is a present from our father."

Liliar placed the ball in her mouth, feeling the fire swirling about, its warmth a pleasant sensation on her tongue. Suddenly the fireball leapt down her throat, sliding down into her belly in a shower of heat. There, it expanded both in size and in temperature. Liliar rocked slowly back and forth as the flames inside her core grew, spreading out into her arms and legs, her fingers and toes. Tehy woke up with a start, feeling her heat envelope him. He sat back, watching as his mate turned a lovely golden red hue, nearly the color of her hair, finally subsiding back to a rosy pink.

"Should I even ask?" Tehy said wryly to Torin.

"I can sing fire now!" Liliar exclaimed. "Our father has given me the tune. Torin, Tehy, it is the only element of creation I've lacked expertise in singing! In the bogs I sang a purifying song for water; remember I told you Mosten fell in one time? And I can bring earth

204

into form and matter into air and back again. But now I will be able to sing the balance of fire. Oh thank you, Torin! I heard our father's voice in the flames, inside myself. What a gift he has given me! And just in time to plant the Great Tree."

"Look who's here!" Rebecca announced from the deck. "Mom and Dad were already en route; some faeries at their office heard from the faeries here in the yard that you had shown up."

Griffin and Auran followed Rebecca out onto the lawn.

"Welcome," Griffin said. "Thanks to the faery hotline we're here on time. We've certainly heard a lot about the two of you."

Tehy and Liliar stood to greet them. Griffin reached out to clasp Tehy's hand, gazing down at his hooves in fascination.

"Welcome to earth and our home," Auran said, shaking Liliar's palm. "We have a tent we can set up back here, or you can bed down in the living room. Whoops," she added, as Haldane narrowly missed stepping on her foot as he tumbled by.

"Is anyone hungry?" Griffin asked.

Tehy and Liliar both nodded, curious to try earthen food for the first time.

"Good timing," Griffin commented as they all sat at the dining room table. Tehy had curled his tail through the back of his chair so as to sit more comfortably. "The Tree will be planted day after tomorrow, so you'll have a little time to play tourists. Of course, you might want to borrow some clothes first."

"I rarely wear garments," Tehy said, munching a bit of bread and garbanzo beans. "But I am curious to explore your city. I would be grateful for some clothes. And we would like to hear all about your adventures here in detail. We have much to tell you as well. Lord Skelric has become even more active in the northern country, attacking the Dwarven folk and freezing the northern-most tributaries of the Merfolk. After aemethra was sung, he sent even more of the Drenics to their deaths in warm climes, simply to attack the Griffin Folk. He makes as little sense as many of the Bolluxes, present ones excepted. Mother is debating calling for all-out war, and thinks to send a mission to the Northern Country to ask assistance from some of the ancient ones, those who have slumbered now for eons. It is time to wake the old ones, now that Thianely is so threatened."

"That's what Rebecca was talking about not too long ago," Griffin commented. "That things may get a bit rough while people decide to serve balance or not. Too bad it has to be so tumultuous. Why can't people have quiet revolutions?"

"We've been calling to the old ones here too," Rebecca said. "And a lot of them are actually children."

Liliar nodded. "The youngest ones have forgotten the least. It makes sense."

"Argh," Tehy muttered, slipping sideways out of his chair. He would have landed on the ground if it hadn't been for the wiry strength of his tail still holding him upright.

Liliar uttered a short burst of notes, and waved a hand in front of his face. Tehy slowly returned to consciousness.

"No more garbanzos for you, Tehy," Rebecca smiled. "You must be allergic."

"I felt like I swallowed cressweed," Tehy said, sipping water to get the sting out of his throat. "At first I was fine, but then my throat went numb and I couldn't think."

"Cressweed," Haldane snorted. "My father eats cressweed for breakfast. It helps Bolluxes curse better."

"But not think better," Liliar added, reminded of her relatives nonsensical arguments. She was still relieved to think that Etestian was not her real father. It was bad enough that Boleria was her mother.

"If everyone's finished," Auran said, "I thought maybe we could decide on arrangements for where you two will sleep."

"Explain to me again about mating customs on earth," Liliar suggested. "I do not quite understand."

Auran looked flustered. "I'll let Rebecca explain to you our customs here. But meanwhile I'll go get some extra bedding."

Griffin shrugged. "We have a pull out sofa, or Tehy could bunk with Torin and Liliar could share with Rebecca. I brought some work home with me that I have to attend to, so I'll see you all a bit later."

After Griffin left the room, Liliar turned a puzzled gaze to Rebecca. "Are your parents uncomfortable with mating? Is this the shame you talked about when we were on Thianely?"

Haldane laughed. "Grandmother Hazel Bollux is even stranger. She poured this tasty soap in my mouth when I asked her if she was too old to mate any more. It made lots of foam and I blew bubbles."

Torin grinned at Rebecca, picturing Hazel's discomfort with the topic. "Remember on Thianely I tried to explain about the idea of shame?" Torin said to Liliar. "It's different than when you realize you behaved badly. Shame is a bad feeling about who you are."

"I am glad I do not understand it." Liliar said, thoroughly confused. "It sounds very uncomfortable the way you described it before."

Torin scratched his head, turning to Rebecca for help.

"Imagine if you had believed all of your relatives that there was something wrong with you for having compassion when not many other Bolluxes ever had," Rebecca said. "Imagine if you took that belief into you so deeply that it colored every action or thought you had about who you are. Imagine if you could not sing creation, had not received so much inner knowing from your abilities, if you did not know who you were or what you were.

Now try to picture that whenever you looked at yourself in a mirror, all you saw were flaws, not just in your appearance, but also in your sense of self. When it comes to sharing your innermost self with your mate, imagine if you thought what you had to share was not good enough, so you always were insecure and doubting yourself. That would affect how you thought of yourself physically as well. On earth, people are worried about not being perfect or looking perfect."

Liliar had listened in shock while Tehy sat aghast that Torin had to overcome such an enormous obstacle in his mate's folk. Compared to such a state as shame, having Bolluxes for relatives seemed well nigh easy.

"But Rebecca," Liliar protested, "surely you are not still under such a force of pressure, after resting in the Great Tree for such a time."

Rebecca shrugged. "Most of it is gone, but to be surrounded by fear and shame and pain again... It is hard here sometimes. I'm not so clear as on Thianely. But in terms of mating, it is my parents who are hesitant. And here parents have some say in their children's behavior, or at least they like to think so. Also, we are worried that if we do mate here, the energy would attract attention from those who would prevent the Great Tree's planting. But you two are already mated, and no one could object to you being together here. It's only a question of space."

"They can have my closet," Haldane volunteered generously. "But Tehy wouldn't really fit."

"You barely fit," Torin reminded him. "But it was a kind gesture anyway."

"Wait a minute," Rebecca said. She closed her eyes for a moment, and nodded, opening them slowly. "There are those at the site of the Great Tree who would like to meet you both. Martas of the Centaurs knows of your mother, Tehy. He welcomes you to earth and to Central Park."

"Centaurs," Tehy repeated in amazement. "I had heard that there were those of our kind who dwelt far from us, distant cousins of the Griffin Folk. I would be honored to meet them."

"I can show you the way," Haldane said proudly. "I am the official weather maker."

"We can all go together once it gets a bit darker," Rebecca suggested. "The park isn't as crowded at night, so we'll have fewer interruptions."

Later that evening they traveled by thought to Central Park where they were greeted by Martas and other faery folk. Tehy still found the mode of transportation, traveling by thought, fascinating, appreciating the lack of wear and tear on his wings. Both he and Liliar were particularly interested in the history of the Centaur Folk, which Martas condensed for them into a two-hour chronology.

Haldane made a cloudburst to clear out the park and give them some privacy. While Liliar, Tehy, Torin, and Rebecca socialized, Haldane amused himself by appearing and disappearing in front of a drunken fellow he found passed out behind a bush. The drunk, who obviously didn't mind getting soaked, was also able to see all of the faery creatures. He merely waved at Haldane blearily and went back to his stupor, prompting a long discussion by Haldane about addictions and other illnesses. Haldane seemed to think he could blast addictions and other illnesses out of people by a particularly tricky bit of lightning, until Rebecca convinced him that he was more likely to incinerate them instead.

The following morning Torin convinced Tehy and Liliar to accompany him on a taxi ride, after Tehy was coaxed into an old pair of Fort's trousers, a pair of shoes stuffed with newspapers to keep them on his feet, and a huge old coat to cover his wings. Liliar couldn't help but laugh at the picture he made, her usually graceful mate bundled up in earth clothes so that he resembled one of her ill-clothed brethren. Rebecca declined to accompany them, as she had some preparations to do before the planting the next day.

Rebecca sat silently after they'd gone, grateful that the trolls were keeping an eye on Haldane outside. With Auran and Griffin at work, she had the house to herself. She checked in with the angels who guarded the house. Feeling their calm presence, she settled deeply into herself, sinking even more deeply still, until she could feel the images of the crystal knowledge moving through her cells. She shifted the images into patterns of energy, resonating inside the structure of her cells, and allowed herself to take on the density and stillness of a crystalline form.

From this place of fullness she allowed her vibration to increase, letting her structure melt into a stream of water, of air, of molten fire, the movement of the earth itself. At last she focused on breathing, assisting the flow of awareness to seep in through her pores and into her lungs as she inhaled. The problems of Thianely and her own planet swirled like tiny galaxies in a vast universe of possibilities.

"It's almost time," she said aloud. "And don't forget," she reminded the earth, "even if it is not sung, your song still exists. Even if your whole form were to disappear, your song would still be sung. Nothing is ever truly forgotten. Your voice is still vast, still powerful, and the Great Tree will soon be here to remind us of that. The Tree will grow so large it will be unmistakable and people will come to see it and they may remember themselves or they may not, but that is up to them. Then we guardians will have played our roles, and acknowledged the freedom of choice that resides in each being. Even when we cannot perceive ourselves so, we are always whole, merely viewing ourselves from smaller perspectives. Soon now, we'll have a Great Tree here."

The next morning Torin and Rebecca met Auran and Griffin coming from the living room, and they visibly trembled as Rebecca stood close.

"Rebecca, what is this? I feel strange, like I'm falling and climbing at the same time."

"It's okay, Mom. Realities are just bumping into each other," Rebecca said, gently touching her shoulder, "It's the intersection of time where the tree needs to be. It's earth time and all times now. How would you like to help us plant it?"

As Rebecca went upstairs to gather a few things that she needed, everyone congregated in the living room.

209

"What is happening?' Torin asked curiously, since the air appeared charged with particles of energy moving very quickly in all directions.

Liliar and Tehy nodded. "We see and feel it too. It's like the area around the Gate of Time."

"Rebecca said it's all time now," Auran said, "Which for some reason makes sense to me even though I don't actually understand it."

"We're in the middle of a Simult," Rebecca explained, as she returned carrying a small sack. "It's a place where all times intersect, where cause and effect can be changed intentionally. The Great Tree has to be planted across all times in order for it to be firmly rooted."

"Okay," Griffin said, "somehow that makes sense, given what you've told us about the tree."

"I'm ready; let's hurry," Haldane informed them. He grabbed Tehy and Liliar by the hands, while Auran, Griffin, Torin, and Rebecca followed suit. In seconds they were once again standing in Central Park.

"Look, Griff," Auran said, noting all of the creatures climbing their way to the top of the Great Hill. "This makes our back yard look nearly empty."

Again the folk of the woods, the faeries, elves, gnomes, tree spirits, unicorns, Martas the centaur, fauns, the animals and birds all made their way toward the planting ground. There were very few people frequenting the area, only a few tourists some distance away. Rebecca bowed to all of the creatures, to each of her parents and companions in turn, then gestured to Haldane to begin his weathering skills. The once clear sky grew dark, prompting those few people in the vicinity to head for their cars. Thunder cracked overhead, followed by some spectacular lightning bolts, although no rain fell since Haldane still didn't like it. Fingering her crystal necklace Rebecca called Meridwen to the Earth.

> By the flow of stream and water's fall,
> Lady of the Trees, attend my call,
> By woods and sky, by thunder's roar
> I call thee Lady, to this shore.
> Out of fire, ash and stone,
> Was borne to Earth this golden bone,
> A branch of the Greatest Tree of all,

Come, my Lady, heed this call.

They stood silently as rippling winds shook the grassy spot, and the air split in two. Meridwen appeared from beyond a green-hued portal and stepped delicately onto the grass. Leva followed her, her usual disheveled green leaf dress replaced with a tattered red one, in marked contrast to the elegance of Meridwen's flame-colored dress of leaves. Auran and Griffin bowed before Meridwen, for there was no mistaking her royal presence and authority. Torin and Rebecca bowed as well, but Haldane merely waved.

"Do not bow to me," Meridwen said kindly. She swayed her arms as gracefully as a tree, and all around them they could hear the murmuring sighs of tree upon tree answering back. Meridwen nodded approvingly, her long hair waving gently from her face.

"See who accompanies me," she said, indicating Leva. "Your friend has been through much and by her efforts with the Gate are we able to stand between times to be here now. Neither of us may stay here long, so greet her as you may and then shall we plant the Tree anew."

Leva hurried to meet her friends, was introduced to Auran and Griffin, and gazed about her wonderingly. "Meridwen speaks true," she said, "I cannot stay in your world for long; it is too far from my own tree and the purple earth that keeps us well. But I am so glad to see you all, and to be here upon the Earth that you call home. I would never have believed that the very ground could be other than purple, or the sky so blue."

She indicated her dress of crimson leaves. "Even now the Tree Folk of Thianely make ready to celebrate the Tree's new birth, for all their leaves are turning to flame and falling upon the ground. Once the new tree blooms, leaves will be green again on Thianely. Meridwen says it has been so with each new Great Tree, and so it will be again. You might think that I would be able to keep my dress clean for once, but no, red is as easily stained as green."

Rebecca laughed and hugged her. "I wish you could stay longer and see more of earth, but I understand you must hurry back. We'll see you again sooner than you might think."

Meridwen welcomed all the magical creatures to the circle that Haldane had seared into the grass with his previous lightning strike. "The ground is ready," she said, "the rooted kindred, the Folk of Wood and Water, Air, Fire, and Earth welcome this golden tree. Do you have the root, Rebecca?"

Rebecca nodded, and took it from a small sack she'd brought along.

Meridwen smiled, and her green skin seemed to smooth and soften before their eyes.

"Wait," Haldane cried, "the creatures from the Bog welcome the tree too. Don't forget the dehydrated bog sprite I gave you, Rebecca!"

"Ah, thank you Haldane." Rebecca said approvingly. "This will protect the Tree from anything harmful. It's a little bit like homeopathy, or an inoculation. Bog sprite energy will deter any nasty creatures from attempting to injure the Tree." She pulled a rather ugly desiccated looking blob from her sack and spit on it. The bog sprite hissed alarmingly, puffed up to the size of a small dog, and then shrank back to a small blob again.

Meridwen smiled. "You and Torin must plant the branch together, Rebecca. Use those gifts which seem appropriate, and it will grow tall and strong. And then, Rebecca, you must enter the tree to place within it the seeds of new crystals, which will grow beneath it just as the old ones did."

"And who will be the Guardian here, as Alphumerian was on Thianely?" Torin asked.

"You will know when it is time," Meridwen said. "Now I will ask the earth to open, and you will plant the branch, for I must soon return to my own trees and my own people."

Rebecca reached into the sack and pulled out the flask of the water of life, the sap Leva had given her, the singing marbles from Liliar, and then pulled the crystal from around her neck and returned it to Meridwen. She held fast to the root as Meridwen, spinning the crystal necklace over the ground, quietly sang the circle of the earth apart.

> "Shift and part and move and sweep,
> Wide and high and smooth and deep,
> Make a place for root to flourish,
> Wisdom hold and knowing nourish,
> Strengthen ground and nurture seed
> Bring the Folk the truth they need,

For all ages and times be found
The highest purpose in this ground."

The ground pulled and pushed itself away from the circle, creating an opening about three feet in diameter. Rebecca bent down and gently placed the root into the center of the hole.

"Here, Torin," she said, handing him the small flask of the Water of Life. Torin knelt and carefully emptied the flask into the hole, saturating the lower part of the root. Then Rebecca asked Haldane to put in the petrified bog sprite, whose shriveled form lengthened a little as it touched the water and then sank down into the ground. Rebecca dripped the sap directly onto the golden branch, which expanded as they watched. Tiny roots sprouted from the lower end and twined their way down into the earth. Around the root Rebecca dropped in the singing marbles and they immediately began humming a melodious tune like one of the leaf lullabies she'd heard on Thianely.

As the onlookers watched, the earth moved to embrace the small golden root, shifting its earthen arms to cradle it, slowly covering it over in layer after layer of soil until it was completely buried, forming a small mound on top of the Great Hill.

Meridwen nodded in satisfaction as Rebecca patted the earth directly over the root. Within moments, they could see the first slim shoots of the tree pushing up through the soil into the air. Soon, it grew higher, thickening even more. Small limbs grew out from the main trunk, reaching and stretching until before them stood a small golden tree, fully formed, about three feet high.

As Rebecca took a deep breath and began to sing, the entire gathering accompanied her,

Tree of Life grow straight and true,
From all creation given you.
The water of life, which heals us all,
The dark of fear, which keeps us small,
The sap of grief and joy in time,
The measure of reason and love sublime.
Now, from all take this gift of stone,
The crystal wisdom, all re-known.

213

When she reached out to the tree, Rebecca seemed to shrink, or perhaps it was the tree that grew, for her head was soon lower than its shortest branches. She embraced the tree; her arms barely holding its circumference, for it grew wider as she held it. As Rebecca slowly dissolved into the thick golden bark, all of the crystal wisdom condensed inside her until she felt solid as stone. Slowly she let the huge record-keeping crystals go, moving from her body and into the tree. One by one the large, crystalline forms burrowed through the tree, beneath the ground, and deep below the tree's roots. Multi-colored light rays cascaded through branch and limb. Finally Torin moved forward and reaching into the tree as if it were air, pulled Rebecca out again. Light continued to dance across the tree's radiant bark, brilliant colors of every hue.

As those who had gathered to watch stood mesmerized, Meridwen motioned to Leva and said, "Farewell, my friends, and may this tree always bear fruit and may the fruit of this tree always be sweet. Farewell, until you come again to us on Thianely."

Leva hugged her friends fiercely, and turning once to wave goodbye, followed Meridwen back through the door inside the air and faded away. Auran, Griffin, Liliar, Tehy, Haldane, Torin, Rebecca, and the others stood quietly, as the Great Tree unfurled green leaves and pink blossoms like tiny fingers, growing golden fruit before their eyes. Rebecca held out her hand and a round golden fruit fell into it. She smiled as each of her family and friends and Folk approached the tree to receive a piece of fruit. The taste was crisp and sweet and sour at once, like the best flavors ever tasted.

"I don't remember the Great Tree on Thianely ever bearing fruit," Torin commented. "I wasn't even sure that it could."

"My mother told me that her mother's great grandmother once tasted an old piece of dried fruit from the Thianelian Tree," Tehy said. "Griffin Queens were often the only ones who received a piece of dried fruit once the tree stopped bearing. But it hadn't borne fruit for many an age."

"My stepfather," said Liliar, referring to Etestian Bollux, "once said that Bolluxes are allergic to Great Tree fruit. His great, great, great, great grandfather lost his bad temper that way. He became so kind they banished him."

"I remember that story," Haldane said. "But look, I'm just as me as I ever was." And he took a huge bite out of the fruit, letting the golden juice drip down his chin and onto his t-shirt.

"Haldane," Rebecca said, "Go ahead and let the sky clear. It's time for everyone to see the Tree."

"One moment," interjected Torin. "I have a gift from my Father." And he spread out his arms to encompass the tree in a radiant shaft of flame that completely encircled it. "Extra protection," he said, and stepped back to admire the ring of fire.

"This is where we part," Martas said. He gazed in gratitude at the Great Tree, thanked Rebecca and her companions, and whistled loudly to the rest of his Folk, who immediately started back to their homes.

"I wonder how long it will take people to notice," Auran said, and soon as she'd finished speaking the first clusters of people began to approach from all directions, drawn by the sight of the magnificent tree and the smell of its fruit.

"What on earth is that?" One woman asked. "I've never seen that kind of tree before."

"Can we eat the fruit?" one old man said. Others wondered too, as Rebecca reached over to touch the tree's golden bark.

"The Tree will give you some if you only ask for it," she said, "Either with your mouth, or your mind, and if you truly want it, the fruit is yours to eat. But it will not be picked before you are ready, no matter how hard you try."

Many people came to eat, though others were content to merely admire from a distance. And some found the sun glinting off the branches too bright for their eyes and avoided the tree altogether. Some that wanted to eat the fruit but weren't quite ready, found that the tree refused to yield up its fruit, and those people had to be content to come back another time. One small child hugged the tree and announced that she was already full.

Later that evening, after Auran and Griffin took an overexcited and kindness-intoxicated Haldane home to bed, Rebecca, Torin, Liliar and Tehy sat under the sunset's palette of colors, sharing the Great Tree's company on the first night of its life on Earth.

"What do you think will happen here on your Earth now that the Great Tree grows here?" Tehy asked.

"I'm not sure, but it can only help," Rebecca said, pillowing her head on Torin's shoulder as they basked in the glow of fire around the Tree to keep warm.

"There will be even more connections between other worlds and here now," Liliar commented. "Many offworlders will come to visit the Great Tree, and its presence will strengthen your planet's song. There will be more harmony, more intunement."

"And the more who eat of its fruit, the better off people will be," Torin added. "Every being has the right to eat of its fruit, although some may doubt their own worthiness. The Tree will not bear for those who demand from it, or those who would eat out of greed. I imagine that children here will eat the most. What happens if a child receives the fruit and gives it to a parent who cannot?"

Rebecca smiled. "I saw that happen actually. But no matter how many times the child offered the fruit to his father, the dad kept dropping it. If he wasn't ready to get the fruit directly from the tree, he couldn't get it from anyone else either."

Some time later, as the sun rose above the horizon, they stretched and stood, preparing to go home. While Tehy and Liliar gathered some fruit for their friends and family on Thianely, Torin ran his hand along the tree's trunk in a gesture of farewell.

"It's time for us to leave now," Liliar said. "I will sing us home through The Time Gate. Thank your parents for us; we enjoyed ourselves here."

"Especially the taxi ride," Tehy said. "I will have much to tell my parents when we return to Thianely. Check in with us soon. As I said before, Mother may have a task for us."

"I'm afraid we'll have to leave Haldane here," Liliar informed them. "Although my Folk are not that smart, they have long memories for revenge. It's still not safe yet for him to return home."

"My grandmother would be devastated to lose him," Rebecca admitted. "He's become sort of a pet project for her."

Liliar smiled. "Your grandmother has made quite an impression on Haldane too. He considers her nearly as good as a Thianelian Bollux."

The friends all bade each other farewell, planning to meet again as soon as they could, and to keep in touch through long distance teling. Before Rebecca and Torin headed for home, they lingered by the Great Tree for one last moment, and heard, through the lilt of the wind, the Great Tree singing to its leafy children:

> In the starlight of the world,
> All is new, my child, my child,
> Like a blossom to unfurl
> For today, my child, my child
>
> Let the universal sound
> Fill you full, my child, my child
> Creation's purpose to abound
> In your soul, my child, my child
>
> And each life that you may live
> Love you well, my child, my child
> A richness given so that you may give
> Your present self, my child, my child
>
> May creation's gift to us all, each other
> Bless you now, my child, my child,
> And that which we create together
> Serve us all, my child my child.

"Do you know who the next Guardian of the Great Tree is?" Rebecca asked Torin, as he stood holding her closely under the canopy of the Great Tree's fruit laden branches.

Torin shook his head, watching the sun's first rays hit the tree's bark and send shimmers of light over Rebecca's face.

"Our first child," Rebecca laughed.